UNDERGROUND U.S.A.

AlterImage

a new list of publications
exploring global cult and popular cinema

UNDERGROUND U.S.A.

FILMMAKING BEYOND
THE HOLLYWOOD CANON

EDITED BY XAVIER MENDIK & STEVEN JAY SCHNEIDER

WALLFLOWER PRESS
LONDON and NEW YORK

First published in Great Britain in 2002 by
Wallflower Press
5 Pond Street, London NW3 2PN
www.wallflowerpress.co.uk

A catalogue for this book is available from the British Library.

ISBN 1-903364-49-3

Printed in Great Britain by Antony Rowe, Chippenham, Wiltshire.

CONTENTS

ACKNOWLEDGEMENTS

The Editors would like to thank all of the writers who contributed so much hard work to this volume. We would also like to offer our sincere thanks Lloyd Kaufman for contributing not only the foreword but also for the endless support and enthusiasm he offered this project. Thanks also to Larry Cohen, Herschell Gordon Lewis, and David F. Friedman for their time and assistance with tracking down illustrative material.

We would also like to thank Melissa Scheld, Stephen Abbott, and Matthew Bucher at Columbia University Press, Christopher Golden, Adrien Glover, The American Museum of the Moving Image (for kind help with stills), Elyse Pellman and Katheryn Winnick, as well as Howard Martin, Kate Cochrane and the staff at OPI Media.

We would also like to express our gratitude to colleagues and friends in the School of Cultural Studies at University College Northampton. In particular, we offer sincere thanks to George Savona, Peter Brooker, and the course team of the Media and Popular Culture degree for their support in establishing the Cult Film Archive and the writing projects which have emerged from this resource.

Finally, we offer our thanks to Yoram Allon, John Atkinson, Hannah Patterson and Howard Seal at Wallflower Press whose assistance and advice with this volume, and the *AlterImage* book series as a whole, remains invaluable.

The images used to illustrate the chapters 'Doris Wishman Meets the Avant-Garde' (with the exception of one image from the personal collection of Michael J. Bowen) and '"Gouts of Blood": The Colourful Underground Universe of Herschell Gordon Lewis' are courtesy of Something Weird Video, Inc and we would like to offer our sincere thanks to Lisa Petrucci who did so much to assist us with finding illustrative material. Readers wishing to access information on the company's extensive catalogue of underground films should contact: Something Weird Video, P.O. Box 33664, Seattle, WA 98133, www.somethingweird.com.

The stills used to illustrate the foreword and the chapter 'A Tasteless Art: Waters, Kaufman and the Pursuit of "Pure" Gross-Out' (Troma images only) are courtesy of Troma Entertainment, for which we thank Doug Sakmann.

The rest of the images contained in the book are the property of the production or distribution companies concerned. They are reproduced here in the spirit of publicity and the promotion of the films in question.

This book is dedicated with love to Nicola.

NOTES ON CONTRIBUTORS

STEPHEN R. BISSETTE was a professional artist, author, editor and publisher in the comic book industry for 23 years. His original novella *Aliens: Tribes* won the Bram Stoker Award in 1993. His film criticism and scholarly articles have appeared in numerous periodicals, newspapers and books, and he is a regular contributor to *Video Watchdog*. Steven is currently working on a history of Vermont films and filmmakers to be published by University Press of New England.

JOEL BLACK teaches comparative literature and film at the University of Georgia. He is the author of *The Aesthetics of Murder: A Study in Romantic Literature and Contemporary Culture* (Johns Hopkins University Press, 1991), *The Reality Effect: Film Culture and the Graphic Imperative* (Routledge, 2001), as well as numerous essays on literature, critical theory and cultural history.

MICHAEL J. BOWEN is a PhD candidate in the Department of Cinema Studies at New York University's Tisch School of the Arts. He has written on exploitation filmmaker Doris Wishman for numerous publications and is currently completing a book about her life.

GARRETT CHAFFIN-QUIRAY received his BA and MA from the University of Southern California School of Cinema-Television. He has sponsored a film festival, taught courses on TV and cinema history and published movie and video reviews. His research interests include pornography and violence, post-War American cinema, representations of Vietnam and the 1970s. He has also managed information technology for an investment bank, had a dot-com adventure and now lives in New York City writing criticism, short-length fiction and his fourth novel.

JONATHAN L. CRANE is Assistant Professor in the Department of Communication at the University of North Carolina at Charlotte. He has published widely on such topics as Top 40 radio, horror film specatorship and music censorship. His book, *Terror and Everyday Life: Singular Moments in the History of the Horror Film*, was published by Sage in 1992.

ELENA GORFINKEL is a PhD candidate in the Department of Cinema Studies at New York University's Tisch School of the Arts. Her dissertation focuses on American sexploitation films of the 1960s.

SARA GWENLLIAN JONES lectures in Television and Digital Media at Cardiff University, Wales. She is currently writing a book titled *Fantastic Cult Television* (Edward Arnold, 2002) and is co-editor of *Intensities: The Journal of Cult Media* (www.cult-media.com).

BENJAMIN HALLIGAN lectures in film at York St John College. He is currently preparing a critical biography of Michael Reeves for Manchester University Press.

JOAN HAWKINS is an Associate Professor in the Department of Communication and Culture at Indiana University, Bloomington. She is the author of *Cutting Edge: Art Horror and the Horrific Avant-Garde* (University of Minnesota Press, 2000).

XAVIER MENDIK is Director of the Cult Film Archive at University College Northampton and the General Editor of the *AlterImage* series. He has published, broadcast and toured cinema events around the themes of psychoanalysis and its application to cult and horror cinema. His publications in this area include (as co-editor) *Unruly Pleasures: The Cult Film and its Critics* (Fab Press, 2000), *Dario Argento's Tenebrae* (Flicks Books, 2000) and (as editor) *Shocking Cinema of the Seventies* (Noir Publishing, 2001). He is currently researching his next book, entitled *Fear at Four Hundred Degrees: Structure and Sexuality in the Films of Dario Argento*. Beyond his academic research in this area, he has also conducted interviews with many of the leading figures of cult cinema as well as sitting as a jury member on several leading European film festivals. Details of his interviews and jury accounts can be found on www.kamera.co.uk where he runs the film column 'Scream Theory'.

ANNALEE NEWITZ is founder of the webzine *Bad Subjects* (www.eserver.org/bs) which is still going strong; and has published two books, *White Trash: Race and Class in America* (Routledge, 1997) and *The Bad Subjects Anthology* (New York University Press, 1998). In 1998, she graduated from the University of California at Berkeley with a PhD in English and American Studies. Currently, she is at work on two books – one about sex and technology, the other about capitalism and monster movies. Her work has appeared in magazines and papers such as Salon.com, *The Industry Standard*, GettingIt.com, *Feed*, SFGate.com, *Gear*, Nerve.com, *The Utne Reader* Online, *Alternative Press Review*, *New York Press*, *The San Francisco Bay Guardian*, *The Metro* and several academic journals and anthologies.

MARTIN F. NORDEN teaches film as Professor of Communication at the University of Massachusetts-Amherst. His articles on moving-image media have appeared in numerous journals and anthologies. He is currently at work on a collection of essays that examine the representation of evil in popular film and television.

BILL OSGERBY is a Senior Lecturer in Cultural Studies at the University of North London and has written widely on youth, gender and British and American cultural history. His publications include *Youth in Britain Since 1945* (Blackwell, 1998), *Playboys in Paradise: Masculinity, Youth and Leisure-Style in Modern America* (Berg/New York University Press, 2001) and a co-edited anthology, *Action TV: Tough-Guys, Smooth Operators and Foxy Chicks* (Routledge, 2001). He has never ridden a motorcycle, but still resents being hassled by The Man.

JACK SARGEANT is the author of *Deathtripping: the Cinema of Transgression* (Creation Books, 1996), *Naked Lens: Beat Cinema* (Creation Books, 1997) and *Cinema Contra Cinema* (Fringecore BVD, 1999); he is the co-editor (with Stephanie Watson) of *Lost Highways* (Creation Books, 2000) and the editor of *Suture* (1998, volume two forthcoming from Amok Books). He has contributed to numerous publications including *Headpress*, *Bizarre*, *BBGUN*, *Panik*, and *World Art*. He has curated numerous film seasons and lectured on underground film and outlaw culture across three continents, as well as acting as an advisor to the British Film Institute on contemporary underground film. He has appeared in numerous television programs discussing underground culture and its manifestations, and has also had cameo roles in several underground films. In addition, he teaches cultural theory, philosophy and film at the London College of Printing.

STEVEN JAY SCHNEIDER is a PhD candidate in Philosophy at Harvard University and in Cinema Studies at New York University's Tisch School of the Arts. He has published widely on the horror film and related genres in journals such as *CineAction*, *Post Script*, *Film & Philosophy*, *Hitchcock Annual*, *Kinema*, *Journal of Popular Film & Television*, *Paradoxa*, *Scope*, *Kinoeye* and the *Central Europe Review*. He is currently co-editing two volumes, *Dark Thoughts: Philosophic Reflections on*

Cinematic Horror (Scarecrow Press) and *Understanding Film Genres* (McGraw-Hill), as well as researching his next book for Wallflower Press, *The Cinema of Wes Craven: An Auteur on Elm Street*.

DAVID SCHWARTZ is the Chief Curator of Film at the American Museum of the Moving Image (New York), where he has programmed numerous avant-garde film retrospectives including 'Films that Tell Time: A Ken Jacobs Retrospective', 'Serene Intensity: The Films of Ernie Gehr' and 'The Art of Vision: A Stan Brakhage Retrospective'.

JACK STEVENSON is an American film-writer, print collector and distributor living in Denmark since 1993. He was a teacher at The European Film College in Ebeltoft, Denmark from 1995 to 1998 and has just completed a book about Lars von Trier, something of a departure from his specialities which centre on American exploitation and underground cinema.

TONY WILLIAMS received his PhD from the University of Manchester in 1974, and is currently Professor and Area Head of Film Studies in the English Department of Southern Illinois University at Carbondale. He is the co-editor of *Vietnam War Films* (McFarland, 1994) and author of *Jack London: The Movies* (Rejl, 1992), *Hearths of Darkness: The Family in the American Horror Film* (Fairleigh Dickinson University Press, 1996), *Larry Cohen: The Radical Allegories of an Independent Filmmaker* (McFarland, 1997) and *Structures of Desire: British Cinema, 1939–1955* (SUNY Press, 2000). His essays have appeared in numerous anthologies and journals. He is currently completing *The Cinema of George A. Romero: Knight of the Living Dead* for Wallflower Press.

NICK ZEDD, crypto-insurrectionary visionary, filmmaker, writer, actor, theorist and xenomorphic magician coined the term 'Cinema of Transgression' to identify the underground movement he spearheaded in New York, directing such movies as *Police State*, *War is Menstrual Envy* and *Thus Spake Zarathustra*. His autobiography, *Totem of the Depraved*, was published by 2.13.61 in 1996.

FOREWORD
I.A.: I-WON'T-SUCK-THE-MAINSTREAM ART

Lloyd Kaufman
President of Troma Entertainment

When I entered Yale in 1964 as a Chinese Studies major, I had expected to become a social worker who would do good things like teach people with hooks for hands how to finger paint. I didn't, of course, because I got infected with the movie bug. My roommates at Yale were co-chairs of the Yale Film Society and it was because of them that I began watching great mainstream movies by Hitchcock, Chaplin, Renoir, Fuller, Lang, Lubitch and others. In my first film, I slaughtered a pig in Chad, Africa, and it was then I realised that offending people was what I yearned to do. By slitting a pig's throat and watching it shit and oink at the same time, I somehow expected to become renowned in the mainstream just like my movie heroes.

It is thirty years later. Michael Herz and I are still expecting. We are an independent team that has tried to hit a home run for the past thirty years. I'm not going to lie – I would cum in my drawers if a Troma film ever became a grand slam in movie history like Hitchcock's *Psycho*. However, Troma is still standing on second base, waiting for one of our pictures to hit us into movie stardom, making our name just as recognisable as Hitchcock's. If you ask someone, "Weren't you scared to take a shower after you watched *Psycho*?" almost everybody would understand your reference to Marion Crane getting slaughtered by the cross-dressing killer Norman Bates. As of now, if you ask someone, "Weren't you scared to ride a bike after watching *The Toxic Avenger*?" you might get a few people who understand that you're talking about the scene in which a young boy innocently riding his bike gets his pre-pubescent cranium turned into kiddy-splat after being crushed by the wheel of an automobile. Perhaps such an image is too graphic for 'the mainstream' to handle. Hollywood prefers to protect human innocence by endorsing movies such as *Pretty Woman*, which should have been subtitled: *Girls who suck will be in luck.*

Troma has never sucked the mainstream. Rather, we have flirted with the establishment as a high school nerd flirts with the idea of being popular. One day, the nerd becomes friends with someone respected by the in-crowd and thinks that he just might be accepted. Troma makes a movie called *The Toxic Avenger* (in which a washroom nerd named Melvin is transformed into a radioactive defender of the weak and powerless). This in turn spawned the children's cartoon show, *The Toxic Crusaders*, a whole lot of lunch boxes and other 'useful' merchandise for kids. Perhaps the mainstream will embrace us. The nerd starts going to parties. Troma visits Hollywood. However, the nerd realises that in order to be popular, he would have to change who he is and leave all of his Melvin-like friends behind. After all, the big shots don't accept the geeks. Troma realises it would have to ditch its underground roots and get Toxie to suck the 'over-ground' snobs in order to be accepted by the mainstream. The nerd decides to stay an outcast and remain loyal to his friends, rather than making a fool out of himself by attempting to ask out the hottest girl, boy or class pet in school.

Troma is that nerd. (Some might say my red bow tie confirms that.) We stay in the underground and remain loyal to our roots. Yes, we've strolled into the mainstream's phoney forest. Luckily, we listened to Hansel and Gretel and left a trail of Toxie crumbs along the way so we'd find our way back home … to a company which stabs movie characters in their hermaphrodite groins (*Terror Firmer*) as opposed to the backs of their employees. We'll leave that to Hollywood.

For me, Troma is an example of underground, micro-budget art that produces macro-violence-vomit-tits-and-more-tits. We have to sleep on the floor, eat cheese sandwiches three times a day and defecate in paper bags in order to make our movies on a non-Hollywood budget. Is this a bad thing? No. In fact, being in the underground is liberating. Not only does this allow us to make the kinds of films we want without mainstream interference, it also allows Troma to distribute movie after movie by artists who have something different to say – something unique and out of the ordinary. If running such a business makes us part of the ostracised underground, so be it. Thanks to the underground and the support and artistic freedom provided and encouraged therein, my career as a film director has been aberrantly prolific.

FIGURE 1 Filmmaking underground style: Lloyd doing his thing

One of my inspirers, Andy Warhol, was able to retain the total creative freedom afforded to him as a member of the underground, but at the same time he came to be embraced by the mainstream media and millions of people around the world. Troma has never been hugged by the mainstream, but we still feel loved! While I will never surrender my artistic freedom, I am always hopeful that one day I will wake to find that millions of people have been able to see beyond the dismemberment in *Tromeo and Juliet* or the de-fetusing in *Terror Firmer* or the head crushing-*cum*-diarrhoea in *Citizen Toxie* and carry me off the battlefield of art on their shoulders … a hero of the underground!

One of the most rewarding aspects of making movies in the underground is knowing that loyal fans genuinely admire you for the work you produce, not because you're in one of *People's 100 Most Talented Actors* editions and worshiped by trillions. One of our fans demonstrated his loyalty on 11 September 2001. That was the day the World Trade Center's Twin Towers collapsed in New York City. When the obscene terrorism occurred, I became stranded in London. I didn't feel like swimming across the Atlantic Ocean to get back home, so I remained stuck in London with very little money and no place to sleep. Luckily, Troma fan Andrew McKay allowed me to stay in his family's house until I was able to leave England. (Andrew is the creator of the official UK Troma fan site, www.toxie.com.) For eight days, he and his parents made me feel at home and became my friends. On the plane home, I thought to myself, "You're a lucky guy, Lloyd. You could have been gutted alive if Andrew were a psychotic fan. You could have been on one of the planes that crashed into the World Trade Center. You could have directed *A.I.*"

We at Troma have survived thirty years in this underground art world despite our history of getting blacklisted and evicted on numerous occasions because we *do* have millions of such people supporting us. It sucks that we have to eat shit to survive and that we never get praised by the BBC, but it's worth it when people of all ages support us at book signings and conventions. They also volunteer to do all sorts of Troma-tic things for free. In fact, when we travel around the U.S. they feed us, house us, fuck those of us who are not married, put on Toxie and Kabukiman costumes and offer to wipe our asses after we take toxic turds. Our fans are the ones who inform and inspire us to do those things that make Troma successful, like being the first film studio to create a website, and the first studio to produce DVDs. Most important, they stand behind us when the mainstream tries to tear us down.

Marcel Duchamp (the guy who hung a urinal on the wall in 1907, with whom I have been compared – well, maybe it was the urinal to which I was compared) stated that "to be an artist of the future, one must go underground." Perhaps I have survived as a film director for more than thirty years because Troma and I have been ahead of our contemporaries. This is because we have total freedom in and control over our art. And it is because Troma has remained underground that I continue to have this freedom. In fact, to be underground is actually liberating because we can stay true to our art and politics. And while the mainstream has never honoured Troma or even considered me for an Academy Award, what greater honour can I receive than being asked to write this foreword for Xavier Mendik and Steven Jay Schneider's superlative tome on underground film? One of the most difficult aspects of being an artist is to follow Shakespeare's admonition: "To thine own self be true … and maybe thou won't bloweth thy brains out." We all need inspiration and support to help us abide by this maxim.

FIGURE 2 Alternative Oscars

For a company so associated with copulation, depravity and excess, it comes as no surprise when I say that making art is very much like having sex. You can go (all) the Hollywood way, allowing the big shots to open you up, jerk you off and prod at your ideas, thereby raping your artistic vision. Or you can go the underground way – and masturbate your art. Only you know all of its hot spots – the places that must be touched in order for it to come to life. The book you are about to read will help you to be brave and masturbate your artistic minds, weather you are filmmakers, film fans or simply interested in peering into the bowels of cinema culture that goes on beneath Hollywood.

In what follows, you will read weird tales of maverick male and female directors who have combined shock value with artistic vision, movie genres that have manipulated Hollywood codes for genuine impact as well as profiles of new independent filmmakers determined to give the mainstream a run for its money. By giving exposure to the American underground, Xavier and Steven's book gives us the courage and wherewithal to band together, proud and erect, to make some art and continue to take that art back from the giant devil-worshipping international media conglomerates and give it back to the people.

Lloyd Kaufman

July 2002

(With thanks to Jamie Greco)

INTRODUCTION
EXPLORATIONS UNDERGROUND: AMERICAN FILM (AD)VENTURES BENEATH THE HOLLYWOOD RADAR

Xavier Mendik & Steven Jay Schneider

Whether characterised by the artistic visions of Andy Warhol or Harry Smith, the art-house erotica of Radley Metzger, the carnivalesque excesses of John Waters or Doris Wishman, or the narrative experiments of Bruce Conner or Abel Ferrara, underground cinema maintains an important position within American film culture. Yet despite its multiple (and not necessarily compatible) definitions as 'cult' and 'exploitation', 'alternative' and 'independent', surprisingly little academic consideration has been given to the modes of production, distribution, exhibition and audience reception of the American cinematic underground. Equally, little research has been undertaken to explain how the social, sexual, political and aesthetic representations of such cinema diverge from and offer alternatives to the traditional, largely conservative structures of the Hollywood machine.

To date, only a few books and edited collections have been produced which critically explore aspects of the American underground scene. Among these are Parker Tyler's *Underground Film*

(1969), J. Hoberman and Jonathan Rosenbaum's *Midnight Movies* (1983), J. P. Telotte's edited volume, *The Cult Film Experience: Beyond All Reason* (1991) and, most recently, Xavier Mendik and Graeme Harper's edited collection, *Unruly Pleasures: The Cult Film and its Critics* (2000). While all significant volumes in their own right, these works have restricted themselves to case studies of various cult and avant-garde texts rather than providing suitable methodologies which examine their historical, economic and cultural emergence within American cinema.

Underground U.S.A.: Filmmaking Beyond the Hollywood Canon strives to extend the merits of such books, while more fully addressing nascent debates in this still under-theorised area of film culture. This volume seeks to examine the stylistic, generic and representational strategies that have emerged in the American underground from the 1940s to the present. Through this examination, *Underground U.S.A.* brings together leading film theorists, journalists, exhibitors and directors, as well as emerging scholars in the field. In a series of specially commissioned articles, these writers situate the various and diverse strands of American underground cinema as a powerful and subversive medium functioning through a fragmentation of official/normative modes of production and distribution. The book takes as its focus those directors, films and genres typically dismissed, belittled or (worst of all) ignored by established film culture.

What unites the articles that follow is the belief that the American underground is a vibrant domain that defies the broad classifications of mainstream cinema. In this respect, many critics in this volume view the underground film scene as a space where art-house stands shoulder to shoulder with spectacle-based atrocity, and where experimentation is a regular feature of exploitation. By collapsing many of the standard dichotomies that continue to plague mainstream cinema, 'Underground U.S.A.' remains a realm where maverick directors, producers and production personnel are able to express offbeat forms of creativity, ranging from the artistic to the absurd.

It is this ability to transgress presumed boundaries between genre-based and art-house products that has marked the career of Abel Ferrara, whose work is discussed by Joan Hawkins. In her article 'No Worse Than You Were Before', Hawkins examines the conflation of art-house and grind-house themes present in Ferrara's 1996 film *The Addiction*. Here, the tale of a philosophy graduate's incorporation into vampirism is used as a springboard to examine wider issues of evil, existential angst and economic power within the contemporary urban landscape. For Hawkins, *The Addiction* represents an example of 'theoretical fictions' which use generic forms to explore theoretical or philosophical concerns. The film's conflation of high and low mirrors the traditions of established gutter poets such as William S. Burroughs, whose concept of the 'Algebra of Need' is used by Hawkins to explore the images of addiction contained in the film. Ferrara's concern with collapsing intellect into the instinctual is seen by the author as key to the understanding *The Addiction*. This explains why the film places its university location in the heart of a black ghetto as well as shedding light on its unsettling ending where the dispossessed and undead rise up to (literally) devour knowledge at a doctoral graduation celebration. With its unexpected combination of high theory and genre motifs as well as its use of disorientating art-house film techniques, *The Addiction* confused and outraged critics and mainstream audiences. However, it found a cult following with underground and 'Indiewood' audiences that lie beyond the Hollywood canon.

While Ferrara used stock vampire motifs as a point of connection with art-house techniques, Metzger combined pornography and avant-garde strategies with startling results. The director's work is discussed by Elena Gorfinkel in her article 'Radley Metzger's Elegant Arousal: Taste, Aesthetic Distinction and Sexploitation'. For the author, Metzger was one of a number of exploitation directors (whose ranks included Russ Meyer, Hershell Gordon Lewis and Doris Wishman) that came to prominence during the 1960s and whose creative input allowed them to escape the traditional ghetto of underground titillation fare. In Gorfinkel's view, it is Metzger's work that represents the most prominent example of an 'exploitation elite' who attempted to erode the traditional boundaries between 'grind-house' and 'art-house'. As she notes, although the director began his career with a failed attempt at social realism, he increasingly turned to Europe (as both a distributor and filmmaker) to provide cosmopolitan polish and personnel to the traditionally stilted genres of American titillation. The end results of these 1960s experiments included works such as *Alley Cats, Therese and Isabelle* and *The Lickerish Quartet,* all of which gained Metzger the 'chic' end of the erotic market as well as the reputation as a director with his own unique and atypical visual style. If Metzger's attempts to produce 'class speciality films' rather than formulaic exploitation works had an impact on the structure of his pictures, they also affected the depictions of male and female sexuality that Gorfinkel discusses in the latter part of her article. Here, she notes that Metzger was innovative in combining the representations of lesbianism that populated many softcore productions of the era with images (or implications) of homosexuality that had been established by American underground auteurs such as Kenneth Anger and Andy Warhol. It was this fusion of the artistic and the erotic that allowed Metzger to provide sensitive and 'aesthetic' images of lesbianism in works such as *Therese and Isabelle* as well as bold, startling same-sex encounters between the male characters of his later film *Score*. Via these strategies, Gorfinkel concludes that Mezger's cinema was able to advance the imagery of alternative sexual identity within an underground format.

Whereas many of the writers in this volume situate Underground U.S.A. as an oppositional or corrective industry to Hollywood, Stephen R. Bissette argues that many of its marginal forms and cycles (such as horror and fantasy) have actually facilitated a shift from independent to mainstream work for several leading directors. While the careers of filmmakers such as David Cronenberg, David Lynch and John Waters are well known, less well documented are the profiles of those earlier directors who used genre templates as a point of transition between these wings of the American film industry. In his article 'Curtis Harrington and the Underground Roots of the Modern Horror Film', Bissette discusses a lost 'alternative' auteur whose later horror films (such as *Who Slew Auntie Roo?*, *Killer Bees*, and *What's the Matter With Helen?*) have been unfairly dismissed as derivative commercial productions. As Bissette reveals, Harrington's roots lay in the West Coast Experimental film circuit as initiated by

3

alternative filmmakers such as Maya Deren (with whom Harrington shared a number of professional and personal links) as well as sharing similar sado-stylistic concerns with the likes of Kenneth Anger and Gregory Markopoulos. As Bissette explains, a key factor which has inhibited an 'alternative' re-reading of Harrington remains the fact that many of his innovative early shorts were in production prior to the current definitions of American underground film. As a result, such filmmakers have been wrongly classified as either experimental (implying a non-narrative focus) or avant-garde (with its distinctly European connotations). Yet, in the case of Harrington, there remains a definite narrative and populist 'pull' in his work that defies such narrow definitions. As the author reveals, the early influence of Edgar Allen Poe on the filmmaker (even down to his directing and appearing in a short film version of *The Fall of the House of Usher* as a teenager) assured a gothic horror dimension to Harrington's work. Following his connections with fellow underground figures such as Kenneth Anger, Bissette also notes how Harrington repeatedly fused supernatural concerns with issues of psychosexual drama and images of annihilation and sexual ambiguity. Bissette explores the director's ability to transcend underground and Hollywood definitions via a study of key Harrington films such as *Fragment of Seeking* and *Night Tide*. While the author's stated aim is to redress Harrington's continued marginalised status as 'a man without a country', he also provides a fascinating overview of a truly 'forgotten' underground figure.

In his contribution 'Special Effects in the Cutting Room', Tony Williams argues for the reclassification of 'guerrilla filmmaker' Larry Cohen's 1984 picture *Special Effects* as an underground rather than simply an independent production. More precisely, Williams sees *Special Effects* as performing many of the self-reflexive, counter-hegemonic functions of the films of Hitchcock. They call attention to the fact that, when originally released, Hitchcock's movies were often viewed by critics and audiences as distinctly 'underground'. This status was seen in the sense that they challenged and subverted prevailing norms, both technical and thematic. Without going so far as to reject those familiar definitions of underground cinema which focus on abstract and non-narrative avant-garde techniques, Williams proposes a more flexible understanding of underground filmmaking. This is one that makes room for independent and radical productions such as *Special Effects* which employ/exploit traditional narrative strategies in order to critique and call into question established gender roles, power relations and ideological structures.

Special Effects is also discussed by Joel Black in 'Real(ist) Horror: From Execution Videos to Snuff Films'. As Black notes, the death film – especially the so-called 'snuff film', in which a killer and/or his accomplice records the actual murder of a victim on video – is surely the most extreme of underground genres. But as public desire for spectacular displays of violence and supposedly 'real-life' drama continues to grow, even while the virtual ban on displaying visual recordings of violent death remains more or less in place, fictionalised snuff has moved slowly but surely from the underground to the mainstream. Black identifies two seemingly opposed cinematic strategies; 'de-aestheticisation' and 'hyper-aestheticisation', evident in realist horror films from low-budget indies such as *Special Effects* and *Henry: Portrait of a Serial Killer* all the way to such commercial Hollywood fare as *8MM* and *Fifteen Minutes*. Despite their budgetary differences, these texts have the same end in view: to 'approach the theoretical limit of *real* horror through their references to, and occasionally their re-enactments of, actual filmed records of murder'.

There is a definite sense in which Abraham Zapruder's amateur film footage of President John F. Kennedy's assassination in Dallas, Texas on 22 November 1963 falls into the underground category of the 'death film' as well. In his essay, 'A Report on Bruce Conner's *Report*', Martin F. Norden takes a close look at another, very different (and distinctly non-amateur) film made about that fateful day in American history. *Report* – the masterwork of experimental auteur and assemblage artist Bruce Conner – creatively combines footage from an abundance of sources, including newsreels, television commercials, classic Hollywood pictures and home videos, to provide a brilliant and disturbing montage of sounds and images. As Norden explains:

> *Report* is perhaps the most outstanding example of the many films – underground and otherwise – that utilise the contrapuntal arrangement of images and sound to create sociological statements in the form of irony, metaphors and analogies. What makes the film special is Conner's ability to intertwine images of fact and fiction to such an extent that a new 'reality' takes place.

Through his insightful analysis, Norden reveals how Conner's 'highly personal meditation' on the Kennedy assassination stands as an original and instantly recognisable merging of underground and avant-garde filmmaking practices.

The theme of pain and suffering is also present in Jack Sargeant's study of the cinematic experiments of Andy Warhol. In his article 'Voyeurism, Sadism and Transgression – Screen Notes and Observations on Andy Warhol's *Blow Job* and *I, A Man*', the author critically discusses some of the sado-sexual practices at play in a variety of the Factory's output. For instance, Sergeant considers the morbid and exploitative screen-testing methods to which Warhol subjected his models, actors and sitters. This required them to stay in the same position for several hours at a time as well as frequently forcing them to reveal painful confessions about their past sexual experiences. While a critical consideration of the sexual morality of one of the American underground's most potent figures is central to Sargeant's quest, it also reveals the extent to which Warhol was not adverse to employing the so-called sensational tactics associated with exploitation cinema in order to get results. This increasing fusion of the commercial and the complex is seen in the gradual alteration of Warhol's film style that Sargeant analyses. For the author, the style associated with Warhol's experimental period centred on the use of long takes and stationary camera positioning. However, this system was gradually eroded by the development of a system that was increasingly narrativised and more coherent and commercialised in form. Thus, soundtrack was introduced to accompany the image track, which itself become altered to include more complex forms of movement and positioning. It is such alterations that the author examines via case studies of films such as *Blow Job* and *I, A Man* before concluding that their stylistic experimentation is coupled with a sexual exploitation similar to the more commercial sectors of Underground U.S.A.

Warhol's underground explorations also provide a point of reference in Michael J. Bowen's work on female exploitation director Doris Wishman, who passed away in the summer of 2002 just before this volume went to press. In his article 'Doris Wishman Meets the Avant-Garde', Bowen seeks to further connect the underground spheres of art-house and titillation via their depictions of sexuality as a zone of shock and transgression. While Bowen admits that accepted underground auteurs such as Warhol framed their sexual experimentations within a complex film form, these textual innovations were mirrored by the 1960s work of Wishman. Although primarily framed as an exploitation figure, Bowen makes a convincing argument for the filmmaker's work as an extension of avant-garde practices. Not only was Wishman a lone female director working in an aggressively male-dominated grind-house arena, but her work has atypically shifted over to the 'legitimate' theoretical circuit as the result of a number of high-profile retrospectives and campus discussions. Bowen extends his analysis of Wishman's avant-garde impetus by dividing his discussion of her work into three key stages. For Bowen, her early work in the 'nudie' cycle of the early 1960s displayed a similar capacity for absurdity and sexual/stylistic deconstruction that marked the work of Warhol and related filmmakers such as George Kuchar. This 'primitive' period of Wishman's development was replaced by her work in the 'roughie' cycle, which began in 1964. For the author, this series of sex-and-sin crime fables remains the director's most accomplished work, which he labels a 'poor man's neo-realism.' Not only did Wishman's roughies lead to frequent comparisons with art-house directors such as Jean-Luc Godard, they also exhibited a similar focus on complex film techniques and problematic and unruly women. While Bowen does concede that Wishman's art-house impetus receded in her 1970s output, he links this to structural and economic changes in the exploitation arena in which the director was operating.

It is a similar series of connections between exploitation and experimental filmmaking that dominates Garrett Chaffin-Quiray's account of director Melvin Van Peebles. In his article 'You Bled My Mother, You Bled My Father, But You Won't Bleed Me – The Underground Trio of Melvin Van Peebles', Chaffin-Quiray questions the extent to which Van Peebles' output within the explicitly populist, 1970s blaxploitation circuit necessarily divorces his work from the avant-garde arena. Not only does the director's work contain explicitly political and counter-cultural themes, but his narratives of racial revolt and role change were also complicated by an unconventional film style developed during his 'training period' in Paris. For Chaffin-Quiray, these thematic and stylistic concerns are evidenced in *The Story of a Three-Day Pass,* Van Peebles' first film as a director. Here, the narrative focus on the failed romantic coupling between a black American soldier and a French female established the theme of failed interracial relations within a white colonial context that the director would develop in subsequent works. Equally, with its emphasis on interruptive jump-cuts, abrupt freeze frames, photo-montage inclusions and multiple non-diegetic music states, this film demonstrates the complex and atypical style that Van Peebles attempted to drag back into Hollywood for his next picture. Although *Watermelon Man* fits into the pattern of 'liberal' race dramas that Hollywood marketed to both black and white audiences during the 1960s, Van Peebles subverted its formula by resisting the standard resolution of interracial integration. Instead, the director pushed the boundaries of diverse ethnic extremism via an absurd comedy of role reversal in which a white male bigot wakes up one day to find his skin has suddenly turned black. In a series of tragic/comic encounters, the film reveals how the protagonist's new-found blackness isolates him from work colleagues, community and family before he is reborn as a coloured militant. According to Chaffin-Quiray, Van Peebles complemented the film's theme of racial alienation by adding complex colour coding to an already un-Hollywood cinematic style. The director's combination of populist and art-house traits reached its logical conclusion with his most prominent feature, *Sweet Sweetback's Baadasssss Song*, which Chaffin-Quiray discusses at the close of his article. The film, which was initially marked as a porn production and distributed as an exploitation flick (before being re-framed as an art-movie) retains an avant-garde air, which for the author demonstrates the director's 'counter-hegemonic style'.

While writers such as Chaffin-Quiray focus on the re-evaluation of specific underground figures, Bill Osgerby considers how the cycle of the biker movie provided a motif of rebellion and transgression for both the experimental and exploitation wings of Underground American film. In 'Full Throttle on the Highway to Hell: Mavericks, Machismo and Mayhem in the American Biker Movie', Osgerby argues that the biker movie came to embody the themes of 'undirected anger and unleashed passion' in a series of films which lasted from the 1950s until the 1970s. For the author, the exploitation roots of this cycle can be traced to an appeal to the rock'n'roll/teen audience market, who were given their definitive role model of rebellion with Marlon Brando's casting in *The Wild One.* The film established the template of a 'nomadic biker gang' who violently undercut the conservative authority of 'Smalltown U.S.A.'. The film's success was emulated by teen movie firms such as AIP as well as experimental auteurs like Kenneth Anger, whose *Scorpio Rising* accentuated the sado-masochism and homo-eroticism implied in Brando's persona. For Osgerby, these works represented an early stage of the biker movie that was violently kick-started in the latter part of the 1960s with the image of the Hells Angel as an anti-social and counter-cultural icon. Although it was primarily within the exploitation traditions of the American underground where these figures gained cinematic exposure in narratives that privileged 'spectacle over narrative, action over intellect', the release of *Easy Rider,* with its experimental style and pseudo-philosophical edge, indicated the biker movie as also attaining a wider import. However, as Osgerby concludes, the film (whose genuine status as biker movie remains a contested fact) very much marked the cycle's decline as new forms and figures of Otherness began to populate the American cinematic underground.

When it comes to Harry Smith (1923–91), generic or artistic labels of any kind, in any combination or conjunction, inevitably fall short of capturing the man or his staggeringly diverse and idiosyncratic creative output. After an eloquent introduction in which he follows P. Adams Sitney in claiming that underground film 'describes what no longer is', Jonathan L. Crane looks at how Smith 'produced work that can be best understood as a cryptic tutorial from a fallen world'. In his article 'The Ideal Cinema of Harry Smith', Crane begins by making apparent the complete and utter novelty of Smith's abstract, labour-intensive film compositions. These eschew the constraints of narrative altogether, and often (especially in his early works) abandon the camera itself in favour of hand-painted drawings on celluloid. He goes on to argue against any understanding of Smith as an 'oppositional' filmmaker whose works possess unambiguous ideological import. Rather, Crane wants to characterise Smith as a cinematic 'idealist', albeit a sensuous one, who 'abjures any direct connection between the screen and the things of the world. … Always challenging us to rethink the foundation upon which we make sense of images, Smith never abandons the hedonistic potential of the screen.'

While Crane deals with an 'idealist' underground figure whose work is gaining posthumous recognition, Benjamin Halligan deals with a contemporary alternative figure whose flourishing reputation is premised on far more nihilistic output. In his article 'What is the Neo-Underground and What Isn't?', Halligan situates Harmony Korine's work (as scriptwriter, actor and director) as a pessimistic 'corrective' to the pseudo-underground tendencies offered by contemporary Hollywood. As defined by recent product such as *American Beauty*, Halligan sees contemporary Hollywood's flirtations with dysfunctionality as transforming underground potential into a far less challenging category of film. It is against this background that Korine has emerged as a potentially subversive voice in alternative American cinema. Through works such as *Gummo* and *julien donkey-boy*, Korine reveals his films to be multilayered visual experiences whose experimental value is matched by their grotesque shock value. For Halligan, it is the director's use of such strategies that prevent his easy assimilation into the contemporary Hollywood version of 'underground'. If Korine's position makes him essentially a 'foreigner' to the dominant American scene, this in part explains why his films are so dominated by similarly 'outside' (i.e. European) influences. Halligan explores these possible precursors to Korine's work via reference to the New German Cinema of the 1970s, noting that directors such as Werner Herzog remain a source of reference to the style of *Gummo* as well as being directly cast in *julien donkey-boy*. For the author, both directors present an environment where contradiction and incongruity overwhelm any drive towards unity and consensus. Both directors also share a penchant for depicting states of the insane and the illogical, which carry as much narrative weight as any grand gestures or dominating world-view. In the case of Korine, this cinematic mismatch is seen in a dichotomy between content (which typically explores the white trash underbelly of American culture) and form (where the unity of the cinematic image is reduced to chaos via the constant overloading with differing mediums of visual representation). According to Halligan, these features result in Korine's work being viewed as a near unintelligible visual language, one whose distortions and deviations act as a corrective to Hollywood's 'Neo-Underground'.

Whereas Halligan holds up *American Beauty* as an example of the conservative nature of the neo-underground, Annalee Newitz offers an alternative reading of this film's importance in her article 'Underground America 1999'. Here, Newitz focuses on two recent pictures, both of which she claims are 'underground', albeit in very different senses of the term: the Hollywood-produced Academy Award-winner *American Beauty* and the independent sleeper hit *The Blair Witch Project*. While holding that *American Beauty* offers a truly subversive vision of US social life, Newitz argues that *The Blair Witch Project* effectively masks its political conservatism under the veneer of stylistic innovation. In her view, *American Beauty*, 'while ... saturated with typical Hollywood flourishes ... nevertheless comes down on the side of "freaks".' *The Blair Witch Project*, in contrast, 'might be a hopeful sign for a flagging independent film scene, in that it has truly been a word-of-mouth sensation, but its content is just a really riveting update on the same old horror movie fears about gender, Satan and rural culture'.

Although the focus of her essay is very different from other contributors to this collection, Sara Gwenllian Jones is also concerned with questioning and ultimately problematising any conception of the cinematic underground as standing in opposition to mainstream filmmaking practices. In 'Phantom Menace: Killer Fans, Consumer Activism and Digital Filmmakers', Jones discusses the example of cel-animation archivist Kevin Rubio's *Cops*-influenced, digitally-produced *Star Wars* spoof *Troops*. The author's case study is used to buttress her argument that 'the interplay between "fans" who produce films, film-producers who are "fans", the ... domestic cultural production between so-called "underground" movements and the so-called mainstream is ... far more complex' than many critics and filmmakers would admit. Jones therefore takes issue with contemporary cultural theory's belief that 'fandom *per se* is the domain of disaffected and marginalised individuals and groups who scavenge for crumbs in the outer reaches of commercial culture'. She illustrates how, in the case of Rubio, a fan 'response' text was strategically made and marketed so as to capture Hollywood's attention and interest.

While many contributors to this volume focus on 'alternative' auteurs, icons or representations, Jack Stevenson considers the crucial issue of independent distribution and exhibition strategies in his article 'Film Co-ops: Old Soldiers From the Sixties Still Standing Against Hollywood Commercialism'. Here, Stevenson contextualises the current signs of underground activity (such as the independent and 'queer' festival scene) against the 1960s formation of film co-ops emerging from the New American Cinema Group. In their polemical nine-point manifesto, the group (whose high-profile members included Emile De Antonio) rejected what they saw as the 'polished' and essentially false nature of Hollywood output. Importantly, the issues of distribution and exhibition were central features of the group's cinematic call to arms. It resulted in the 1961 formation of the New York Filmmakers Co-op, whose aims and influence Stevenson outlines in detail. The formation of this body (and the other associated American and British organisations the author discusses) resulted in a crucial public exposure for those movies deemed too non-narrative or nonsensical to reach mainstream movie houses. The importance of the co-ops can be measured by the fact that underground notables such as John Waters, Paul Morrissey and Paul Bartel were attracted to their ranks. The co-ops also gave crucial exposure to short works and cine-experimentations during a volatile period when the 16mm camera functioned as 'a weapon of provocation and subversion'. Stevenson laments the loss of this vibrant scene in a contemporary film culture that finds film co-ops unable to economically sustain themselves, and in which the term 'independent production' is used mainly to indicate a Hollywood dry run. The author's sentiments are all the more marked due to the sudden closure of one the organisations under review, soon after his article was submitted.

While the 1960s was a period in which film co-ops re-wrote the processes of independent exhibition, it was also the era in which maverick director Herschell Gordon Lewis revolutionised underground American horror. In the interview 'Gouts of Blood: The Colourful Underground Universe of Herschell Gordon Lewis', the director recounts how he gained notoriety (and the label of the 'Godfather of Gore') via a series of lurid and gory productions such as *Blood Feast, 2000 Maniacs* and *The Gore-Gore Girls*. These films were infamous for their gruesome scenes depicting male exotic caterers and lethal country bumpkins eager to dispatch those who stumble upon their activities. Beyond their blood-red construction and obvious shock value, Lewis' films gained merit for their frenzied image tracks, surreal silent cinema influences and experimental soundtracks which the director frequently scored and performed himself. Through his long association with exploitation producer David F. Friedman, Lewis sought to construct a horror Hollywood outside the control of established movie moguls. This resulted in him functioning as a pivotal figure able to work closely with other notable exploitation and independent filmmakers of the era, as well being a director whose influence is still felt in contemporary movie-making circles. In this exclusive interview conducted in its entirety for *Underground U.S.A.*, Lewis talks to Xavier Mendik about his colourful cult universe, the influences on his film style and structure, and current trends in underground horror cinema.

In the 1985 issue of *The Underground Film Bulletin*, edited by Nick Zedd (under the pseudonym Orion Jeriko) – founding member and still-denizen of Manhattan's Lower East Side post-punk film underground – there appeared the 'Cinema of Transgression Manifesto'. Its declaration began with the line, 'We who have violated the laws, commands and duties of the avant-garde; i.e. to bore, tranquillise and obfuscate through a fluke process dictated by practical convenience, stand guilty as charged.' This calculatingly provocative statement of purpose and passion resulted in increased media coverage (and potential distribution) for such New York underground filmmakers as Kembra Pfahler, Beth B, Richard Kern and Zedd himself, as well as for sometime-associates Jon Moritsugo, Jeri Cain Rossi and others. In his 'Theory of Xenomorphosis', Zedd offers yet another reconceptualisation of the underground in terms of a *breakdown* (rather than a construction or maintenance) of neat and simple, ideologically motivated cultural oppositions. Defined as 'the process through which negation of the fraudulent values, institutions, mores, and taboos of consensus reality is accomplished', xenomorphosis is a cinematically achieved 'neurological re-engineering' whereby 'the life/death, win/lose, right/wrong dichotomy imposed by the dominant hierarchy is revealed to the … mind as a false equation. This false dichotomy is the method by which social control is maintained.'

When held up against the self-proclaimed underground and transgressive cinema movements of the late 1970s and 1980s through to today, the avant-garde-influenced New York City underground of the 1960s can seem positively tame, though no less personal or creative, by comparison. In his short piece, 'Visions of New York: Films From the 1960s Underground', David Schwartz emphasises the historical if not conceptual truth of the very oppositions challenged by so many of the contributors to this volume. It was by 'rejecting the factory-style artifice of Hollywood films, whose worlds were literally built from scratch on empty soundstages', that underground filmmakers of the period – Ken Jacobs, Ernie Gehr, Andy Warhol, George and Mike Kuchar, Jack Smith, *et al.* – 'found their reality in the world around them. The city's buildings and streets became a vast impromptu studio in which personal, idiosyncratic movies were made – movies as eclectic and varied as the city itself'. However, in contrasting the distinctive and culturally-specific New York film underground of the 1960s with the contemporary independent film scene, Schwartz too may be read as arguing on behalf of a fresh, more complex understanding of underground cinema in the United States today.

No collection of writings devoted to the radical and heterogenous practices of American underground filmmaking would be complete without some consideration of the improbable, unforgettable productions of John Waters on the one hand, and Lloyd Kaufman's Troma Studios on the other. In the final contribution to this volume, Xavier Mendik and Steven Jay Schneider investigate what can only be considered the 'anti-aethestic' sensibilities of both these underground icons. 'A Tasteless Art: Waters, Troma and the Pursuit of "Pure" Gross-Out' applies the lessons of such cultural theorists and philosophers of art as Mikhail Bakhtin, Noël Carroll and William Paul to Waters' most notorious 1970s films, notably *Pink Flamingos* and *Desperate Living*, as well as to Troma's shockingly successful *Toxic Avenger* series. Contrasting the construction and presentation of disgusting depictions in these films with their tamer, more generically-situated Hollywood counterparts, Mendik and Schneider suggest that 'the difference between underground and mainstream cinematic gross-out [may be] not just a matter of *degree* but rather a matter of *kind*.' For Mendik and Schneider, the work of both directors proves distasteful because its draws on notions of the carnivalesque, grotesque body that Bakhtin studied in popular activities and marginal forms. It is not merely the fact that both Waters and Kaufman focus on an excess of physical abnormality and 'gross-out' bodily acts that makes their work of interest. Rather, it is the fact that these unruly images are presented in narrative forms that parody the norms, ideals and values associated with the American dream. This leads Mendik and Schneider to conclude that the grotesque works of such directors exist as a 'pure' (rather than hybridised or qualified) gross-out genre, one which bears an essential connection to the aesthetics and practices of underground filmmaking.

The articles presented in this book thus investigate the phenomenon of American underground cinema from a variety of perspectives, as well as incorporating filmmakers' commentaries and exhibition strategies alongside 'traditional' academic approaches. In this respect, *Underground U.S.A.* represents part of a larger examination of global cult and popular cinema currently being undertaken at the Cult Film Archive at University College Northampton, UK, which will be published regularly through the *AlterImage* book series.

Since its inception in 2000, the Cult Film Archive has rapidly grown to become an established research centre, as well as a venue with an international reputation. From the outset, the Archive has sought to develop a critical understanding of cult, trash and underground film and its audiences for both academic and commercial projects. This is central to the Archive's belief that, while trash can be taken seriously, cult and exploitation cinema requires a multiplicity of interpretations that combine 'traditional' academic thought alongside an appreciation of production practices and subsequent interpretations by differing fan and user groups. This philosophy of integrating academic with critical and fan-based approaches to cult and 'marginal' film forms has proven a key feature in the rapid and successful growth of the Archive, to the extent that it now enjoys important links with key academic and commercial film organisations (both nationally and internationally). In terms of its commercial links, the Archive enjoys a longstanding relationship with the leading UK television production companies, including OPI Media, (who currently produce Channel 5's cult film series *OutThere*). The growing reputation of the Cult Film Archive has also meant that its staff have been able to draw upon exclusive interviews with key cult filmmakers. These have included Paul Verhoeven, Nic Roeg, Brian Yuzna, Alex Cox, Lloyd Kaufman, Jesus Franco, Jean Rollin, Herschell Gordon Lewis and Takishi Miike, and transcriptions of this work will be available in future volumes of the *AlterImage* series.

From the outset, the Archive's mission has been to promote its research via a credible academic publisher, and this is facilitated through the long-term association we have with Wallflower Press and the *AlterImage* series. This series reiterates the Archive's objective of integrating theoretical with critical and production accounts of cult film and its audiences. Each edition of *AlterImage* will be themed and contain 12–15 key academic articles alongside shorter critical accounts and interviews with cult filmmakers and exhibitors. Further details on future editions of the book series are available from both the editors and the publisher.

CHAPTER ONE
'NO WORSE THAN YOU WERE BEFORE':
THEORY, ECONOMY AND POWER IN ABEL FERRARA'S
'THE ADDICTION'

Joan Hawkins

Abel Ferrara occupies an unusual niche within the American underground. Although the edge of his work has continually appealed to downtown underground audiences (he is something of a hero at San Francisco's Roxy Theater, for example) he has also garnered more mainstream acceptance than the other underground filmmakers to whom he is frequently compared in the alternative press (Nick Zedd, Amos Poe *et al.*). For this reason, his work – or at least its reception – highlights many of the tensions surrounding the dividing line between avant-garde, underground film and the cinema derisively labelled 'indiewood' by downtown cinema fans.

The Addiction (1995) stands as something of an interesting anomaly in Ferrara's oeuvre. A vampire film peppered with references to Nietzsche, Beckett, the My Lai massacre and Burroughs, the film seemed tailor-made to appeal to both an underground and a mainstream audience. But, as Xavier Mendik points out:

Mainstream critical reaction to *The Addiction* was at best mixed. Although writers such as Gavin Smith [*Sight and Sound*] praised the complex nature of the film's construction and style, the narrative's continual shift from scenes of excess 'necking' to narrations on Nietzsche frequently lead to claims that it was both pretentious and greatly distilled its reading of European philosophy.[1]

While the much tamer *Wolf* (Mike Nichols, 1994) was praised in the mainstream press for its implicit critique of corporate downsizing and capitalist greed, *The Addiction*'s explicit retooling of vampirism as another example of Burroughs' junk pyramid did not elicit the critical commentary it deserved.

The film that should have cemented Ferrara's status with both mainstream 'independent' and underground audiences, then, had the reverse effect of solidifying his status as a primarily underground director. The very things that made *The Addiction* a difficult viewing experience for mainstream critics endeared it to underground audiences. As Tom Charity notes:

> This is one wild, weird, wired movie, the kind that really shouldn't be seen before midnight. … Shot in b/w, with an effectively murky jungle/funk/rap score, this is the vampire movie we've been waiting for: a reactionary urban-horror flick that truly has the ailing pulse of the time. AIDS and drug addiction are points of reference, but they're symptoms, not the cause. … Scary, funny, magnificently risible, this could be the most pretentious B-movie ever – and I mean that as a compliment.[2]

In this essay, I plan to discuss the significance of *The Addiction*'s success as an underground film and to analyse the way it retools vampirism as addiction, economy and power. As the subtitle indicates, I am particularly interested in the way the film uses theory to get its point across. Because of its 'narrations on Nietzsche', *The Addiction* belongs to a growing body of underground work which I have described elsewhere as 'theoretical fictions', the kind of fiction in which 'theory becomes an intrinsic part of the "plot", a mover and shaker in the fictional universe created by the author'.[3]

It is the prominent position of theory in *The Addiction* which made reviewers on opposing sides of the cultural divide label the film as 'pretentious' (a word that took on both derisive and celebratory nuances, depending on the user's cultural point of reference). It is the prominent position within the film of a theoretical discourse that intellectuals critiqued (for greatly distilling a reading of European philosophy) which problematises some of the assumptions that academics tend to make about the cultural uses of theory itself. Like Charity, I think this is 'one wild, weird, wired movie,' the vampire movie underground audiences have been waiting for. I hope in this article to demonstrate why.

THE TROPE OF ADDICTION

The film begins with a philosophy lecture on the My Lai massacre – a series of atrocity slides with a voiceover explaining when the attack occurred, what happened in that place and the nature of US national reaction to the horror. As Kathleen (Lili Taylor) and her friend Jean (Edie Falco) leave the lecture, they discuss the central moral problem which the My Lai trial of Lt. Calley seems to illustrate. That is: how can you hold one man responsible for the crimes and guilt of an entire nation, and how do you separate what happened at My Lai from what happened during the rest of the Vietnam War? 'What do you want me to say?' Jean asks Kathleen. 'The system's not perfect.' As Kathleen leaves her friend, she encounters a woman dressed in an evening gown ('Casanova', played by Annabella Sciorra), a real vamp who drags her into a subway station and bites her neck.

There is a certain grim logic in going from one kind of bloodlust (war crimes) to another (vampirism) here. And there is a way in which the hunger for blood – in all its manifestations – is disturbingly figured in the film as addiction. Throughout the movie, Kathleen keeps returning to images of atrocity – an exhibition of Holocaust photographs, documentary footage of a massacre on the evening news. In part, this continual return serves to remind us of the ethical questions posed at the beginning of the film. Who exactly is responsible for this constant replay of inhumane violence and brutality? To what extent are we all complicit in a world system which seems to need blood as much as vampires do? But, as the last question suggests, Kathleen's continual return to a kind of 'primal scene' of historic atrocity also serves to link war crimes – crimes against humanity – to a trope of physical dependency and sickness, vampirism. 'Our addiction is evil,' Kathleen says at one point, meaning that our addiction is *to* evil, as well as being evil in and of itself. 'The propensity for this evil lies in our weakness before it,' she continues. 'You reach a point where you are forced to face your own needs and the fact that you can't terminate the situation settles on you with full force.'

If war crimes are linked to vampirism and addiction, blood itself is continually linked to junk. This is most clearly manifest in Kathleen's emerging vampiric 'hunger', as the need for a 'fix' makes her physically ill and as the lines between the substances of blood and narcotics are continually blurred. Kathleen's first 'fix' is literally that – a fix. Walking down the street, she sees a junkie with a needle still in his arm. She draws blood up into the syringe, and once home shoots this blood-drug mix into her vein. Later, she initiates her graduate advisor into vampirism by seducing him first with drugs. Inviting him to her apartment, she kisses him and then disappears into the kitchen to fix 'drinks'. What she brings out, however, is a tray with two syringes, a candle and a spoon. 'Dependency is a wonderful thing,' she tells him. 'It does more for the soul than any formulation of doctoral material. Indulge me.' It is only later, after he has succumbed to one potentially addictive substance, that she takes a bite out of his neck and turns him into a vampire. And Peina (Christopher Walken),

15

FIGURE 3 Kathleen gets a fix in *The Addiction*

the vampire 'guide' Kathleen encounters in the street, continually conflates the language of blood with that of drugs. He mixes terms like 'fasting' with 'shooting up' to describe his attempts to control 'the hunger', and pointedly asks Kathleen if she has read William S. Burroughs' *Naked Lunch*.

The repeated commingling of blood and junk, as well as the direct reference to *Naked Lunch*, invites the viewer to 'read' vampirism in *The Addiction* as yet another example of Burroughs' 'Algebra of Need'. In the Preface to *Naked Lunch*, Burroughs draws a picture of what he terms the 'junk pyramid', in which the traffic in heroin – and here, blood – becomes the distilled model of the entire capitalist system. The idea is to 'hook' the consumer on a product that s/he does not initially need, in the secure knowledge that once hooked the buyer will return for ever-increasing doses. Burroughs writes:

I have seen the exact manner in which the junk virus operates through fifteen years of addiction. The pyramid of junk, one level eating the level below (it is no accident that junk higher-ups are always fat and the addict in the street is always thin) right up to the top or tops since there are many junk pyramids feeding on the peoples of the world and all built on the basic principles of monopoly: 1) Never give anything away for nothing;   2) Never give more than you have to give (always catch the buyer hungry and always make him wait); 3) Always take everything back if you possibly can. The Pusher always gets it all back. The addict needs more and more junk to maintain a human form … buy off the Monkey.[4]

The analogy which Burroughs draws between addiction, capitalism, evil and power in *Naked Lunch* is drawn in *The Addiction* as well. Like many US urban universities, the university which Kathleen and Jean attend is located in the heart of what we euphemistically call the 'inner city' (the film was shot in and around New York University's Washington Square, before it was 'cleaned up'). An enclave of privilege, it is surrounded by streets that stand – as Robert Siegle points out – 'as one of the most potent demystifiers of the illusions in which most of us live'.[5] The economy here is based, it seems, on junk. The first time we see Kathleen walk down the street, young men approach her, hoping she will buy, and 'I want to get high, so high' plays on the soundtrack. It is in these mean streets that Kathleen is first accosted and then turned into a vampire, and it is to this neighbourhood – as well as to the University itself – that she continually returns, looking for blood.

The geographic construction of Ferrara's New York is a junk pyramid, then, with the higher-up 'pushers' – those who push knowledge and a certain ideology – living off the addicts in the street. In case we do not get the economic/class point, Ferrara includes a doctoral dissertation defence party that plays like some vampiric reworking of May 1968, where the working class and student hordes rise up to attack the power elite. After successfully defending her doctoral thesis, Kathleen invites the faculty to a small gathering at her home. There, the loose coalition of vampire students, street people and one 're-formed' graduate advisor, stage a blood bath – as they gorge themselves on professors and 'unturned' students. The class barriers between the University and the streets break down as soon as the underclass unmasks itself at Kathleen's party, and begins drawing blood.

The subsequent vampire banquet is both a revolt and a final levelling of class structure. 'The face of "evil",' Burroughs writes, 'is the face of total need.'[6] One of the disturbing things about this film is its insistence that reducing everyone to the 'total need' level of the addict on the street is a necessary precursor to meaningful sociopolitical, economic change. As Peina darkly tells Kathleen, the first step toward finding out what we really are is to learn 'what Hunger is.'

THE WILL TO POWER

If blood/junk 'is the mould of monopoly and possession', as Burroughs asserts in *Naked Lunch*,[7] it is also – as Allen Ginsberg testified at the *Naked Lunch* trial – 'a model for … addiction to power or addiction to controlling other people by having power over them.'[8] In *The Addiction,* Ferrara makes this explicit by substituting tropes of domination for the traditional vampiric trope of seduction. 'It makes no difference what I do, whether I draw blood or not,' Kathleen thinks as she gets ready for a vamp-date with her thesis advisor. 'It's the violence of my will against theirs.' The fascistic nature of vampirism is hammered home early in the film with the pointed use of a sound bridge. In a key scene shortly after she has been bitten, Kathleen goes to an exhibit of Holocaust photographs at the University Museum with her friend Jean. A speech by Hitler plays in the background. In the next shot, Kathleen is slumped on the floor of her apartment – in a posture we have come to associate with her vampiric sickness. We still hear Hitler's voice, echoing now, it seems, in her head. In the next shot, she is on the street, looking for blood.

While vampirism is cinematically linked to a Nietzschean 'will to power', the vampiric attack itself is figured as existential drama. Most vampiric encounters in *The Addiction* begin with a pointed invocation of individual responsibility. 'Look at me and tell me to go away,' the vampire tells the victim. 'Don't ask, tell me.' And when the victim – overcome and traumatised by the violence of the unexpected attack – *asks* the vampire to leave her (usually her) alone, the vampire is quick to assign blame. 'What the hell were you thinking?' Kathleen asks an anthropology student. 'Why didn't you tell me to get lost like you really meant it?' When Kathleen herself is first bitten by Casanova, she is called a 'fucking coward' and 'collaborator'.

The question of who bears responsibility for the vampiric attack mirrors the ethical questions surrounding the prosecution of Lt. Calley, raised in the opening scenes of the film. Only here it is not the entire nation that stands culpable for war crimes, but the victim herself – the 'fucking coward', the 'collaborator' – who is somehow responsible for her own victimisation. The fact that so many of these victims are women and that they are seemingly punished for being too polite, too nice, too passive, only adds to the discomfort that many viewers experience watching a movie which – in the words of J. Hoberman – 'insists on blaming the victim.'[9]

Furthermore, there are the recurring shots of atrocity photos within the film itself – shots of the My Lai massacre, the Holocaust, Bosnia – which only serve to increase the ethical stakes of raising the responsibility question at all. Are *these* victims, too, responsible for what happened to them? Were they too nice, too passive in the face of American/German/Serb aggression? In the face of such horrific brutality, does it even make sense to ask who is responsible, who holds the moral high ground?

Yet the film consistently does invite us to ask the question. The ongoing philosophical quarrel in the film – raised repeatedly by different characters – is the old quarrel between determinism and existentialism, the old dilemma governing the kind of guilt we choose to embrace. Are we evil because of the evil we do, or do we do evil because we are, in the last analysis, evil? In the universe of the film, the constant presence of evil is the only issue on which all Western philosophers seem to agree. Before biting Jean, for example, Kathleen pointedly sets an impossible philosophical task: 'Prove there's no evil and you can go.'

What made so many critics and reviewers uncomfortable about watching this film, then, is precisely what was *supposed* to make them feel uncomfortable. *The Addiction* mounts what Avital Ronell has called a 'narcoanalysis' of society, that is, a mode of analysis in which 'substance abuse' and 'addiction' name 'the structure that is philosophically and metaphysically at the basis of our culture.'[10] 'Addiction,' Ronell writes, 'has everything to do with the bad conscience of our era.'[11] To get the point of Ferrara's film, one need only add 'vampirism' to 'addiction' in the above quote.

THE STATUS OF THEORY

As most critics note, theory and theoretical discourse are a heavy presence in the film. This is usually credited to the fact that Kathleen is a philosophy graduate student and that much of the film is set in academe. What is interesting, however, is that Kathleen does not really start speaking theoryspeak until *after* she has been bitten. When she discusses Lt. Calley's case with her friend and fellow graduate student, Jean, in the opening sequences of the movie, she formulates questions using much the same language that any savvy watcher of the six o'clock news might use:

> The whole country, they were all guilty. How can you single out one man? How did he get over there? Who put the gun in his hand? They say he was guilty of killing women and babies. How many bombs were dropped that did the exact same thing?

Once bitten, however, her manner of speaking begins to change. When she runs into Jean after her long absence from school, Jean asks if the infirmary gave her 'something to take'. 'Medicine's just an extended metaphor for omnipotence,' Kathleen answers. 'They gave me antibiotics.' In fact, in this film the emergence of theoryspeak becomes another sign that someone is 'turning'; like loss of appetite and aversion to sunlight, it is a sign that the vampire virus is at work.

Like any sickness or physical addiction, the vampire virus plunges Kathleen into an awareness of the absolute materiality of the body. Soon after she has been bitten, she has to leave a philosophy lecture on determinism and rush to the bathroom, where she vomits blood. After she is released from the infirmary she begins to question the wisdom of doing a dissertation on philosophers who 'are all liars'. 'Let them rot with cancer,' she tells Jean, 'and we'll see what they have to say about free will.' The emergence of theoryspeak, then, seems to coincide with an awareness of mortality, of the absolute materiality of life. This is perhaps odd in a film that is also so resolutely and unabashedly metaphysical. But it foreshadows one of the important distinctions that the film insists on making between 'academic' philosophy and the theoryspeak of real life.

There are two textual canons which are given to Kathleen in the course of the film. The first is, of course, the reading list for her philosophy seminar: Sartre's *Being and Nothingness,* Heidegger's *Being and Time*, Husserl, Kierkegaard's *Sickness Unto Death*, Nietzsche's *Will to Power.* The list always gets a laugh from the audience, since the titles seem to play like double entendres – a further indication of the ways in which vampirism is categorically linked to existential despair ('sickness unto death') as the key sickness-metaphor of the time. This canon is not much use to Kathleen, however, as she tries to manage living-with-vampirism. So, she is in pretty bad shape when she meets Peina, who tries to teach her how to control the hunger.

Kathleen's encounter with Peina is one of the crucial episodes of the film and central to their interaction is the fact that Peina operates according to a canonical logic of substitution and contamination. That is, Peina provides both an alternative canon and a deconstructive means for reading the old one. 'Have you read *Naked Lunch*?' Peina asks Kathleen early in their encounter. 'Burroughs perfectly describes what it's like to go without a fix.' Later he tells her again: 'Read the books. Sartre, Beckett. Who do you think they're talking about? You think they're works of fiction? "I felt the wind of the wings of madness" – Baudelaire.' He also cites Nietzsche. 'You think Nietzsche understood something? Mankind has striven to exist beyond good and evil from the beginning. You know what they found? Me.' This is the vampire who will later drain Kathleen dry in order to teach her about pain and reveal her true nature.

With the exception of Sartre and Nietzsche, who appear on Kathleen's philosophy seminar syllabus, the works in Peina's canon are associated with literature; all the texts he mentions are works that have been privileged by those who 'do' theory – Kristeva, Cixous, Derrida, Ronell. Here, they emerge not only as key texts for Kathleen's survival ('Who do you think they're talking about? You think they're works of fiction?'), but as key texts for 'reading' philosophy. It is after her encounter with Peina that Kathleen begins serious work on her dissertation, which seeks to reposition the philosopher him/herself in the text. 'Philosophy is propaganda,' she tells her dissertation committee:

> There is always the attempt to influence the object. The real question is what is the philosopher's impact on other egos. ... Essence is revealed through praxis. The philosopher's words, his ideas, his actions cannot be separated from his value, his meaning. That's what it's all about, isn't it? Our impact on other egos.

Kathleen's dissertation comes down, then, on the side of existentialism ('essence is revealed through praxis'), which she insists on reading through a vampiro-theoretical lens ('philosophy is propaganda'). More importantly, however, the fact that she writes the dissertation after her encounter with Peina – an encounter which marks her painful initiation into theory and into learning the nature of the hunger – recalls the link between drugs (addiction) and writing that Derrida sees in the *pharmakon*. Certainly the writing pours out of her at this point, as she tries to deal with 'a metaphysical burden and a history' which, Derrida tells us, 'we must never stop questioning'.[12]

As even this sketchy outline will show, Ferrara does not supply the viewer with a neat theoretical package, a logical argument leading to one final conclusion. Given the often contradictory discursive theoretical registers invoked during the course of the film, it is easy to see why academics disliked what they saw as a reductive reading of European philosophy and theory. And just as easy to see why people with no theoretical background at all might find the film 'pretentious' or confusing. But the very split which the film posits – the split between academic philosophy and a kind of savvy streetwise theory (where the real teachers emerge from the shadows) – is reflected in the reception the film received from underground, as opposed to academic, audiences. In fact, *The Addiction*'s positive reception as an underground film problematises some of the assumptions that academics tend to make about the cultural uses of theory itself.

A quick glance at alternative culture productions and publications (*Bomb, CTheory*, and the *Frameworks Online Experimental Filmmakers* listserv, for example) reveals that many of the distinctions academics routinely make between academic discourse (particularly theoretical discourse) and 'lay' discourse are problematic. People outside the academy read theory and they use it as an intrinsic part of their work – they do not always read it the same way academics do, and they certainly use it differently, but the received wisdom that only academics can understand theoretical language or concepts simply is not true.

To take one example, there are strong connections between poststructuralist theory and techno/electronic music. DJ Spooky – an African-American spin master whose real name is Paul Miller – has done gigs with Baudrillard, for example, and talks about DJing as a mode of deconstruction. One of the German labels that regularly records American DJs is called *Mille Plateaus*; it was specifically named after the famous work by Deleuze and Guattari – and one of its best selling compilation CDs is a memoriam for Gilles Deleuze.[13]

Within the experimental work of late twentieth-century culture there is a whole cultural formation that deals with theory in ways that mean we are ultimately going to have to redefine what we call theory – what counts as theory. There are a lot of works – literary, artistic, musical and cinematic/video – that I am beginning to call 'theoretical art'. It is the audience for particularly this kind of underground theoretical culture which responded so positively to Ferrara's film – who laughed out loud at the funniest academic pretences of *The Addiction* and did not find its theoretical contradictions disturbing at all.

REDEMPTION OR THE SEVENTH CIRCLE

The end of *The Addiction* is notoriously hard to read. It does not follow the formulaic folklore pattern that Carol Clover ascribes to most contemporary horror; that is, it does not seem to restore order.[14] Or rather, it restores order, but it is difficult to say exactly what kind of order is being restored. In the words of one reviewer:

> After the grand guignol hilarity of a faculty party/bloodfeast, Ferrara has the guts to go for the jugular. The final scenes of *The Addiction* are religious in the most unforgiving sense of the word; once again, Ferrara writes as a soul doomed to redemption.[15]

Following the bloodfeast, Kathleen is sick from overeating. Stumbling down the street, smeared with blood, she is taken to a nearby Catholic hospital by a good Samaritan. Once admitted to a room, she asks the nurse to let her die. When the nurse assures her that nobody is going to let her die, Kathleen asks her caregiver to open the blinds and let in the sunlight.

So far, so good. This is classic vampire movie fare, where we expect to see the vampire go up in a puff of smoke (as Christopher Lee does at the end of Terence Fisher's 1958 film, *Horror of Dracula*). As soon as the nurse leaves, however, and Kathleen begins to pant and moan, the room suddenly darkens as the blinds quickly close. There is a cloud of smoke all right, but it is coming from Casanova's cigarette. 'The Seventh Circle, huh?' she asks Kathleen. 'Dante described it perfectly. Bleeding trees waiting for Judgement Day, when we can all hang ourselves from our own branches. It's not that easy.' Casanova leaves Kathleen's room; a few minutes later a priest enters. The credits reveal that this is Father Robert Castle, who also provides the voiceover narration for the My Lai sequence which opens the film. Father Castle hears Kathleen's confession (her acknowledgement of guilt and request for forgiveness). Shortly thereafter we see Kathleen's grave. A woman, dressed in lightly coloured slacks and blouse, her hair neatly pulled away from her face, is standing in front of the grave. It is Kathleen. She puts a flower on the gravesite. In voiceover narration, she says 'to face what we are in the end, we stand before the light and our true nature is revealed. Self revelation is annihilation of self.' She leaves the churchyard and the screen goes black. The credits roll.

On one level, this seems to be a nod to Brian De Palma's *Carrie* (1976), whose shock graveside ending established the pattern for many horror movies to come. Only here, the Final Girl who survives the school party-turned-bloodbath is not the altruistic good girl who encouraged her boyfriend to take the school's dowdy scapegoat to the prom. Rather, it is a reconstructed and resurrected vampire who appears to have finally learned, in Peina's words, to control the hunger, blend in and 'survive on a little'.

On another level, however, this scene is, as Peter Keough maintains, 'religious in the most unforgiving sense of the word.' Kathleen's assertion that 'self-revelation is annihilation of self' seems

FIGURE 4 Elegant evil: Casanova at the blood feast in *The Addiction*

a repudiation of the arguments she made during her dissertation defense: 'That's what it's all about, isn't it? Our impact on other egos.'

Here, by way of contrast, she seems to be moving toward the kind of Christian mysticism espoused by Simone Weil – a woman so dedicated to tearing down her ego that she literally starved to death. 'If the "I" is the only thing we truly own,' Weil wrote, 'we must destroy it. Use the "I" to tear down the "I".'[16] As if this were not already confusing enough, the music which plays on the soundtrack during this sequence is an instrumental piece, 'Eine Sylvesternacht' (a New Year's Eve Night), beautifully played by Joshua Bell and composed by the 'beyond good and evil' philosopher himself, Friedrich Nietzsche.

If the ending is perplexing, it is appropriate. One of the major stylistic aspects of *The Addiction* is its *trompe l'oeil* visuals, in which perspective – both historical/empirical and ethical – is repeatedly called into question. From the earliest shots in which we watch Kathleen watching, we are constantly challenged to think about perspective, to wonder whose point of view we are occupying and/or what exactly it is we are seeing. This emerges most pointedly in confusing or *trompe l'oeil* shots, the first of which occurs shortly before Kathleen encounters Casanova. As Kathleen walks down Bleecker Street, the screen goes black. Then we get what first appears to be a wipe, moving left to right. But there is a funny 'hook' at the bottom of the screen, the edge of a building, indicating that this is not a wipe, but a lateral tracking shot (right to left). Someone is coming from the shadows of a building, but who? Not Casanova, whom we see in long shot. Not Kathleen. This kind of Eye of God, point-of-view shot recurs several times during the course of the film, helping to visually establish a mystical/religious feel to the whole movie.

In addition, what appear initially to be unattributed associational shots/edits invite comparisons between vampirism and real brutality. This happens most frequently in the shots which show atrocity photographs. When Kathleen goes home with the anthropology student, for example, we see the women cross the street together. Then we get a shot of mutilated bodies. It takes a while before we realise that this is news coverage of Bosnia which Kathleen, blood still smeared on her lips, is watching on television – not a slaughter which she herself carried out.

Ferrara also repeatedly challenges traditional expectations of space. The scene during which Kathleen is working on her dissertation unravels as a lateral tracking journey through space and time. But here Kathleen seems to be literally butting heads with herself, as she appears frame left (facing right) in one shot and frame right (facing left) in the shot immediately following. Finally, Peina's loft is an impossibly ethereal space. At once tiny apartment and cavernous loft, it changes shape and dimension, depending on the framing of each shot (there is a curious shot in which words appear on a wall behind Kathleen, a shot which somehow simultaneously invokes an art gallery, church and street graffiti). It is also notable that it is hard to tell where exactly in the city Peina's loft is located; 'someplace dark', he tells Kathleen.

The fact that we are not continually exclaiming at these jumps and shifts, as we might during a Godard film, is a function of both the way we watch horror and of Ferrara's genius for *apparent* continuity. But it is a mistake to read the confusing nature of the film's end as somehow *different* from what came before. If this film is about anything, it is about the fact that – as Peina tells Kathleen – we are nothing, we know nothing; nothing, that is, except the fear of our own death.

It is interesting that the final 'word' of the movie – the song that plays on the soundtrack as the credits roll – takes us back to the opening sequences of the film (My Lai and our responsibility to and for the world). 'Eine Sylvesternacht' segues into a rap song about black-on-black violence, and the film ends with the vampire refrain 'forever is a long time'.

CONCLUSION

'Every age embraces the vampire it needs,' the book jacket copy for Nina Auerbach's *Our Vampires, Ourselves* proclaims.[17] This applies not only to ages, but also to subcultures within each age. For while it is true that *The Addiction* had 'the ailing pulse' of its time, as Tom Charity wrote, it is also true that it did not find popularity among a mainstream independent or horror niche market. Instead it drew its audience from the underground, from a subculture of viewers who were not put off by its peculiar drug-theory blend, or obtuse vocabulary, or pointed socio-economic commentary. And while it did not cement Ferrara's reputation with a mainstream 'indie' crowd, it did extend his fan base within the underground itself. *The Addiction* is an alt.film Goth lover's delight, and so patrons (particularly women) who had not been attracted to Ferrara's earlier work found him through this 'vampire tale told Ferrara style'.[18]

The film that should have cemented Ferrara's status with both mainstream independent and underground audiences, then, had the reverse effect of solidifying his status as a primarily underground director. But it also expanded his fan base within the underground, extending it beyond the audience for films like *Bad Lieutenant* (1992) to the audience for films like *Nadja* (Michael Almereyda, 1994) and the ever-popular *Night of the Living Dead* (George A. Romero, 1968). Its visually arresting style and 'wild weird wired' story confirmed Ferrara's reputation as 'one of contemporary American cinema's most challenging and consistently innovative underground directors'.[19] Finally, its 'narrations on Nietzsche' helped to situate Ferrara within a larger downtown artistic tradition ('theoretical fictions') that was already trading heavily on theory. For all these reasons, it has emerged as a key text in the history of contemporary underground US cinema. It is also, as I hope I have shown, a spectacular film. As Peina might say, 'See it. Read the books.'

Special thanks to Chris Dumas, Nicky Evans, Skip Hawkins, Xavier Mendik, Steven Schneider and the students in my graduate horror seminar (C592).

CHAPTER 2
RADLEY METZGER'S 'ELEGANT AROUSAL': TASTE, AESTHETIC DISTINCTION AND SEXPLOITATION

Elena Gorfinkel

Irena: Where've you been?

Lesley: Where've I been? Around the world in eighty ways, that's where.

The Alley Cats (1966)

It is now a commonplace to view the 1960s as marked by the public sphere's saturation with sexual representations. These were representations that had up until that time only circulated within underground, marginal viewing spaces. The debates which coalesced around this putatively pornographic visibility were concerned as much with questions of taste and the exceedingly blurred boundaries between art and obscenity as with the possible responses of an untrained 'low-brow' public to the products of savvy sexual entrepreneurs and 'smut peddlers'. One such place where the shift from underground to 'above ground' occurred was in the genres and cycles of the sexploitation film. Independent filmmakers such as Russ Meyer, Herschell Gordon Lewis, Doris Wishman, Michael and Roberta Findlay, Andy Milligan and many others produced profitable cycles of nudies, roughies and kinkies to capitalise on the inability of the courts to empirically define and legislate against obscenity.[1]

Marked by their low budgets, oppositional stance towards Hollywood, amateur (if not 'impoverished') aesthetics and 'crude' transcriptions of dystopian sexual fantasy, simulated violence and soft-core sex, sexploitation films provide a shadow history to the cultural and social events of the turbulent 1960s. As 'the capitalist impulse seized upon sexual desire as an unmet need that the marketplace could fill',[2] sexploitation films deployed a rhetoric of erotic consumption made prevalent in the public sphere of the 1960s.

The film work of Radley Metzger plays a significant role in the history of this independent mode of production. This is because it mediates between the high culture status of the foreign art film and the rough-hewn, low-cult material of the sexploitation feature. Metzger's work can be seen in terms of its attempts to dissociate from its sexploitation neighbours through a process of cultural distinction, mapping the move from underground to aboveground along an axis of sexual, and cinephile, taste. Shot in Europe with European actors on lavish and 'cultured' locations, Metzger's cinema of the 1960s attempted to school its public in the erotic pedagogy of continental life.

Bringing 'art-house' legitimacy to the economic and narrative degradations of the American sexploitation film industry were films such as *The Dirty Girls* (1964), *The Alley Cats* (1966), *Carmen Baby* (1967), *Therese and Isabelle* (1967), *Camille 2000* (1969), *The Lickerish Quartet* (1970) and *Score* (1972). With these works, the director introduced a component of market segmentation into the field of erotic consumption. Metzger's talent as a 'creative distributor' facilitated the importing of European films with sexually suggestive content – films such as the infamously auto-erotic *I, A Woman* (1966), as well as *The Fourth Sex* (1961), *The Twilight Girls* (1956), *Sexus* (1964), *The Frightened Woman* (1968) and *The Libertine* (1969) – to American theatres.

HISTORY, INDUSTRY, RECEPTION

Metzger began his career in films as an editor, with a brief stint as a film censor, cutting out offensive footage from *Bitter Rice* (1948) for RKO. He moved on to editing and making trailers at Janus Films, a major distributor of European art cinema. European films had garnered a substantial audience in American cities in the late 1940s and early 1950s in the emergent exhibition context of the art-house theatre.[3] After making the relatively unsuccessful film *Dark Odyssey* (1959), about Greek immigrants in New York City, Metzger decided to start a distribution company with Janus co-worker Ava Leighton, which they named Audubon Films. The 1960s began with the buying of US rights to risqué European films, repackaging them – via dubbing, liberal editing and sensational ad campaigns – before distributing them in art-houses in urban and suburban locales. The Danish *I, A Woman* (1966), directed by Mac Ahlberg, concerning the unsatisfied and auto-erotic desire of a young woman played by Essy Persson, was the most successful and notorious of these imports. It was credited with expanding the contexts in which erotic films could be screened in the United States, prior to Vilgot Sjoman's controversial *I am Curious [Yellow]* (1969). Exemplary of the Audubon art-porn hybrid aesthetic, *I, A Woman* was seen to 'break down the distinction between sex-violence films and conventional films'.[4] This breaking of barriers came at a price, as Metzger's soft-core films can be understood as setting the scene for the emergent circumstances of hard-core 'porno-chic' in the early 1970s by validating, for audiences, the exhibition of sexual content in more conventional theatres.

In the mid- to late 1960s, when the availability of European product dried up due to more stringent censorship codes established in Europe, Metzger, while still importing films, shifted gear and began filming his own features in extravagant continental settings such as mansions, castles and swish European apartments, with cast and crews culled from other European productions. Renowned cinematographer Hans Jura worked with Metzger on a number of films, including *Therese and Isabelle* and *The Alley Cats*, giving the films a glossy aesthetic which utilised processes as Ultrascope and 3 strip Technicolor. As the decade progressed, Metzger's budgets grew larger, from five to six figure sums. As a result, his features took up the florid and modern excesses of 1960s fashion via set design and costume to impart a polished and streamlined look to his filmic locations and his characters' upper-class lifestyles. Many of the films were adapted from novels, short stories and plays, according to Metzger a compensation for his lack of skills as a storyteller.[5] *Score*, filmed in 1972, was the bridge between Metzger's soft-core and hard-core product, the latter directed under the pseudonym of Henry Paris.

Metzger's studied cinephilia, garnered from years of his editing work, film viewing and childhood bouts in the summer air conditioning of New York City movie theatres, found an apt object in the aesthetic and editorial construction of his films. The logic of the cut, a mark of the censors classification and judgement as well as of the manipulation of flow, movement and economies of visual desire, defined the cinema of Metzger in both his authored and 'curated' projects. Metzger himself claimed, in allegiance with the marketing angle, 'I'm never going to make a shot that I couldn't use in the trailer. And I think that rule gives the scenes an intrinsic movement.'[6]

This stylistic and conceptual synthesis of the commodity status of the cinema with its new cultural value as art, not only exemplifies the ethos of the sexploitation film, but also speaks to the particular predicament of the American cinema at the crossroads of the 1960s. Specifically, one granted free speech protection by the 1952 *Miracle* case, and capable of enlightenment, yet still bound to the travails of the free market.[7] The film trailer, the lynchpin of the sexploitation industry's appeals to its audience and mode of address, held the key to the experience of sexually explicit films, as one of condensation. Vincent Canby noted that 'exhibitors of these film find that the trailers advertising their coming attractions are as eagerly awaited as the feature films. On one Monday night, a Manhattan sex-violence house devoted no fewer than 20 minutes to its trailers for future films.'[8]

28

We can look at one of Metzger's own trailers to see their effectiveness in condensing a cinematic experience and promising pleasures ahead. In the trailer for *The Alley Cats*, Metzger's editing style – reused in the *Camille 2000* trailer – stacks a series of quickly-cut freeze frames from the film in a synchronised crescendo, a movement which is arrested by the intruding flow of the moving image. This stop and start method, in which sexual scenarios are catalogued and archived as cinephilic moments or screen memories of auratic female sexuality, stilled and put in motion, reveals all of the narrative and spectacular trajectories of the film itself. The condensation of sexual action, and the condensation of the action of the film into a commodity form, itself enacts a certain mnemonic function at the same time that it provides promise of a future ahead of it, of footage that will exceed what has been shown. The finale, which zooms in staggered fashion on main character Leslie's (Anne Arthur) face and parted mouth, with moaning voiceover, seems to presage the facial displacements of the hard-core genre that would soon follow. Signaling a kind of completion in the aural acquisition of female orgasm, the double play on 'COMING!' and 'COMING ATTRACTIONS' performs a textual joke on the structure of the trailer itself and the temporal structure of viewer desire. Metzger's success can thus be partly attributed to his creative and skillful workings of the art-erotica hybrid in all arenas of film production, promotion and distribution.

The lesson of the economic success of independents such as Metzger and the lesser-budgeted sexploitation mavericks was not lost on the major Hollywood studios. In an attempt to alleviate its economic slump, Hollywood began to compete with sexploitation features, art-house films, foreign imports, underground and experimental films and independent films for a share of the commercially lucrative arena in sexual suggestiveness.[9] By the latter part of the 1960s, Metzger was complaining of the danger Hollywood's poaching strategies posed to his business, as he asked, 'How can we compete with Elizabeth Taylor's dialogue in *Virginia Woolf* or undraped stars in many big-budget films with our unfamiliar starlets?'[10] Positing difference and distance from the rabble of sexploitation in the aspirational trajectory towards a more middle-class audience did not necessarily alleviate the fuzzier distinctions between *Camille*, *Carmen*, *Therese et al.* and the majors.

At a point when sexualised narratives and Hollywood features with 'mature' themes seemed to blur the lines between 'smut' divined by community standards and 'film art', Metzger's 'high class' productions introduced distinction in their upper class pedigree and representations of the sex lives of the decadent bourgeoisie. The relationship between classification of 'art films' and sex films has a detailed history,[11] and Metzger's pictures took advantage of the slippages, misrecognitions and overlaps between the grind-house and the art-house to maximise audience attendance. In the early 1960s, for example, the debate over the classification of films as 'adult' or designated for 'adults only' met with consternation from conservatives such as Martin Quigley, the editor of the Motion Picture Herald,[12] and with exasperation on the part of art-house proprietors such as Walter Reade.[13] This was because 'adult films' included films that ranged from foreign imports, mature family melodramas produced by Hollywood, underground and avant-garde work and sexploitation fare. Metzger's films intervened to re-inscribe the battle over adult sexuality and its fantasmatic dangers along the lines of taste cultures and edified publics.

By positing a classed hierarchy between his own features and the sexploitation market, Metzger's films made a claim for the 'average' audience and purportedly deflected the more 'prurient' viewer who was out to see flesh regardless of the finer points of story, sentiment and ambience. Metzger preferred not to term his pictures 'exploitation films' but rather 'class speciality films',[14] or 'class sex', and tried to 'appeal to the sophisticated filmgoer, not to the skinflick audience … he conceived of his audience as consisting of "sophisticated married couples in the mid-30s" rather than of ageing insurance salesmen with their finger poised behind their suitcases.'[15] These intentional modes of address to a particularly classed audience produced a speculative, if not successful, alibi of a middlebrow spectator who wants, presumably, to be educated and edified more than entertained or aroused.

It is evident that Metzger's film work engaged with and produced a unique discourse of taste around the consumption of sexual images. Looking at the historical reception contexts and the directorial and marketing strategies of Metzger, I want to ask how sexuality and sexual taste gets classed in the films he both directed and re-directed, through distribution, for an American audience. What are the specific aesthetic and ideological strategies deployed to create this art-erotica/soft-core hybrid, and what are its characteristics and effects? As Mark Jancovich notes:

> [T]he study of pornography … requires us to acknowledge that sexual tastes are not just gendered but also classed and that, as Bourdieu argues in relation to the aesthetic disposition more generally, sexual tastes are not only amongst the most 'classifying' of social differences, but also have 'the privilege of appearing the most natural'.[16]

The rhetoric of taste is deployed in Metzger's 1960s films on numerous levels, on the level of aesthetics, decor, sexual content and performance, and in the films' marketing and distribution.

'MIDDLEBROW PORNOGRAPHY' AND SEXUAL TASTES

Agnes: I like you because you're always … *ready*.
The Alley Cats

The historical and aesthetic complication of Metzger's output, which in the 1970s expanded from soft-core into hard-core pornographic product, is an interesting test case for understanding the economically destabilised film market of the 1960s. It also clarifies the debates over obscenity, classification, taste and aesthetic judgement that gained prominence at the time. 1968 saw the emergence of the CARA ratings system and the final sloughing off of the spectre of the arcane and obsolete Production Code Administration, which had regulated the visibility of licentious subject matter in Hollywood films since the early 1930s.[17]

Margot Hentoff, writing in 1969, pointed to one element of the saturation of the marketplace with sexual imagery:

> There is almost no one left in town who is not an expert on sex, going from film to theatre to newsstand to bookstore – talking and writing about what he has seen. Everyone knows which theatrical coupling was real and which was simulated. Everyone tells us how sexually healthy he is and how non-erotic the performance, the performer, the book. The *New York Review of Sex* advertises in these pages. *Screw* and *Pleasure*, two of the other raunchy commercial offshoots of the old love-drug-revolution press, are read for fun by people I know. One turns the pages of these papers, sees a naked girl whose legs are spread, and says very *Yellow Book* – 'What bad teeth she has!' We are apparently developing a new genre of middle-class pornography: one which stimulates no one at all.[18]

Hentoff's ironic reading of the contemporary scene is concerned with the ways in which the seeming underground has lost its sense of transgression and taboo. In the hands of a middlebrow, middle-class audience for whom aesthetic distancing, just short of boredom, is the hermeneutic strategy *tout court* for reading sexual representations, sex is evacuated of its secret thrills. Her wit, in the final line, proclaims null and void the experience of sensual shocks and affective inscriptions on the viewer's body. This is an experience diluted and denigrated by the light of day and the codes of propriety, knowledge and taste that rule middlebrow consumption. No one can acknowledge their own arousal, a function of a border policing and regulated sexuality which distinguishes middle-class bodily response from the excesses of the lower-class lower body. In the context of over-stimulation, arousal is transformed into boredom.

In an attempt to make arousal 'elegant', Metzger's films can be seen as part of this branch of a middle-class pornography, a niche market expanded to include less the maligned all male 'raincoat brigade' – envisioned as the true audience of sexploitation – but more the newly targeted 'date crowd'. A reviewer, sceptical of their aesthetic innovation, commented that:

> Metzger's films allow middle-class people who have been conditioned to abhor pornography but who secretly crave it, to indulge their erotic fantasies with the firm conviction that what they are witnessing on screen is somehow more 'serious', more 'uplifting', than the crudely made quickies designed for the proles.[19]

Contrary to the work of Meyer, his competitor at the time, to whom Metzger was often compared, Metzger's films refuted the more overt appeal to the low cultural sensibilities of the 'cold-beer and grease-burger gang'.[20] Whereas Meyer revelled in the inept physicality of his spectator and the boorishness of a stereotypical underclass, Metzger promoted an aspirational project, both in terms of genre and narrative, classing his films in terms of the already available and upper-middlebrow tenets of the art-house patron.

As Pierre Bourdieu notes, tastes manifest and justify themselves in the negation of the tastes of other groups, and are constituted as much through distaste and disgust as through a positive identification. As he writes:

> [A]version to different lifestyles is perhaps one of the strongest barriers between the classes
> … the most intolerable thing for those who regard themselves as the possessors of legitimate
> culture is the sacrilegious reuniting of tastes which taste dictates shall be separated.[21]

Continually described in terms of his stylistic elegance, aristocracy, sophistication, distinction and refinement, Metzger remarked in an interview that:

> We didn't start out to be elegant. I was taught in college that the reason comedies are about
> rich people is because you shouldn't have to worry about how they make a living … if you
> want people at leisure, they have to have resources.[22]

Lifestyle, particularly sexual lifestyle, defined by a utopian notion of sexual liberation becomes the landscape upon which Metzger unites the particularly apposite fields of youth culture and bourgeois living. Metzger's films embraced the counter-cultural cache of the image of the 'swinging sixties' and sexual experimentation, of which his party scenes are the utmost apotheosis. These included images of women jumping fully clothed into swimming pools with men, a prison-themed bourgeois orgy replete with jail cell and a nightclub where a strip poker game leads to a female player's removal of her underwear in full view of the club crowd. Yet Metzger managed to cloak such tactical screen debauchery in the patina of respectability, attempting to unravel sexual practice from its moralising and pathologising vestments. In Metzger's films, narratives of erotic ennui and sexual existentialism piggyback on the fashionable pop-psychologised rhetoric of social malaise and youthful disinvestment. In *The Lickerish Quartet*, the disaffection of a family is disrupted by their pursuit of a circus performer, played by Silvana Venturelli, whom they are convinced starred in a stag film they have just screened. Her spectral appearance and disappearance spurs psychological rediscovery on the part of the father, mother and her son. In *Therese and Isabelle*, Therese (Essy Persson) returns to the site of her first love, a lesbian romance, at a now decaying and abandoned school for girls, in which her present experience of the space mixes fluidly with the recollection of her amorous entanglements with the elusive Isabelle (Anna Gael). The erotic listlessness of Metzger's female protagonists is tinged with memory and melancholy – Marguerite Gautier (Danièle Gaubert), the relentless playgirl of *Camille 2000*, is

FIGURE 5 Making pornography middle class in *The Lickerish Quartet*

haunted by her mysterious illness, which in deadly combination with her debauchery, prompts her demise at the end of the film. Monique (Reine Roman) wistfully pines for the icy Laurence, who we realise is actually Nadia, in the end of *The Dirty Girls*. And Leslie in *The Alley Cats*, on the heels of her rejection by her lovers and fiancé, considers suicide off the balcony of a church, only to be deterred by the lesbian artist Irena (Sabrina Koch).

These scenarios intermingle the prototypical gesture of refusal, sported by youth cultures with the literary pretensions of alienation and psychic torment. The literary sources of many of Metzger's works – from Dumas to Merimee, from LeDuc to contemporary theatre – authorised the sexual liberties taken on screen. It also veiled them in the impulse of a modernised and utopic desire, a sensibility that necessitates a contemporary yet aloof viewpoint on the world and historical events. The preference for fantasy, chosen over the depredations of material necessity, gave Metzger's films the structure of fables, erotic melodramas set against the eminent yet denied contexts of 1960s social change.

Metzger's work therefore draws attention to the historicity of taste and its relation to sexual pleasure. If an understanding of taste is always reckoning with ways it can negotiate and train the body, in the Kantian project of distanciation, abstraction and aestheticisation, the location of eroticism in the act of consumption has no better model than sexploitation film and pornography. Russell Lynes, whose book *The Tastemakers* (1954) introduced the lexicon of 'highbrow, lowbrow and middlebrow' to the American public, reverts to gendered and sexualised analogies to lament the loss of pleasure in the pursuit of taste for taste's sake within the post-war leisure economy. He writes, 'a great many people enjoy having taste, but too few of them enjoy the things they have taste about. Or to put it another way, they are like a man that takes pleasure in his excellent taste in women but takes no pleasure at all in *a* woman.'[23] This point, about abstraction of pleasure from its object, takes on another meaning in the context of 1960s public sexual culture. Sexual taste is coded into the structure of consumption, and it appears the most irrefutable of processes and preferences, aspiring to its own invisibility. Metzger's films, as artefacts of a middlebrow trajectory, attempt to have it both ways, in taking pleasure in the aestheticisation and abstraction of sexual pleasure itself, in an erotic reflexivity.

STYLE, GESTURE, DÉCOR: CONSUMING SEX

Metzger's films contributed to what Margot Hentoff identified as the inundation and overexposure of sexuality in the public sphere, coded in the same principles of access, but still embedded in the logic of the 'tease'. As Thomas Waugh notes, 'The tease, an erotic enunciation orchestrated like a tantalising power game, was still the characteristic erotic rhetoric of 60s public culture, the sexual revolution notwithstanding.'[24] Metzger's cinema is full of what would become generic soft-core aesthetic motifs which generated and refined the art of the tease in its narrative and *mise-en-scène*: focus on decorative objects such as sculptures, glass bottles, furniture and mirrors, and creative attention to off-screen space.

It is in the aesthetics and syntax of Metzger's films that we can see the articulation of the paradox of art-house erotica. This is a place where the tease is held in tension between the edification and abstraction accorded to art and the materiality of arousal and an embodied spectator. Likening his films to the equivalent of foreplay, the representation of sexual acts and physical pleasure is met with the challenge of attempting to create a metaphor of pleasure into an aesthetic experience, between exhibition and concealment. These works move against the realist ontological function attributed to pornography as the limit of the representable. As Fredric Jameson claimed, 'the visual is essentially pornographic, which is to say that it has its end in rapt, mindless, fascination.'[25] However, Metzger's images arrest the motion towards representational truthfulness of the sexed body in favour of presenting sex as aesthetically mediated or dematerialising. Many examples of this tendency can be seen in the texts, in which the *mise-en-scène* serves to make manifest a psychic function or process of desire, arousal and pleasure.

In certain films, actual physical objects within the set take on the role of lenses through which the sex act can be seen. In *Carmen Baby*, coloured glass bottles on a ledge become the telescoping filter to the imaging of sex between Carmen (Uta Levka) and her lover. The camera slowly pans along the length of their reclined bodies through the mediating tints and mildly distorted perspectives of the bottles' organic contours. A similar device is used in *Camille 2000* to serialise and fragment the sex between Marguerite and Armand Duval (Nino Castelnuovo) in her futuristic, all white, mirrored boudoir. Sex on a clear plastic bed is seen only reflected through the series of vertical mirrors which encircle Marguerite's bed, as the camera pans across slowly and the image the viewer sees is broken up into a repetition of frames within the frame.

Representing the inner experience of primarily female sexual pleasure is also organised through this interface with the décor and decorative objects. In *The Dirty Girls,* Monique's lesbian sexual longings are temporarily satisfied by a bout of masturbation with her own reflection in the mirror, in which her image is reduplicated in the frame and she appears to be kissing her own likeness. In *The Alley Cats*, Metzger frames Leslie's face during an oral sex encounter with Christian (Harald Baerow) by a mirror against which she has her back. As she is being stimulated, a montage of shots of her point of view of the rococo ceiling and her bear rug which has been blindfolded are rapidly edited together. As Leslie nears orgasm, her head shaking back and forth in close-up, the ceiling, replete with curlicue details and gilt angels, begins to spin, alternating more rapidly with the bear's head, and on cue with the non-diegetic sound of the film's score and her moaning. Another heterosexual sex scene in *The Alley Cats*, between Logan (Charlie Hichman) and Agnes (Karin Field), uses a deliberate and distorted blurry focus, a mode of dematerialisation, to signify sexual pleasure. The physical gestures and facial responses of Agnes, astride Logan, appear fogged, as if the lens is smudged or out of focus, thereby cueing the spectator to the relationship between perceptual clarity and physical release, the parallel between the corporeality of sex and the recession of the image into a literalised 'bodylessness.' This performs an indexical move despite itself – attempting to allegorise and conflate the pleasure of sex with the impulse to watch, from outside oneself.

A comparable scene in *Camille 2000* focuses exclusively on Marguerite's face, in the background, and a vase of camellias, in the foreground. As Armand performs oral sex on her – implied off-screen – Marguerite's moans punctuate an alternating focus of the camera, from her face to the camellias. The screen is split into two fields, as the flowers and Marguerite's expression get fuzzy and then come into sharp view, in time with her accelerating orgasm. The temporality of pleasure is coded, through visual clarity and rhythm, to represent the unrepresentable female clitoral orgasm, cloaked in the excesses of a lavish *mise-en-scène* and the organic associations of the highly arranged flora.

These examples, a choice few among many, dramatise the trajectory towards abstraction which orient Metzger's films to a discourse of taste. Attributable to Metzger's signature style, it is *style itself* that is being eroticised. Such scenes are themselves easily abstractable from the films they are in. They emphasise the extent to which his films are ready-made for a cinephile sensibility, constructed of rhythmically adept fragments which operate, like the ambulatory and swerving route of fantasy, independently and often unmoored from their narrative content, capable of being re-arranged by the viewer.

Such is the guiding trope of *The Lickerish Quartet*, which depends on the misrecognitions of desire, as the metacinematic film screen, on which are screened stag films – thus becoming the mediating site for the operations of fantasy. The back of the screen, set up in the living room, becomes

FIGURE 6 The cluttered erotic frame: *Camille 2000*

the physical and psychic space of traversal (by the camera and the viewer), mobilising the distance between a husband, his wife and his stepson through an erotic character who seems to emerge from the screen, from the stag film, to rearrange their fantasies and their memories. Metzger commented on the idea for the film:

> It came from *Dark Odyssey* days. Whenever we screened the picture the film looked different for different audiences. I didn't understand this, there's nothing more permanent than film. Once its developed, it cannot change. And yet depending on the audiences, the film would actually change. The actor's timing would change, the performances would change. Depending on who was in the theatre at the time. ... And I wanted to kind of get that across, when we have a piece of film that is never the same, its different every time you run it.[26]

The mutability of the film image resembles the mutability and plasticity of sexual fantasy. Again we can see the importance of the cut, of the editorial signature, in Metzger's films, as it allows for the camp reappropriation of images and scenes, gestures and dialogue, the standard of curation and the instrument of classification.

TASTE AND (SEXUAL) PREFERENCE

The camp value of Metzger's films emerges from their flaunting of social change, and particularly female sexual liberation, as transformations in the consumption and economy of lifestyle. Taste, as Bourdieu reminds us, is emblematic of what one has and who one is in relation to the classifications of others and how one is classified by others.[27] That a 'modernised' female sexuality became available for consumption by heterosexual men in the burgeoning sex industry of the 1960s is another commonplace of cultural history. We can see this hitoricist cliché transcribed into a scene in *The Alley Cats*, as Christian writes 'GREAT!' on Leslie's naked back while she sleeps, assessing her previous night's sexual performance and manifesting classification as body graffiti. The body becomes a vehicle, a prop like the décor itself, a material which requires evaluation, and through this evaluation it can be distanced from its physicality into style. It is also a mark of Christian's appetite, an inscription of his *own* sexual taste, which has been sated by Leslie. The 'GREAT!' on Leslie's back serves as an impetuous move signifying Christian's defiant cad persona as well as a mode of address to the audience, a complicity to appreciate and consume Leslie, and the film itself, as a pure, fantasmatic surface.

The emergence and availability of particular sexual preferences – such as lesbianism and bisexuality – coded as consumer preferences, comes as a unique effect of the relationship between capitalism and sexual identities as they were mutually constituted in the 1960s. For Metzger, this offering up of alternative sexualities within his filmic narratives – from the lesbianism of *Therese and Isabelle*, *The Alley Cats* and *The Dirty Girls*, to the bisexuality exhibited in *The Lickerish Quartet* and *Score*, becomes the premise for an aesthetic 'elevation' rather than degradation of his films. Here, such images are filtered through his particular style and *mise-en-scène*. What Metzger's films lack in comparison to his more 'crude' sexploitation competitors is an attribution or designation of pathology to its sexually and emotionally voracious characters.

In the 1960s, sexploitation films capitalised on lesbianism as a safe way to present sexual content without the incriminations associated with full frontal male nudity. Lesbian sex became a legal loophole, and as Kenneth Turan and Stephen Zito claim about sexploitation, 'there is a great deal more explicit activity in the lesbian scenes than in the heterosexual ones, because it is much easier to fake sex between two women than between a woman and a man'.[28] Despite the spurious assumptions in their analogy between sexual visibility and simulated sex, their logic makes clear how lesbian sexuality became a staple of adult film product, a token benchmark in the 'progress' of sexual liberalism.

Whereas gay male sexual cultures became accessible in part through the avant-garde film work of the New York underground, in the likes of Kenneth Anger, Jack Smith and Andy Warhol, images of lesbian sexuality had a more marginal existence as an accessory or indulgence of heterosexual male fantasy. Janet Staiger and others have credited the visibility of non-traditional sexuality in the avant-garde films of the early 1960s with opening up a space for the later flourishing of the soft-core and hard-core film market.[29] Metzger's popularity came on the heels of the waning of the New York underground in the mid- to late 1960s. Indeed, it is interesting to periodise the declining years of the underground, as well as the falling fortunes of the foreign film, in relation to the economic boom years of sexploitation, 1966–70.

Therese and Isabelle became the first sustained exploration of lesbian romance, adapted from Violette LeDuc's 1964 memoir, *La Bâtarde*. One of the most 'sensitive' of Metzger's portrayals and subsequently one which shows a minimum of bare flesh, *Therese and Isabelle* was a landmark film in its non-pathological portrait of lesbian sexuality. Couched within the art-house erotica mould, lesbianism became a consumable and aestheticised experience, heavy on sentiment, and sexual experimentation was positioned from a classed space of exploration and safety. Lesbianism was a stage passed through, a refutable yet pervasive melancholia haunting the now presumably straight and adult Therese. Literary voiceovers and the structure of memory which frames the narrative, in Therese's adult return to the site of adolescent sex, buffer the impact of a film entirely devoted to lesbianism.

Lesbian relationships work in many of Metzger's features, both his own and in the Audubon imports, as a structure of 'diversification' of the sexual commodity. Women, unmoored from traditional marriage and work, could be pictured in the extremity of their autonomy. In *The Alley Cats*, the artist and socialite Irena mediates between Leslie and her philandering fiancé Logan, ultimately through a seduction, delivering the emotionally harrowed Leslie back into her fiancé's arms. And in *The Dirty Girls,* lesbianism, the surprise ending which reveals that the prostitute Monique's affection rests with a woman, is more subtly mediated by an American john who has just had a sexual encounter with Monique. A shower scene in which the lesbian lovers are reunited is intercut with an image of the john reminiscing about Monique as he sits on the train, with a recurring male voiceover questioning, 'Who is a dirty girl?' The john becomes the authenticated spectator, the voyeur who haunts the unravelled 'mystery' of Monique's inner life.

These films depict alternative sexualities as a refinement of sexual taste and a 'sign of the times,' as well as a gesture of pedagogy, in which sex is treated without guilt. Participating and forwarding the trend of 'bisexual chic' in his films, Metzger's *Score* was one of the few films to present same-sex scenarios between both men and women. Indeed, the film's male-male scenes caused a considerable stir in its initial release, as the straight male audience for sexploitation was considered too squeamish to sit through gay sex.[30] *Score*'s status as a film which bridges the soft-core and hard-core stages of Metzger's work is substantiated by the existence of both hard and soft versions of the film, as censorship and regional distribution necessitated different sells. As a result, a crucial five minutes of hard-core footage was pared down, excised or reinserted in a number of the prints of the film. Starring gay porn icon Cal Culver*, Score* featured a seduction of one married couple by another older, more experienced one, as husbands and wives pair up with each other in a play of erotic education, the learned initiating the naïve into sexual knowledge. *Score*'s innovation came at the waning days of the sexploitation genre, as hard-core pornography, enjoying widespread public exhibition, had begun to eclipse the now dated novelty of the soft-core sexploitation tease. Metzger went on to direct a number of highly popular hard-core porn features such as *The Private Afternoons of Pamela Mann* (1975), *Barbara Broadcast* (1977) and *The Opening of Misty Beethoven* (1975), and acceded to auteur status in the acquisition of his films by the Museum of Modern Art.

CONCLUSION

Having operated on the cusp of the underground and in pursuit of legitimacy and larger audiences, Metzger's films of the 1960s represent an expansion of the sphere of acceptable consumption in a period of re-stratifying public taste. 'Sexual liberation' is allegorised through a Continental and fairytale elsewhere of lush homes and bodies pliable to the plasticity of fantasy. In assessing Metzger's work in the present, one is struck by its capacity for camp reading as well as its auratic textures, as the diversions of the tease are redirected onto other surfaces – décor, objects, bodies. The soft-core predicament in the conditions of its production – the prohibition of the explicit sexual act – requires strategies of association to link it back to that act. The paradox between the aesthetic sensibility, for a person who has taste, or is looking for taste, is always contravened by the ways in which abstraction, in Metzger's *mise-en-scène*, leads back to pleasure. The soft-core predicament is turned into an asset, as style becomes a mode of cultural capital, justifying sex while re-eroticising it through mediation, reflection and atmospherics.

If Metzger's films 'date' in the present, they are coded as archives of the fluctuating American film industry, as the very hybridity which he pioneered is today a mark of its place within film history, addressed to an audience classed by their sexual tastes for 'sophisticated' erotica. By paying attention to the soft-core work of Metzger in the 1960s and early 1970s, we can begin to see how erotic films were legitimised and began to circulate amongst a wider audience, and what the impact of such a move up from the underground could and did yield within its own historical moment.

CHAPTER 3
CURTIS HARRINGTON AND THE UNDERGROUND
ROOTS OF THE MODERN HORROR FILM

Stephen R. Bissette

In the years 1927–28, after directing a small number of films in Switzerland, France and the United States, Robert Florey interrupted his Hollywood career as a gag writer, publicist and assistant director to direct a quartet of non-narrative, expressionistic short films. The most famous of these remains *The Life and Death of 9413 – A Hollywood Extra* (1928), which Florey made with Slavko Vorkapich for the princely sum of $96. This expressionistic short caught the fancy of many of Florey's Hollywood associates; Charlie Chaplin himself arranged for the film to play on Broadway, opening it to wider venues.[1] Its success eventually attracted the attention of Paramount Studios, launching Florey's mainstream directorial career. This included his aborted pre-production work on Universal's *Frankenstein* (1931), before helming genre classics like *Murders in the Rue Morgue* (1932) and *The Beast with Five Fingers* (1942).

Thirty years later, a young Californian underground filmmaker named Curtis Harrington made the more difficult move from the American avant-garde cinema to directing features in Hollywood. Like Florey before him and David Cronenberg, John Waters, David Lynch and E. Elias Merhige after, Harrington's preoccupation with dark fantasy inspired him to use the horror genre as a generic bridge to mainstream filmmaking. After completing a total of nine underground short films from 1942 to 1955, Harrington made his feature directorial debut with the atmospheric *Night Tide* (first shown as an independent/underground effort in 1961, opening wider in 1963). Harrington continued directing feature films for over twenty years, mining his distinctive vein of stylish suspense and horror in any and all venues that presented themselves. His work encompassed the drive-in and grind-house exploitation circuit (*Queen of Blood* (1965), *Who Slew Auntie Roo?* (1971), *The Killing Kind* (1973), *Ruby* (1977)) and medium-budget projects with major studios (Universal Pictures' *Games* (1967), United Artists' *What's the Matter with Helen?* (1971)), along with a brood of made-for-television features (*How Awful About Allan* (1970), *The Cat Creature* (1973), *The Dead Don't Die* (1974), *Killer Bees* (1974) and *Devil Dog: The Hound of Hell* (1978)).

Harrington also directed numerous television episodes for popular programmes like *Baretta* (1975), *Charlie's Angels* (1977–78), *Dynasty* (1983) and *The Colbys* (1986). Some of his television output in this era were genre efforts, including *Lucan* (1977) and the final episode of *Logan's Run* (1977). These credits extended to self-contained entries for anthology programmes like *Tales of the Unexpected* ('A Hand for Sonny Blue', 1976), *Darkroom* ('Makeup', 1981) and *The Twilight Zone* ('Voices in the Earth', 1986).

Thus, Harrington was one of the few true underground filmmakers to actively engage with mainstream media venues, savouring the occasionally rich opportunities to further explore his own particular visionary and thematic obsessions and interests for a much broader audience. As such, Harrington is one of the genre's true pioneers, a stature that has not, as yet, been properly acknowledged. Whereas the 'underground to mainstream' careers of Cronenberg, Waters and Lynch are considered as equally vital components in their richly personal oeuvres, Harrington has not yet received such critical attention. To date, no one has considered his experimental films as vital, organic and integrated elements of his more commercial directorial vision and career.

HORROR UNDERGROUND?

Part of the difficulty with assessing the link between Harrington's underground and commercial works remains the presumed cultural and critical gap between the narrative and non-narrative cinema. Specifically, the avant-garde and underground movements of the twentieth century in all their permutations, from the Surrealists to the recent 'Cinema of Transgression' – have cut the horror genre away from some of its most vital roots. Genre scholars are forced to acknowledge Robert Weine's *The Cabinet of Dr. Caligari* (1919) and David Lynch's *Eraserhead* (1977) as two landmark crossovers between the schools of underground experimental and mainstream horror. But between these landmarks lay many seminal works: Dimitri Kirsanov's *Menilmontant* (1924) opens with a horrific axe murder that anticipates the very editing techniques Alfred Hitchcock wielded with such perfection for the shower murder in *Psycho* (1960). Luis Buñuel and Salvador Dali's *Un Chien Andalou* (1929) was the first graphic, cold-blooded, calculated 'Audience Assault', and as such the forefather of all modern horror films. Equally, Maya Deren's underground masterpiece *Meshes of the Afternoon* (1943) can be seen as the true 'midwife' to a whole series of later horror 'trance' films. These have included John Parker's *Dementia* (aka *Daughter of Horror*, 1953/55/57), Herk Harvey's *Carnival of Souls* (1962), Roman Polanski's *Repulsion* (1965) and *The Tenant* (1976), as well as Adrian Lyne's *Jacob's Ladder* (1990) and E. Elias Merhige's *Begotten* (1991).

We have been denied – and denying – the full breadth and depth of the horror genre's cinematic legacy, conceding to the artificial walls between perceived modes of intent, expression, production, marketing, distribution and exhibition. These differences are crucial to the artists and central to the very identities of the various avant-garde and underground movements, wherein the films are personal works of art, not industry-driven products designed for commercial exploitation. But it is necessary for film scholars and historians to consider the entirety of cinema as a cohesive, communicative medium, and the vital function of genre as language within that medium. Within the cinema and any given genre, it is the cross-pollination of ideas, content, approaches, images, kinetics and emotional textures between permeable 'walls' (defined, most often, by venues of exhibition, distribution and the respective industry issues) that must be studied and assessed.

Much of this process can be traced through popular culture's voracious appetite for the 'new', prompting an interminable cannibalisation of richer resources from outside the mainstream. Thus, elements of Harrington's *Queen of Blood*, Lynch's *Eraserhead* and Tobe Hooper's *The Texas Chainsaw Massacre* (1974) are digested and regurgitated into the mainstream via the example of, say, Ridley Scott's *Alien* (1979). On a wider scale, the visionary personal cinema of prior generations has been distilled into either the meditative calm of the computer 'screensaver' or the frenetic kinetics of the music video form. This process is ongoing and organic, in its way.

The process is particularly compelling when embodied in an individual artist's career. The exchanges between these perceived, permeable 'walls' are particularly revealing when an individual artist is actively, intimately and consciously involved with that ongoing osmosis, as was Florey, Harrington, Cronenberg, Waters and Lynch. Harrington is arguably the genre director whose deserved prominence remains most compromised by the unforgivable critical and scholarly refusal to mesh underground and mainstream cinema into a coherent weave. The half-a-century critical 'blind spot' between *Caligari* and *Eraserhead* remains sadly unilluminated, casting a shadow over the very period in which the young Curtis Harrington worked. Though the context is different, Amos Vogel's statement that 'the crucial importance of such filmmakers as Sidney Peterson, the Whitney Brothers … Maya Deren, Curtis Harrington, and James Broughton remain unknown or unanalysed trivia in the ideological development of the new generation' is as true today as it was in the 1960s.[2]

This can be attributed in part to the relative inaccessibility of Harrington's underground work. Accurate descriptions of Harrington's experimental films are difficult to find. Except for ready access to his 1949 film *On the Edge*, I only have the memory of seeing *Fragment of Seeking* (1946) in the early 1970s to work with. Indeed, the sketchy synopsis in some of the books and catalogues cited herein conflict with my viewings of *On the Edge* and my memories of *Fragment of Seeking*. Nevertheless, the effort must be made to contextualise this crucial body of creative work within its genre and the director's subsequent mainstream feature productions.

EXPERIMENTATION AND EXCESS

Harrington emerged from the West Coast experimental film renaissance which began with Maya Deren and Alexander Hammid's seminal *Meshes of the Afternoon* (a film properly revered by the underground, but still an unsung classic of the fantastic cinema) and continued for a little more than a decade. In *Meshes of the Afternoon*, Deren herself played the troubled dreamer, haunted in and about her own home by a faceless figure, a key, a knife and her own doppelgänger. Though inspired by the surrealist filmmakers before her, Deren's precisely calculated structure of the waking dream that plunges into nightmare was a revelation. In *At Land* (1944), Deren played an almost elemental being who emerges from the sea, crawling over surf, sand and a banquet table to flirt with a game of chess and then follow one of its spilled play pieces over the rocks, back into the water.

Deren was a potent figure in the underground cinema movement, indelibly shaping its language and potential. Harrington subsequently struck up a relationship with Deren: 'Whenever she'd come to Los Angeles, I'd throw a little party for her and provide bongo drums so that she could dance. Maya loved to dance.'[3] Indeed, Deren was the first to make dance movement the absolute expressive focus of her films. *A Study in Choreography for Camera* (1945), *Meditation on Violence* (1948) and her final film, *The Very Eye of Night* (1958), established a fresh cinematic vocabulary for others to follow.

Vocabulary of another kind was problematic; throughout the 1940s and 1950s, the term 'underground film' did not even exist (the moniker was not coined until 1959, and at that time it had a much more specific meaning than it has in the title and scope of this book). Deren's works, like those of her fellow filmmakers – including Harrington – were referred to as 'experimental films', a clumsy label implying amateurism, which at least signified such films' daring nature and distinction from mainstream Hollywood fare. The European term 'avant-garde film' was also adopted, but the works of Deren and her peers were distinctively American. *Meshes of the Afternoon* and *At Land* had been shot in Los Angeles before Deren's move to New York City. It was there in the City of Angels that Harrington and his friends Kenneth Anger and Gregory Markopoulos began to create their own stylised, personal 16mm works that were central to the experimental film renaissance.

Harrington, Anger and Markopoulos were a unique trinity in the history of avant-garde cinema, their childhood fascination with the artifice of Hollywood's manufactured opulence and the medium of cinema blossoming into three distinctive, artistic voices. Harrington notes his formative readings of L. Frank Baum and Edgar Allan Poe – 'I was very much into the imaginative fiction when I was a mere toddler'[4] – and the first horror film Harrington recalls seeing was Edgar Ulmer's *The Black Cat* (1934), though Harrington saw it during a later re-release.[5] At the age of 14, Harrington made his first 8mm short film, *The Fall of the House of Usher* (1942), playing the dual roles of Poe's doomed siblings, Roderick and Madeline Usher, himself; thus, the gender issues so central to Harrington's work were manifest from the beginning. *Usher* was followed by two other 8mm efforts, *Crescendo* (1942) and *Renascence* (1944). Harrington later studied at the University of Southern California film school which, at that time, did not incorporate 'the idea of really making student films, though it had been done at points in the history of the USC cinema school … [as] a standard part of the curriculum.'[6]

If Harrington sounds prodigious, consider his similarly gifted companions. Anger claims to have appeared in Hollywood features since he was a baby (boasting Max Reinhardt and William Dieterle's delirious adaptation of Shakespeare's *A Midsummer Night's Dream* (1935) among his childhood credits). He began making films at age nine, his ambitious early films including *Prisoner of Mars* (1942, shot with miniatures) and *The Nest* (1943), a tale of incest. Markopoulos shot his own 8mm films in Toledo, Ohio, beginning at age 12 (including a version of Dickens' *The Christmas Carol*), and enrolled at USC in 1945, where he met and reportedly lived 'across the hall'[7] from Harrington, on whose *Fragment of Seeking* he later worked as a camera assistant. As Sheldon Renan notes, 'All three had made films as children. All three made works that were obviously very personal. All three made works that were almost confessions.'[8]

These dreamlike 'confessions' were implicit and explicit expressions of male love and sexuality, both narcissistic and homoerotic. Harrington's potently manifested, fearful images of female sexuality and matriarchy marked thematic obsessions which would remain essential to his later mainstream narratives. Where Anger's literally explosive *Fireworks* (1947) overtly embodied the homoerotic tensions in a sadomasochistic beating, evisceration and implied rape – culminating in the titular image of a sailor's penis as a sparkling Roman candle – Harrington and Markopoulos favoured less explicit expressions of their shared themes. Harrington's first 16mm film was *Fragment of Seeking* (originally entitled *Symbol of Decadence* (1946, approx. 15 min.)), suggested by the myth of Narcissus. A youth (Harrington at age 17) urgently seeks the object of his own desire; the tension builds with his search, culminating in his embracing a young woman who is revealed to be a female version of himself, before dissolving into a grinning skeleton with a blonde wig.

Nevertheless, *Fragment of Seeking* and *Fireworks* were companion pieces, though they were not consciously designed as such. 'They were virtually simultaneously made, within a month or two [of each other],' Harrington later noted. 'We really were embarking on similar projects at the same time. … But I don't think there's anything sensational about [*Fragment of Seeking*]; it deals with adolescent narcissism. But Kenneth Anger's film was more explicit in its sexuality, and was very disturbing to people.'[9]

The overt homosexual content of *Fragment of Seeking* and the especially aggressive imagery of *Fireworks* was still quite taboo at the time of their production; *Fireworks* in particular later became a fixture of screenings of homoerotic 'art' films organised by the gay urban subculture of the 1950s and early 1960s. Recalling a 1947 screening for 'the *crème de la crème* of Los Angeles artistic intelligentsia at that time,' Harrington recalls: 'I'll never forget it, it was an extraordinary experience … when the screening was over, not a single person would even speak to us, they were so shocked by these two films. These people were truly shocked. … The irony is within one year of this incident, Kenneth left for France and of course was instantly hailed by Jean Cocteau as being the young genius of filmmaking in the world.'[10]

There is further irony in the fact that Harrington and Markopoulos were arguably closer in spirit to Cocteau. Anger (his name accurately conjuring the abrasive power of many of his films) initially embraced the 'shock cinema' tactics of Buñuel and Dali's *Un Chien Andalou*. Applying the phantasmagoric vocabulary of Cocteau's own *The Blood of a Poet* (*Le Sang d'un Poet*, 1930) to their cinema, Harrington and Markopoulos created consciously mythic evocations of atmosphere and dread, which further linked their films with Deren's fantastique poetics. However, Markopoulos was cinematically and kinetically closer to Anger, proposing 'a new narrative form through the fusion of the classic montage technique with a more abstract system … [that] involved the use of short film phrases which evoke thought-images',[11] while Harrington chose a more accessible, linear approach to his dreamlike shorts.

Harrington's next 16mm effort was *Picnic* (1948, 22 min.), reportedly a satiric but nonetheless personal work, while *On the Edge* (1949, 6 min.) – Harrington's personal favourite of his early films – was an authentic Freudian nightmare. Here, seething tar deposits steam and bubble beneath the titles. A dour, middle-aged man wanders a desolate landscape and arrives at what appears to be an abandoned dock or shipyard. He is drawn to an older woman sitting in a rocking chair beneath the ruins, knitting, the ball of yarn at her feet turning slowly in a glass jar. She is oblivious to him, but he seems mysteriously bound to her. The man bolts, now attached to her by a length of her yarn slung over his shoulder, and runs away. He plunges into the magma-like substance seen under the opening titles, the length of yarn protruding from the bubbling mass the only evidence of his passing. The final image is of the dispassionate matron rewinding her yarn.

The Assignation (1952, released in 1953, 8 min.), Harrington's first colour work, was a matured refinement of Edgar Allan Poe's source material, shot in Venice. *Dangerous Houses* (1952), filmed in London, was an overt return to the mythological realm. Specifically, it was a reinterpretation of the tale of *Odysseus* (specifically, his episode with Circe and subsequent trip to Hades). Harrington describes it as 'the only so-called "experimental" short that I made out of will rather than inspiration', because he was attracted to the romantic, bombed-out, post-war ruins of St. John's Wood.[12] At 18–20 minutes in length, *Dangerous Houses* is the longest of Harrington's shorts, but was deemed 'a lifeless artefact' by its maker and never distributed. *The Wormwood Star* (1955) was also in colour, focusing on the mystical paintings of Cameron (Parsons), who later appeared in Harrington's debut feature as 'The Woman in Black'. She is cast here as an alluring figure that appears to sideshow mermaid Mora (Linda Lawson) and seems to beckon her back to the sea (she also appeared in Anger's *Inauguration of the Pleasure Dome* (1956)). *The Wormwood Star* reportedly offered a portrait of 'painter Cameron and her work … achieving an alchemical transmutation.'[13] Given the rich use of colour in Harrington's later narrative works, this final underground effort is of particular interest.

MONSTROUS MUSINGS, MONSTROUS WOMEN

What is striking, even from blurred memories and descriptions, are the shorts' visual and thematic anticipations of Harrington's later narrative works, with their femme fatales, smothering matriarchs and alienated, androgynous 'heroes'. The wan male leads of *Fragment of Seeking* and *On the Edge* and their tormented psychodramas of narcissism, troubled sexual identity and mother-fixation clearly delineate the tortured persona John Savage portrays in *The Killing Kind* (1973). Dominant female power is central to all Harrington's works, with men trapped in or consumed by their orbit of that power.

The lead male characters in nearly all of Harrington's features are passive, almost hapless figures. Indeed, these depictions reveal a pantheon of male victims (the spaceship crew which provide sustenance for the alien in *Queen of Blood*; James Caan and Don Stroud in *Games*; Anthony Perkins in *How Awful About Allan*; Savage in *The Killing Kind*). When not victims, Harrington's males are, at best, kept 'drones'. This is literally manifest as such in *Killer Bees*, with a quartet of drones led by Craig Stevens tending to every need of their 'queen bee' Gloria Swanson, and young Edward Albert accepting the role of 'head drone' once his fiancée Kate Jackson mystically assumes Swanson's central matriarchal role. As Tim Lucas has asserted, even *Voyage to the Prehistoric Planet* (1966) 'is surprisingly consistent with themes already evident with Harrington's earlier films … [given] its emphasis on one cosmonaut's obsessive reaction to the sound of an unseen female's siren song.'[14] However, Harrington's creative participation on this 'patch job' for producer Roger Corman was minimal, dubbing and directing minimal additional footage for an American version of the Russian science fiction film *Planeta Bura* (*Planet of Storms*, 1959) under the pseudonym 'John Sebastian'.

In fact, Harrington left the Russian film essentially intact. The director's similar, but far more extensive and inventive, revision of another Soviet science fiction film, *Mechte Navstrechu* (*A Dream Comes True*, 1963), yielded another monstrous female figure: the fascinating Queen of Blood. The film stars the Slavic actress Florence Marley as an alluring, green-skinned alien who transfixes her exclusively male victims with a hypnotic stare, drinking their blood and secreting her throbbing eggs in the hold of the ship.

Any displays of male power prove to be either illusory and/or ultimately self-destructive (Caan in *Games*; Savage in *The Killing Kind*), with the exception of his surrogate 'Hansel' (Mark Lester) in *Who Slew Auntie Roo?* (aka *The Gingerbread House*, 1971) and those works Harrington had little creative control over: the pulp hero (George Hamilton) of *The Dead Don't Die*, the put-upon patriarch (Richard Crenna) of *Devil Dog: The Hound of Hell* – both made-for-television movies – and the vengeful male spirit in *Ruby* (1977). Though Harrington practically disowns the risible *Devil Dog*, it too echoes the gender tensions at the heart of his best work. Namely, the satanic cult which sired the titular menace is led by Martine Beswick, and the first manifestation of its malignant influence over Crenna's wife (Yvette Mimieux) is dramatised by the sudden, 'uncharacteristic' awakening of her sexual appetite. It is interesting to note that most made-for-television movies of the period reflected patriarchal unease with the growing feminist movement with surprisingly vivid scenarios in all genres; *Devil Dog*, *The Cat Creature* and especially *Killer Bees* snugly fit this mould, the latter most imaginatively.

The malicious male energy in *Ruby* – the restless spirit of a murdered gangster (Sal Vecchio) – is directed at and through female characters, notably manifesting (via possession) in the autistic daughter (Janet Baldwin) to lash out at her mother, another monstrous matriarch (Piper Laurie). The ensuing mayhem satisfies a dynamic common to Harrington's work. Thus, the climactic spectacle of a young woman destroying a monstrous mother echoes similar eruptions in *Queen of Blood* (in which the sole female astronaut accidentally kills the haemophilic alien Florence Marley with a mere scratch) and *Who Slew Auntie Roo?* (Chloe Frank's surrogate 'Gretel' also survives her encounter with surrogate 'witch' Shelley Winters), though it is more typical for the matriarchy to 'devour' its own (Simone Signoret/Katherine Ross in *Games*, Shelley Winters/Debbie Reynolds in *What's the Matter with Helen?*, Gloria Swanson/Kate Jackson in *Killer Bees* and even the pack of felines which tear the mummy-cat-woman to shreds in *The Cat Creature*).

The links between Harrington's underground short films and other notable genre works outside of Harrington's subsequent features are also apparent. The derivations from Hollywood and Germanic femme fatale archetypes seem obvious, and it is tempting to suggest *Fragment of Seeking*'s subliminal shot of Harrington's female surrogate over skeletal remains as a prophetic inversion of the double-exposure of Norman (Anthony Perkins) and Mrs Bates' faces at the close of *Psycho*, 13 years later. A common source for this imagery may lay in Leon Frederic's painting 'Studio Interior' (1882), in which the central figure is a seated, bearded male, propping a skeleton in his lap rendered suggestively feminine via the star-patterned dress it wears. Both Harrington and Hitchcock were connoisseurs of fine art, and the association with Frederic's painting is evocative. More contemporary echoes can be found in Lynch's own experimental short *The Grandmother* (1973), anticipated in both tone and substance by *Fragment of Seeking* and particularly *On the Edge*. It is a kinship Harrington once responded to, hopefully forwarding a video copy of *On the Edge* to Lynch with the aim of directing an episode of Lynch's television series *Twin Peaks* (1990–91).

Before his segue into narrative cinema – as an assistant producer to Jerry Wald at 20th Century Fox – Harrington played *The Cabinet of Dr. Caligari*'s Casare the Somnambulist in the second act of Kenneth Anger's grandiose underground epic *Inauguration of the Pleasure Dome*. 'The inspiration for what I did came out of a party,' Harrington recalled, 'a "come as your own nightmare" party or something. I decided that my nightmare would be a scene from *The Cabinet of Dr. Caligari*, and Kenneth was so taken with that [it became] a part of his concept for the film, and he included me in that guise.'[15]

In white gaunt makeup and clad in black tights, Harrington's Cesare struts zombie-like through one of the film's most impressive tableaux. He is seen wandering past a row of glittering candles and into a dark wall embellished with Egyptian cats, and on into a dreamlike realm of silk and light (which, in the revised version, Anger embellishes with a superimposed sketch of Aleister Crowley's face). In the sanctum within, Cesare pours an elixir for the gathered magical beings, and the film dissolves into a non-linear and progressively denser and frenzied hallucinogenic experience. This fascinating iconic conjugation of German expressionism, the West Coast American experimental film movement and the horror genre consummates one of the richest periods of American cinema with a consciously alchemical intensity.

AFTER THE UNDERGROUND

Harrington's underground works were erratically distributed at best, but they were seen. Maya Deren, ever the heart of the movement, co-founded the first of many filmmakers' co-operative networks in the 1940s, programming theatrical showings of their own works through New York's Provincetown Playhouse, Amos Vogel's 'Cinema 16' and others. In 1957, Harrington's films found their first distributor in the Creative Film Society, founded by fellow West Coast filmmaker Robert Pike when he was unable to find a distributor for his own work;[16] most of them remained available from the CFS and Audio Brandon well into the 1970s. The American underground cinema was introduced to Europe at the 1958 Brussels World's Fair, followed shortly thereafter by New American Cinema Group representative David Stone's presentation of 'fifty-four independent productions to the 1961 Festival of Two Worlds in Spoleto, Italy.'[17] This was a retrospective that included the works of Markopoulos and a print of Harrington's just-completed first feature, *Night Tide*. Shortly thereafter, Markopoulos 'publicly dissociated himself from the term "underground"';[18] even as vocal acolytes and advocates of the movement began to disassociate from Harrington's *Night Tide* and subsequent works.

Harrington scripted and directed *Night Tide*, raising the necessary funding himself, much as he had before, though on a grander scale. Harrington expanded upon his own unpublished short story 'The Secrets of the Sea' and drew his title from Poe's poem 'Annabelle Lee', and he is not idly boasting when he notes that 'it has had an astonishing life for a little $50,000 movie.'[19] *Night Tide* synthesised elements of the underground (e.g. Deren's *At Land*) and the popular (through Jacques Tourneur's celebrated *The Cat People* (1942)). The film tells the tale of a forlorn sailor (Dennis Hopper) who falls for Mora (Linda Lawson), an alluring young woman who appears in a beach side-show as a mermaid – and believes she is, in fact, a siren, responsible for the drowning deaths of her previous suitors. The similarities to Tourneur's doomed shapeshifter Irene (Simone Simon) are obvious – including the fleeting presence of an enigmatic older woman to suggest the troubled heroine may indeed be linked to an ancient hybrid race. However, *At Land*'s elemental (played by Deren) is also a kindred spirit. Emerging from the ocean to engage in a procession of dreamlike encounters, she elliptically vanished into the sand dunes, an eerie predecessor to Harrington's haunted Mora.

The fact that Harrington's underground shorts were known among the Hollywood scene aided immeasurably in financing and casting the production. Harrington notes that Dennis Hopper had seen and admired the underground films, and as a result was eager to star in *Night Tide*. Equally, co-star Luana Anders similarly cited how Harrington's reputation as 'a director of what we used to call "art" films' attracted her as 'a rebellious young Hollywood actress wanting to be creative in what I felt was a climate of stifling conformity'.[20] Roger Corman arranged for the film's distribution via Film Group, aiding in post-production funding and deferrals while ensuring wider public exposure than any of Harrington's previous work had enjoyed.

In *Film Culture* no. 21 (1960), critic Parker Tyler's article 'Two Down and One to Go?' dismissed both Harrington and Markopoulos' work, specifically reflecting the underground movement's disdain for Harrington's shift into independent theatrical narrative features. Jonas Mekas, the evangelical *Village Voice* critic for the underground cinema, passionately rose to Harrington's and Markopoulos' defence. In *Film Culture*, Mekas cited *Night Tide* as one of the films 'which, in one way or another … have contributed to the growth of the new cinema, and … should be mentioned in any survey of this kind.'[21]

Note that both these articles predated *Night Tide*'s subsequent distribution into exploitation's venues, primarily as a second-feature for *Battle Beyond the Sun* (1962), another of Corman's patchwork dubbed-Russian science fiction films incorporating new footage (this time shot by a young Francis Ford Coppola). Many seemed suspicious of *Night Tide*'s overt genre trappings, despite its fidelity to Harrington's personal vision and previous work. The mainstream 'grind-house' and drive-in venues *Night Tide* was consigned to, and its association with as exploitative an effort as *Battle Beyond the Sun*, only further alienated underground film purists and ghettoised Harrington's breakthrough feature. Thus, the first 'battle lines' were drawn between subcultural perceptions of underground and exploitation films – a distinction this collection of essays blurs and explores, forty years later.

Some aficionados remained steadfast in their interest in, and defence of, Harrington's work. Through interviews conducted by Mekas, Markopoulos himself defended Harrington's work. 'Sometimes, through sheer accident, I do come upon a very important commercial work,' Markopoulos commented in Mekas' 14 April 1966 *Village Voice* column. 'I am thinking of Curtis Harrington's [*Queen*] *of Blood*. … It is excellent, and fascinating, that Curtis Harrington was able to put so much of his own work into the science [fiction] motion picture. There must have been rapport between the producer and himself. And I do know from personal experience [*Serenity*, 1955–60] how difficult this is.'[22]

Harrington did indeed nurture his bond with *Queen of Blood* producer George Edwards, and together they carved a unique niche in the post-modern Hollywood Gothic that thrived for a time in the 1960s and 1970s. Sadly, Harrington's fortunes dwindled under other producers; both *What's the Matter with Helen?* and *Ruby* suffered from extensive re-edits by their respective producers, though *Ruby* went on to become Harrington's strongest box-office hit. *The Killing Kind* suffered an abortive release theatrically and on video, and has become almost impossible to see today, though it remains perhaps the strongest of Harrington's features. Television censorship further truncated Harrington's best work, including made-for-television features like *The Dead Don't Die*; the most compelling of Harrington's television films, *Killer Bees*, remains in syndication, but it (along with *The Cat Creature*) has never been released on video in any form. Producer Steve Katz further tampered with the television version of *Ruby* (credited, after the final credits, to 'Alan Smithee'), rendering it almost incoherent; unfortunately, this subsequently became the primary cut available on video.

Harrington directed his last feature, *Mata Hari*, in 1984, and his frequent television series work dried up shortly thereafter. He was unable to mobilise financing for his planned feature *Cranium* in the 1990s, though his friendship with James Whale led to his acting as an unofficial consultant for Bill Condon's *Gods and Monsters* (1998). At the age of 72, Harrington returned to his personal filmmaking roots to remake *The Fall of the House of Usher* (2000, 36 min.) As he stated, this was 'simply to make a film, just like I made the short films at the beginning of my career.'[23] Once again, Harrington played Roderick Usher.

Today, Harrington's underground work is long out of circulation and nearly forgotten – the underground movement disowned him in the wake of his commercial features, just as the mainstream critics' vehement rejection of the underground shorn Harrington from his own creative roots. Harrington remains a 'man without a country', an important genre director who has rarely enjoyed the critical attention and acclaim he long ago earned. Like Edgar Ulmer, Riccardo Freda and Mario Bava, Harrington created imaginative, visually rich, even lavish, masterworks of the genre within the parameters of often ridiculously tight budgets and schedules, a skill he had refined with his underground efforts.

The renewed availability of Harrington's underground films is essential to the recovery of his identity as a filmmaker, and his historic identity as an innovator. Attempts in the late 1980s to release Harrington's short films through Mystic Fire Video sadly evaporated. The majority of his features have been released on video (though often in substandard transfers from dubious labels) and a few have appeared on DVD. However, they are still unfairly dismissed as being overly derivative of *Psycho* and *Whatever Happened to Baby Jane?* (1962) rather than the vital culmination of his own formative, thematic obsessions which – as these 1940s experimental films prove – predated their mainstream 'archetypes' by over a decade.

CHAPTER 4
'SPECIAL EFFECTS' IN THE CUTTING ROOM

Tony Williams

The films of Larry Cohen have long been an interesting anomaly in American cinema. Cohen has made pictures on budgets which would be entirely impossible in today's mega-million buck industrial climate. He has also operated in a manner very akin to the techniques of underground cinema by the ways he finances and shoots his films. As an independent commercial director, he describes his role as that of a 'guerrilla' filmmaker.[1] Cohen and several of his collaborators use this term to describe the director's particular method of making films, one often involving minuscule budgets and a type of risk-taking not found in mainstream cinema today. Although Cohen's style differs from most examples of Hollywood mainstream and independent cinema, his very *modus operandi* and synthetic inflections of motifs taken from diverse sources parallel certain practices associated with American underground filmmaking.

Any case for defining Cohen's work in relation to the cinematic underground must consider the nature of the dominant discourses surrounding the usual definitions of independent cinema. Generally, as in the work of Wheeler Winston Dixon,[2] these involve concepts that historically define American experimental cinema as arising from the development of an avant-garde tradition emerging from New York and/or California in the 1960s. More often than not, this movement is associated with key names such as Andy Warhol, Jack Smith, Ron Rice, and several others. Also, the theatrical venue often forms an influential role in conceptions of underground cinema by defining relevant examples as those having had premieres at the New York Underground Film Festival or various independent campus locations. Most popular definitions of underground film usually encompass those works which eschew narrative in order to operate in a totally avant-garde manner which will preserve both formal purity and radical intentions from contamination by the dominant ideology.

However, these definitions tend to be too rigid in terms of understanding how cinematic movements operate in particular fluid ways. Although narrative and independent films tend to be regarded as mutually exclusive, this is not often the case in certain realms of cinematic practice. For example, Soviet independent films such as Lev Kuleshov's *The Extraordinary Adventures of Mr. West in the Land of the Bolsheviks* (1924) engaged in a satire of both Hollywood cinema and Western ideological misconceptions of a new society by merging comedy techniques, circus acrobatics, avant-garde acting styles and documentary shots within a highly heterogeneous formula.

Also, the Andy Warhol Factory films often engaged in interrogating the nature of Hollywood formulas, using them for their own mode of satire. This was particularly the case with those films directed by Paul Morrissey. Although Morrissey altered Warhol's avant-garde practices into more structured directions, thereby incurring the wrath of purists (similar to those who criticised Bob Dylan's use of electric instruments in the late 1960s, as well as Miles Davis' jazz explorations in the same decade), Warhol-produced films such as *Heat* (1972), *Andy Warhol's Frankenstein* (1974) and *Andy Warhol's Dracula* (1974) did not entirely depart from their subversively satirical, underground use of Hollywood formulas. For example, *Heat* was a reworking of Billy Wilder's *Sunset Boulevard* (1951) starring Factory alumni Joe D'Allesandro in the William Holden role and Sylvia Miles as Gloria Swanson. (Both Miles and Morrissey had appeared separately in John Schlesinger's *Midnight Cowboy* (1969), which also featured aspects of New York underground life.) Not only did the film transform Wilder's original into another 'Day in the life of Joe the Hustler', as in *Flesh* (1968) and *Trash* (1970), but it ended with the hero escaping his predecessor's fate by not falling into a Hollywood swimming pool after a rejected lover fires a gun at him. We must also remember that Wilder had attempted his own version of an 'underground', non-Hollywood mode of discourse in the original cut of *Sunset Boulevard*, where Joe Gillis' dead body engaged in voiceover conversation with other occupants of the morgue. Preview reactions led to the elimination of this scene.

An underground film may operate in an essentially fluid manner and does not necessarily involve the jettisoning of either narrative or influential mainstream films for referential purposes. Certain examples may, however, update and interrogate the premises of the original mastertext in a manner which, although not abandoning narrative, can resemble certain practices of underground cinema by adding new inflections both stylistically and thematically.

HITCHCOCK AND COHEN: A COUPLE OF RADICALS

My point concerning the films above is not to argue for demolishing the usual convenient classifications concerning the nature of underground cinema. It is rather to argue for a more flexible interpretation which recognises occurrences of this phenomena in areas where it would not otherwise be considered. This is specifically so with respect to two films Cohen shot in New York during 1984: *Perfect Strangers* and *Special Effects*. Although formally narratives, they rework cinematic conventions in very much the same manner as the best examples of underground cinema. Furthermore, not only did Cohen shoot these films on the kinds of low budgets common to this type of cinema, he also understood their specific kinship. Speaking of shooting both films back-to-back with the same crew, he remarked on the former's use of 'all kinds of New York people who'd worked in underground movies,' people who were not 'even in the Screen Actors Guild.' Cohen enjoyed working with Eric Bogosian, Zoë Tamerlis and others on *Special Effects*, describing them as 'all highly offbeat people who lived in strange basements, had no money, but were highly talented.'[3] On *Perfect Strangers*, Cohen worked with Anne Carlisle, whose only previous role involved playing both male and female characters in *Liquid Sky* (1983), directed by Eastern European alternative filmmaker Slava Tuskerman. Although *Perfect Strangers* is an accomplished work in its own right, *Special Effects* is really the more 'underground' of the two.

Special Effects is particularly significant in terms of its use of self-reflexive techniques usually associated exclusively with underground cinema. It continues Cohen's interrogation and extension of motifs contained within the films of Alfred Hitchcock, but they are here mediated within the mode of the former's cherished 'guerrilla cinema'. Despite its narrative structure, *Special Effects* contains several self-reflexive elements characteristic not only of Hitchcock's cinema, but also Hitch's fascination with those earlier avant-garde moments in European cinema such as German expressionism and Soviet montage which he often incorporated into his own films. Although Hitchcock later became identified with the Hollywood studio system, he was also influenced by the 'underground' films of his day which were first screened at the London Film Society from 1925 onwards. Although many of these films later became classified as 'Art Cinema', at the time of their original exhibition they were considered dangerously subversive works, especially those belonging to Soviet Cinema that received their only public screenings at Workers' Film Societies both in Britain and America. Furthermore, both Hitchcock and Douglas Sirk subtly attempted to inflect their Hollywood narratives with non-mainstream cinematic expressionistic flourishes in their later careers within the studio system.

Since underground cinema is often associated with radical movements interrogating the status quo, *Special Effects* offers an interesting example of how a narrative film may provide the viewer with oppositional strategies often exclusively associated with independent cinema. For example, during the heyday of *Screen* theory in the 1970s, the avant-garde was thought to be the only salvation for viewers seeking to escape from a supposedly oppressive form of gendered visual pleasure associated with a particular rigid definition of narrative cinema. However, this strategy soon became redundant with the emergence of a diverse number of theories associated with the fluid nature of visual spectatorship, as well as the later translations of then-unknown Russian narrative theorist Mikhail Bakhtin.

Although, to her credit, Laura Mulvey noticed an 'uneasy gaze' and 'disorientating voyeurism' in the Hitchcock films she singled out for criticism, her influential 1975 essay led to a rallying call for an oppositional avant-garde non-narrative cinema (which, supposedly, would lead viewers in radical directions) that went unanswered.[4] Furthermore, as critics such as D. N. Rodowick have since revealed, this original essay is highly rigid and reductive in nature.[5] *Special Effects*, however, is particularly instructive in showing how a low-budget underground film using a narrative structure can interrogate the negative effects of the male gaze and, at the same time, deliver a form of visual pleasure that is not compromised by the dominant ideology.

It is also possible to argue that *Special Effects* provides a specific reply to the third formulation of Mulvey's theory in terms of its radical use of narrative interrogation. Whereas in 'Visual Pleasure' Mulvey championed the avant-garde, her second follow-up essay (entitled 'Changes') saw possibilities within a Bakhtinian carnivalesque narrative strategy.[6] May not an independent cinematic use of narrative space contain a potentially transgressive Bakhtinian conflict involving visual technique, self-conscious practices and humour, one that leads to a particular cinematic pleasure as challenging to the audience as the pointing figure of the jester in the climax of *Blackmail* (1929)? One might question whether a particular inflection of the Hitchcock text belongs in any definition of underground cinema. But if Warhol's Factory could appropriate and rework *Sunset Boulevard* in *Heat*, then Cohen has every right to do the same thing in *Special Effects*. Furthermore, both counter-cinema and the underground are at their best operating against a dominant narrative and providing alternative counterpoints. This may not necessarily be formal; it can also be both narratively thematic and oppositional. As Sally Potter's *Thriller* (1979) demonstrated, a Hitchcock text may be used in many counter-cinematic ways. The same is true for productions belonging to that now-lost era of creative British television, as seen in the later works of Dennis Potter and *Artemis 81* (1981). Directed by Alastair Reid from a teleplay by David Rudkin, the latter merged allusive references to Hitchcock films within a generic framework indebted to British television productions such as the *Quatermass* series (1953–57) and *A For Andromeda* (1961), while challenging viewers to respond actively in a manner resembling practices associated with avant-garde techniques by the very nature of its allusive narrative structure.

SELF-REFLEXIVITY IN 'SPECIAL EFFECTS'

Special Effects is based upon a screenplay written at the same time Cohen attempted to interest Hitchcock in directing *Daddy's Gone A Hunting* (1969), based on another Cohen script. Universal Studio politics succeeded in thwarting this ambition, and the project ended up in the less creative hands of Mark Robson. Already disillusioned by the way his West Coast television projects usually ended up on the small screen, Cohen then decided to control his work by directing it whenever possible. This led to his first film, *Bone* (1972), which he shot in a manner resembling an independent, underground film. The original title of *Special Effects* was 'The Cutting Room', self-reflexively specifying certain parallels between film editing and violence. Cohen's later involvement in the world of New York independent cinema finally led to the filming of this project.

Special Effects engages in a self-reflexive cinematic examination of the murderous gaze within a narrative plot partly indebted to *Vertigo* (1958). But it also evinces Cohen's fascination with the oppressive nature of patriarchal, family-defined identity. These were themes already present in his early teleplays, such as the 1963 *Arrest at Trial* episode 'My Name is Martin Burnham', and the January 1965 opening episode of *Branded* (entitled 'Survival'), as well as his later scripts for both film and television. *Special Effects* also contains several humorous moments, not just Hitchcock-influenced, but part of Cohen's strategy whereby comedic moments often disrupt coherent operations of traditional narrative cinema. This strategy can be observed in many Cohen films, including such successful and not-so successful instances as *It's Alive III: Island of the Alive* (1986) and *Wicked Stepmother* (1989).

Special Effects opens with a scene which uncannily foreshadows Bill and Monica's escapades in the White House. A scantily clad woman poses half-naked in the Oval Office, providing a particular form of visual pleasure before leering male photographers. It takes a moment to realise that the scene is not 'realistic', but a studio recreation of the now-infamous Clinton 'Oral Office' set up for voyeuristic purposes. Abandoned Okie husband Keefe Waterman (Brad Rijn) arrives to find his erring blonde wife Mary Jean (Zoë Tamerlis) positioned upon a revolving dias. As this opening sequence shows, appearances can be both deceptive and devastating. Mary Jean has not only abandoned her traditional subordinate role as Oklahoma housewife, but (to Keene's disgust) has taken on a new identity as 'Andrea Wilcox' in order to begin realising her dreams of fame and fortune in New York. Furthermore, the opening shot tracks Andrea by performing a 360-degree camera movement. This not only calls to mind the dominating cinematic mechanisms used to depict the complex romantic agonies of *Vertigo* and Brian De Palma's *Obsession* (1976), but also the patriarchal system's exploitative use of the female body as seen in Hitchcock's *Notorious* (1946) and *North by Northwest* (1959). Here it is worth remembering that although Hitchcock's techniques have over time become appropriated as Hollywood 'cultural capital', they were originally regarded as the equivalent of today's underground filmmaking techniques in the conservative world of British cinema, which reacted adversely against the infiltration of European techniques such as German expressionism and Soviet montage into their productions. The same problems affected the work of Powell and Pressburger.

Returning to her sleazy apartment, Keefe forces Andrea to watch a 16mm film of their 31-month-old son. While Andrea objects that the child will no longer recognise her, Keefe callously replies that as an actress she can easily play the mother's role (a line that will foreshadow the film's climactic airport scene). A blurring of identities occurs early on, as Keefe acts like a dominating director making his lead actress watch a cinematic example of the part he wishes her to perform. Andrea also engages in her own form of fantasy role-playing by lying to Keefe that twice-busted Hollywood director Chris Neville (Eric Bogosian) wants her for his new film. She manages to escape from her husband and arrive at Neville's apartment. After auditioning for a different type of role, she becomes outraged when she discovers him filming their lovemaking. By verbally humiliating Neville's sexual and creative powers, she provokes her own death at his hands under the eye of a camera concealed behind a mirror. Falsely accused of her murder, Keefe finds himself bailed out of jail by Neville, who wishes to use him in a 16mm re-creation of Andrea's life and death. This will obviously be a picture made under underground filmmaking conditions, to be blown up into 35mm for general release.

Neville's circumstances not only echo the plight of directors who have experienced flops within the mainstream film industry and who wish to keep working in the low-budget independent field, but also anticipates the contemporary predicament facing once major talents today. During 2001, some British newspapers reported the plight of television and film director Ken Russell; now exiled from both industries, he continues making films on video in his garage with the aim of distributing the finished product on the Internet. Under these circumstances, boundaries between mainstream and underground talents as well as divisions between narrative and avant-garde techniques become very blurred – a contemporary phenomenon Cohen's *Special Effects* superbly foreshadows.

Supposedly firm boundaries between the 'law' and exploitation also become blurred in a manner evoking Hitchcock motifs in works as diverse as *Easy Virtue* (1927), *Champagne* (1928), *Notorious* (1946), and *Vertigo*. Detective-Lieutenant Philip Delroy (Kevin O'Connor), the officer who arrested Keefe, becomes so fascinated by cinematic techniques that Neville appoints him as technical advisor on his film. Such a blurring of boundaries also echoes the high degree of contemporary involvement of New York police on television productions such as *Law and Order*, *Law and Order: Special Victims Unit*, *N.Y.P.D. Blue*, *Third Watch* and *100 Centre Street*. As one critic remarked in a recent *New York Times* article, 'So many New York badges glisten in the lights of the cameras these days, it might behoove the police brass to think about recruiting from the drama schools.'[7]

Failing to find a suitable actress, Keefe accidentally discovers lookalike Elaine Bernstein (also played by Tamerlis) whom Neville transforms into the dead Mary Jean/Andrea in a manner resembling the techniques Scotty (James Stewart) uses on Judy (Kim Novak) in *Vertigo*. After losing footage of Andrea's death, Neville decides to recreate the original murder according to the improvisation techniques of underground cinema. But he rewrites the screenplay so that *Keefe* supposedly kills Elaine, with Neville killing him in turn. After realising that Neville intends to make him 'The Wrong Man', Keefe escapes from the police and removes all the fuses from Neville's apartment to frustrate his plans. Engaging in a struggle with Neville, Keefe throws him into his indoor pool along with a studio light which electrocutes him – a punishment he would have received before the days of lethal injection. Elaine unknowingly becomes Keefe's accomplice by plugging the fuses back in, an act which leads to Neville's electrocution. She thus becomes the underground equivalent of Hitchcock's 'guilty woman'. *Special Effects* concludes in an ironic manner, with Delroy before the media announcing his intention to complete Neville's unfinished film while Keefe flies home to Oklahoma with Elaine, whom he now renames Mary Jean.

Special Effects might appear to be a mere derivation of *Vertigo* were it not for the fact that the source is incidental to a plot centered upon identification and the cinematic machine. These elements not only occur within Hitchcock's British and American periods, but also within various works of underground cinema. *Special Effects* also emphasises the self-reflexive components contained within the low-budget world of independent cinema much more radically than any of Cohen's previous or subsequent films. In addition, the dislocation of Hollywood cohesive narrative structures echoes the challenging nature of his screenplay for *Bone*, which was written at the same time as *Special Effects*.[8] The latter film uses the *Vertigo* references more radically than does De Palma's *Obsession*; although both utilise Hitchcock's recognition of the oppressive nature of gender roles, Cohen's treatment brings this issue to the forefront by formally employing underground cinematic techniques. Ultimately, the *Vertigo* narrative becomes as marginal to the construction of *Special Effects* as the scene showing Mary Jean/Andrea's dead body in a car parked in the abandoned Coney Island winter landscape. Like Marion Crane (Janet Leigh) during her drive to California in *Psycho* (1960), Andrea's eyes are wide and staring, the only movement being the swish of the windscreen wipers turning back and forth. Mary Jean's journey to New York ends in brutal violence. She is the victim of a power relationship in which two impotent males attempt to dominate her.

(DIS)HONEST ABE ZAPRUDER

If the themes of *Special Effects* were not extraordinary enough, Cohen's particular manner of cinematic treatment is also exemplary insofar as it blurs numerous boundaries. This blurring involves sound as well as vision. The opening of *Special Effects* resembles that of Hitchcock's second sound film, *Juno and the Paycock* (1929), in that it contains voices against a black background before the visuals actually begin. Although such practice became commonplace in the later sound era, Cohen restores this 'disruptive' opening to the very radical avant-garde intentions employed by Hitchcock in his early sound productions. While Hitchcock emphasises the monologue of Barry Fitzgerald's Orator at the beginning of *Juno*, Cohen employs a dialogue between the unseen figures of Neville and reporters after his firing from a multi-million dollar production. Dismissing accusations of wasting money, Neville responds that his movies make millions of dollars in video rentals – a common situation for many directors who never gain theatrical release today – in a distribution system which functions as an alternative means of seeing different types of films (depending of course on the location).

As a special effects director, Neville acclaims 'honest Abe Zapruder' as his mentor in a manner acknowledging transgressions of real-life boundaries between fantasy and reality. Although Zapruder shot the only footage of the Kennedy assassination on an 8mm camera, questions of documentary reality often clash with issues of interpretation, as films such as Oliver Stone's *JFK* (1991) reveal. Despite being a 'real-life' documentary shot like a family home movie, the Zapruder footage is open to as many interpretations as the best examples of avant-garde and underground cinema. Neville actually dismisses Andrea's belief in the reality of the news footage documentation of Lee Harvey Oswald's death, viewing it instead as make-believe.

The original title of *Special Effects* – 'The Cutting Room' – emphasises editing, a process which denotes not only the manipulation of reality, but also murder, as demonstrated in such classic examples as *Battleship Potemkin*'s (1925) Odessa Steps Massacre and the shower scene in *Psycho*. In *Special Effects*, Neville embodies William Rothman's definition of Hitchcock's 'murderous gaze' by committing murder wearing editing gloves and attempting another with editing scissors.[9] (Significantly, Jeff Costello [Alain Delon] in Jean-Pierre Melville's 1967 *Le Samouraï* wears editing gloves as part of his murderous profession.) Neville's fascination with the Kennedy and Oswald assassinations also reinforces the connection between the real-life world of documentary and violent fantasies revealed by Hitchcock in the opening scenes of *The Lodger* (1927) and *Blackmail* (1929). The subversive blurring of boundaries between reality and imagination is thus present not only in the more familiar examples of underground cinema, but also in the work of Hitchcock and Cohen.

Neville inhabits an apartment decorated with rose imagery, the rose fascinating him because it combines opposing emblems of beauty and violence. Roses also have thorns that can injure. During his assault on Andrea, Neville scratches her back with thorns. Also, at various points in the film, rose thorns prick the fingers of both Neville and Keefe. These oppositional realms of beauty and death complement intertwining associations of sexuality and violence occurring throughout *Special Effects*. After Neville's interview segment in which he acclaims the death-conveying 8mm Zapruder home movie footage, *Special Effects* opens (as discussed above) with a low-angle shot of Andrea posing before male viewers in the sleazy Oval Office set. When Keefe brutally assaults the organiser who attempts to stop him from pursuing Andrea, an exhilarated voyeur immediately gets over his disappointment in losing 'girly shots' by avidly photographing Keefe's victim. Later, when Neville films a bedroom scene between Keefe and Elaine (the latter now cast in Andrea's fictional role), he coaxes the prudish husband into coupling as he remembers his earlier violent bedroom assault upon Andrea.

In one striking scene, Cohen films Neville from a high angle as he casually walks over the photos of hundreds of willing actresses eager to audition for the role of a murdered woman. Oblivious to (or uncaring about) her death, even Andrea's own agent sends Neville a still! The imagery here superbly illustrates certain deadly psychoanalytic mechanisms contained within the cinematic medium, mechanisms which parallel the sadistic nature of the director's murderous gaze with the masochistic submissiveness of willing victims eager to lend their bodies to passive reproduction on the screen. Significantly, this scene also depicts the world of cinema as an art of dangerous ideological illusion trapping males and females within deadly, power-dominated roles. It is a revelation usually defined as belonging to the anti-mainstream movement of non-narrative underground cinema. But here we find this device employed within a narrative film.

The unequal nature of power relationships between males and females occurs at different points throughout *Special Effects*. When Keefe chases Andrea out of the 'Oval Office', he first encounters a lookalike who plays upon his fantasy. Keefe's former reality of his Oklahoma wife and mother of his child is an illusion, since Mary Jean has now become Andrea. The lookalike propositions Keefe: 'My name is Mary Jean. I can be whatever you want me to be.' Keefe angrily replies, 'You're not Mary Jean. You're not my wife!', to which the woman significantly responds, 'Are you sure?' Later, while Keefe compulsively gazes at the 16mm image of their young son, Andrea expresses alienation. Frustrated by his puritanical nature, she rejects the role of wife and mother. Unlike Margaret (Peggy Ashcroft) in Hitchcock's *The 39 Steps* (1935), Andrea has managed to escape to the city but only finds disillusionment, sexual exploitation and death there. Keefe's aggressive attitude parallels that of crofter John (John Laurie) in the earlier film. But Keefe finds his true shadow self in director Chris Neville, who will carry the violent implications within his possessive gaze to their logical conclusions.

Like other oppressive Hitchcock figures, such as Millie (Margaret Leighton) and the pre-repentant Charles Adare (Michael Wilding) in *Under Capricorn* (1948), Ben McKenna (James Stewart) in *The Man Who Knew Too Much* (1955), Scotty in *Vertigo* and Lil (Diane Baker) in *Marnie* (1964), Keefe's possessiveness and denial of Andrea's real personality drives her into the bed of a man she actually dislikes. She complains to Neville about her husband, 'He wanted me to be Mary Jean, not Andrea.' The climax of *Special Effects* has Elaine exhibiting reluctance about playing her next role as long-lost mother when she travels to Oklahoma with Keefe. While she speaks of Keefe's son – 'I wonder if he'll recognise me. It's been so long' – the camera zooms in to Keefe's dominating gaze as he replies: 'Don't worry about it. You look just like your picture.' The scene ends with Elaine realising her new entrapment under another director who will groom and direct his contracted actress for another dangerously oppressive role, one that exists within the same patriarchal system her predecessor attempted to flee from in vain.

Neville and Keefe appear as dominating males in *Special Effects*. But they are both role-players whose everyday performances conceal deep insecurities. Keefe has lost Mary Jean while Neville has lost two major films. Both characters resort to violence to compensate for their loss of power. Keefe also becomes insecure when Neville casts him as himself in the movie *Andrea*, directed by Neville. In one humorous scene in a nightclub, Neville kisses Keefe briefly and undermines the Oklahoma husband's gendered security. This scene also reinforces the line a taxi driver utters while driving Keefe to Neville's apartment. Perhaps recognising the hidden sexual ambivalence within his violent passenger, he twice unsuccessfully attempts to interest him in visiting a transvestite bar: 'You can't tell them from the genuine article.' This line also echoes those spoken by Andrea's lookalike several scenes earlier.

Andrea too engages in several masquerades. Discarding the role of Oklahoma wife and mother Mary Jean, she poses in the recreated Oval Office as a Presidential Playmate, passes herself off to Keefe as a successful actress, pretends to be a New York University student trying to write a paper on Neville's films and plays her last role as unwilling corpse. Additionally, Keefe's flight to Neville's apartment duplicates that of Andrea's on the previous day. Neville also shoots both partners on film, his camera recording Andrea's death as well as Keefe's arrest. As for Elaine, she confesses to having several personalities, none of which she actually likes. She engages in Salvation Army work, feminist activities and teaching new maths in Harlem in very much the superficial manner of Melanie Daniels (Tippie Hedren) in *The Birds* (1963), finally becoming a voyeuristic object for both Neville and Keefe. Like Hedren's eponymous Marnie, Elaine is a victim of 'feigning and falsehood',[10] seeing in masquerade an escape from her personal dilemma.

Like Sir John (Herbert Marshall) in *Murder* (1930), Neville intends to direct his own project and nearly succeeds in accomplishing this aim. As with Hitchcock's theatrical performers, he plays directly to the camera. Before killing blackmailing laboratory technician Gruskin (Richard Greene), Neville decides against using a knife. He speaks to the camera: 'No, it's been done.' Finding a pair of editing gloves, he puts them on and strangles Grushkin with celluloid. Neville concludes by praising his own performance to the audience, 'Now that's fresh!' At one point Elaine remarks to Neville: 'You don't do things. You rehearse them,' complementing an earlier line – 'You don't talk to people. You do routines' – when they are in a restaurant overlooking a theater advertising *A Chorus Line*. After murdering Andrea, Neville exclaims 'That's a take,' before the screen displays Neville's imagined credit, 'Andrea. A Film by Chris Neville'.

Cohen's technique here and elsewhere breaks up established techniques of narrative diegesis. After Keefe accidentally destroys Neville's footage of Andrea's murder, mistakenly believing it to be his family home movie, Neville envisages another scenario. This one is mediated on the cinema screen in script captions that describe Elaine's murder and Neville's accidental killing of Keefe as the supposed murderer. Throughout Cohen's film, everyone becomes hooked within a cinematic scenario they are powerless to prevent. Ignoring Keefe's moral objections during a sex scene, Elaine responds, 'I don't care. I'm hooked and so are you.'

Special Effects concludes ironically, with the unhappy couple flying away to Oklahoma after the airline attendant informs them that the flight has 'a complimentary luncheon and a movie'. This line not only satirically reflects Hitchcock's frequent associations between food and violence, but also compliments the shot revealing Andrea's dead body, one which shows a sign prominently displaying 'Golden Fried Chicken'. Another parallel can be found in the 'Cold Meat' advertisement Richard

Hannay (Robert Donat) sees in the newspaper announcing Annabella's (Lucie Mannheim) murder in the crofter's cottage in *The 39 Steps*, as well as the many visual associations between food and violence occurring in Hitchcock's *Frenzy* (1972). As the plane flies away, the credits 'A Philip Delroy Film' appear, before the 'real' film credits roll.

As a director Neville may be a master manipulator, but he never lacks for willing victims. Top criminal lawyer Wiesenthal (Steven Pudenz), whom Neville hires to represent Keefe, is often mistaken for infamous media-conscious McCarthy attorney Roy Cohn. He helps Neville because he wishes a movie to be made of his life one day. Neville seduces not only Andrea and Elaine, but also Keefe and Lt. Delroy. Delroy in fact becomes fascinated by the movie business, ignoring his partner's pleas to return to their normal work, and eventually becoming Neville's associate producer (with his own car and free advertising). In the penultimate scene of *Special Effects*, Delroy informs news reporters – among whom is Cohen in an uncharacteristic Hitchcock-like cameo appearance – that he intends to complete Neville's picture himself. Unlike Detective Frank Webber (John Londgen) in *Blackmail*, who avidly views Scotland Yard movies such as 'Fingerprints' to see if the director gets the facts wrong, Delroy believes that his 'skill and insight and knowledge of police procedures' will make for 'one hell of a picture'.

CONCLUSION

Special Effects uses many of the self-reflexive techniques associated with underground cinema to engage in a dialogical re-working of the Hitchcock mastertext in the manner suggested by Mulvey in her 1985 'Changes' essay. Although her original 'Visual Pleasure and Narrative Cinema' manifesto championed the supposed radical claims of independent cinema, her subsequent revisions revealed a number of blind spots in her premises. For example, a narrative film may employ techniques associated with the supposedly alternative world of underground cinema. Furthermore, Mulvey's original argument lost sight of the fact that directors such as Hitchcock also employed certain techniques within their films which were once associated with the contemporary version of the underground. *Special Effects* is a low-budget film interrogating narrative mechanisms in very much the spirit of underground cinema. Neville explains his methodology (and the film's title) to Delroy in the following manner, also defining Cohen's principle of underground filmmaking: 'People assume that special effects means taking models, miniatures, tricking them up, making them look real. I'm taking reality and making it look like make-believe. That's a special effect too.'

In very much the same spirit as Hitchcock's explorations, Cohen's film interrogates the mechanisms of narrative cinema, breaking down supposedly rigid boundaries between the mainstream and underground worlds. It examines the supposedly distinct realms of fiction, fact, fantasy, documentary, news reporting, sex and politics, revealing them all as belonging to a system needing interrogation and eventual rejection. As Keefe and Elaine fly away towards an undisclosed marital future as bleak as that facing Frank and Alice (Anny Ondra) in the climax of *Blackmail*, two director's credits appear, 'A Larry Cohen Production' following 'A Philip Delroy Film'. These credits contrast a reality and fiction both of which have been revealed as deadly illusions.

Special Effects is a challenging film. Consciously employing different styles and techniques, it suggests one possible avenue for achieving Mulvey's idea of a 'transformative potential'[11] within areas of popular culture, one that combines a self-aware textual pleasure within a narrative format that remains uncompromised by the very nature of the exploration achieved by its its director. It is an interesting and maverick experiment in underground filmmaking that deserves more acclaim.

This is a revised version of a paper originally presented at the 'After Hitchcock' Panel at the March 1995 Society for Cinema Studies Conference in New York.

CHAPTER 5
REAL(IST) HORROR: FROM EXECUTION VIDEOS TO SNUFF FILMS

Joel Black

> If it is real, I'd be a fool to admit it. If it isn't real, I'd be a fool to admit it.
>
> Allan Shackleton, about his film *Snuff*[1]

> You could take the best expert today on moviemaking and he wouldn't be able to tell if it's real or not. The only thing is if you find the victim.
>
> Israeli investigative journalist Yoram Svoray on snuff films[2]

THE SHOCK OF THE (UN)REAL

Without a doubt the most extreme form of underground cinema is the death film. Up to now, non-fictional footage of executions, assassinations and ritual sacrifice of the sort featured in the *Mondo*

Cane and *Faces of Death* series have enjoyed a limited, cult following. Yet there are growing signs that this form is gaining more widespread public acceptance, and is emerging from the underground to appear in more mainstream forms of entertainment.

The principal reason why 'real life' death films have traditionally been an underground subgenre is because of the virtual ban on visual records of death, and especially violent death. As a result, the movies have found it not only necessary but profitable to adopt a variety of conventions for simulating loss of life. This was not always the case. In the early years of cinema, scenes of actual death were as likely to be encountered as their simulations. It was not President William McKinley's 1901 assassination, after all, that Thomas Edison's studio re-enacted on film, but a recording of the *actual* execution that same year of his killer, the anarchist Leon Czolgosz. With its depiction of the condemned man approaching the electric chair, being strapped down, blindfolded and finally electrocuted while staring directly into the camera, Edison's *Execution of Czolgosz with Panorama of Auburn Prison* elicited a voyeuristic response in the viewer rather than surprise at a time when cinema was a 'medium of shock and excitement and stimulation'.[3] As such 'spectacle films' evolved from a documentary record of actual events into a form of fictional entertainment, simulations of violence increasingly became the norm while actual recordings of violent death tended to be marginalised, in effect going underground.

Although today executions have become a fairly routine occurrence in contemporary American society, they are sealed off from public view and are no longer the spectacles they once were, satisfying either the masses' demand for justice or their appetite for violence. (The last legal public execution took place in the United States in 1937.) Now the public must turn to movies, television and video games for their dose of realistic – as opposed to real – violence. Such simulations thrive principally in the genre of horror cinema: first, in stylised and expressionistic monster films from *Nosferatu* (1922) to *Frankenstein* (1931), and later in increasingly realistic representations of serial killers and other outwardly normal sociopaths that are often based on actual individuals. Unable, and supposedly unwilling, to see the *real* thing, American spectators have turned to thrillers and horror movies for the next 'best' thing – realistic simulations of murderous violence that afford many the luxury of seeing and experiencing what they profess to abhor.

Recently it seemed that the real-life death of convicted Oklahoma City bomber Timothy McVeigh in June 2001 might become the most watched American execution in well over a half-century. Yet although McVeigh himself wanted his death broadcast nationally, the country's first closed-circuit television broadcast of a federal death sentence was seen (besides by the actual witnesses in Terre Haute, Indiana) by an audience of only 232 survivors and family members of victims who gathered to watch the event at a secure site in Oklahoma City. And despite last-minute efforts of lawyers in an unrelated death penalty case to allow McVeigh's execution to be videotaped in order to show that the death penalty violates the Eighth Amendment's ban on cruel and unusual punishment, no visual document of the execution was made since federal regulations prohibit such recordings.

As it turned out, witnesses of the death by lethal injection of the unrepentant McVeigh reported no evidence of pain or suffering on his part, and little satisfaction on theirs. 'It was almost like the Devil was inside him looking at us,' said one observer who had lost an uncle in the blast.[4] Glaring up at the camera suspended from the ceiling at the moment of his death, McVeigh was both the star and the director of his own underground film. To the 'grieving people' watching him die he was 'more [a] manipulator ... than an offering to them.'[5]

The unsuccessful efforts by McVeigh to have his execution broadcast on national television, and by the attorneys who sought to have his execution videotaped, were essentially an attempt to bring back the practice of public execution in the age of electronic mass media. It was an attempt to show the real thing rather than a simulation. In effect, an underground genre of visual reality would have suddenly erupted into the mainstream of cinematic illusion, exposing the latter as such in the process. Even if such executions were made visible to mass audiences, however, this ultimate form of Reality TV is bound to be as contrived and artificial as any of the other so-called 'reality shows' that have saturated the air-waves in recent years (although this could change as such ratings-driven shows continue to 'to push the envelope farther and farther in order to make them interesting ... even if something terrible happens, even if someone gets killed').[6] As Wendy Lesser has foreseen, televised executions 'would give us a false experience, a substitute experience, while leading us to imagine we had had a real one. ... Watching on television as our government eliminated someone in a prison death chamber would seem like just another form of reality programming.' The principal reason in Lesser's view that such actual killings would seem so false is because, like most deaths on television (or, for that matter, in the movies), they are 'almost always expected'. Lacking the element of surprise, a fully-anticipated event like McVeigh's execution has virtually none of the shock value that could enable anti-death penalty advocates to argue that executions are a cruel and unusual punishment. Nor, for that matter, would live broadcasts of executions have the shock value we (paradoxically) look for in horror movies, and that we occasionally experience on live television when death is least expected, as in Lesser's examples of Jack Ruby's shooting of Lee Harvey Oswald or the Challenger space shuttle explosion.[7]

If we cannot find the shock of 'reality' in live broadcasts or videotapes of actual executions in which, even if they could be shown, the public display of inflicted death would strip it of its actual horror and neutralise it into a 'false experience', where then is such visual horror to be found? Once again, it seems, we must turn from underground visual records of actual deaths to commercial media fictions. By exploiting elements of suspense, surprise and spectacle, the fictional violence depicted on television and especially in the movies may elicit, as Lesser suggests, a greater sensation of horror in viewers than underground visual recordings of real-life violence.

Yet what if the sensational aesthetic elements of suspense, surprise and spectacle in mainstream fictional films were to be incorporated in episodes of real-life violence? Would this not produce the ultimate 'horror effect'? It is not surprising, then, that a number of commercial filmmakers have adopted the strategy of incorporating what seems to be authentic death-film footage within their cinematic fictions. Steven Jay Schneider has noted this convention in films like *Special Effects* (1984), *Mute Witness* (1994) and *Urban Legends: Final Cut* (2000), which begin by first presenting some obviously fake 'horror movie' material and then switching to a supposedly real 'snuff' mode.[8] Here I would like to pursue this observation, and to offer my own sampling of feature films that use this technique to push the envelope of what Cynthia Freeland calls 'realist horror'.[9] The films I have in mind attempt – either through apparently de-aestheticising techniques or though the opposite use of *hyper-aestheticising* strategies – to approach the theoretical limit of *real* horror through their references to, and occasionally their re-enactments of, actual filmed records of murder. Through their incorporation of amateurish, homemade snuff sequences, this subgenre of ultra-realist horror films reveals the concept of realist horror in underground as well as in mainstream fictional films to be a relative, aesthetic notion – at once an oxymoronic impossibility and a cinematic and cultural necessity.

USING SNUFF TO MAKE HORROR REAL

We may begin by briefly considering the film that has occasioned perhaps the most debate concerning the concept of realist horror: John McNaughton's *Henry: Portrait of a Serial Killer* (1990). This commercial movie, which has spawned its own cult following, is loosely based on the actual serial killer Henry Lee Lucas, but is more a fictional narrative than a documentary presentation. While various explanations have been offered as to why the film is so disturbing – because of its 'attitude of neutrality toward Henry',[10] because Henry 'defies external exegesis' and 'never comes to an ethical reckoning with his own savagery'[11] – the movie is especially problematic because it presents murderous violence in a way that seems both real and staged. The most disconcerting and frequently discussed scene in this film is a sequence in which Henry (Michael Rooker) and his partner Otis (Tom Towles) view their slaughter of a suburban family that they have recorded on a stolen camcorder. In this sequence, which has been called 'the scariest home-movie footage ever to make it to the big screen',[12] viewers see the killings not *as* they happen, but afterwards as we find ourselves watching the taped footage of the slaughter. As Freeland notes, what makes the camcorder sequence so disturbing beyond the brutality of its content is the viewers' discovery that

> we are watching this footage alongside the killers. … Point of view and real time are
> wrenched in a disconcerting way, with contradictory effects. On the one hand, the scene
> distances viewers and makes the murders seem less awful. The effect is as if we were just
> watching something on TV. The people in the family are already dead, depersonalized, not
> individuals. On the other hand, the amateur camera also makes the murders seem more
> real: things happen unexpectedly, everything seems unplanned and awkward. The view-
> point is not standard, and the murders are not cleanly centered for our observation.[13]

In Freeland's view, it is the combination of our identification with the killers in the act of reviewing the video of their deed and the 'grainy, tilted ... amateur' appearance of that home video that 'makes the murders seem more real'. The viewer has the uncanny experience of watching a snuff film – a visual record of a murder filmed (and viewed) by the killer or his or her accomplices. (Small wonder, as David Kerekes and David Slater note, that in some edited versions of *Henry*, 'an edit insert makes it clear *much earlier on* that Otis and Henry are watching a re-run of the murder on their television set. There seems to be some comfort in establishing that it is the two protagonists who were watching a snuff film and not us, the public.')[14] Only at the end of the snuff-film-within-the-film is it made clear that Henry and Otis are in fact the principal viewers. It is their emotionless, *affektlos* reaction to the video that provides such a stark contrast to what is presumably our horrified reaction at watching the identical footage. And the horror we experience is the result of the grainy realism of the snuff tape and the editing of the frame film, which bring about a temporary suspension of disbelief whereby we momentarily forget we are watching a fictional movie. For just a moment we think we are witnessing an actual snuff film: the horror we experience stems from our capacity – in contrast to Henry and Otis – to empathise with the terror of the apparently real victims.

Although it is certainly possible to consider 'this snuff movie within a movie to be John McNaughton's self-reflexive commentary on the lurid nature of his own movie',[15] the snuff sequence is first and foremost a means of giving a heightened sense of reality to the film as a whole. Yet for all its vaunted realism, the fictional snuff sequence in *Henry* hardly seems true to life if we compare it with footage of an actual sexually abused and terrorised victim in the hours and moments before she is killed. Even in the brief, heavily edited footage of Leonard Lake and Charles Ng's treatment of their victims shown in the 2000 A&E documentary *The California Killing Field*, the inert, passive state of the actual bound women contrasts sharply with the thrashing and screaming of the fictional bound woman in McNaughton's film. It would seem that claims about the realist horror of *Henry* are undercut by comparing the theatrical hysteria of the actress playing the part of the female victim in Henry and Otis' video with the frozen terror of the actual victims in Lake and Ng's tapes. As Irene Brunn of the San Francisco Police Department comments: 'You hear about movies, and you read about books and sadistic things that some people do to others, but [when] you view it unexpectedly it is just a total shock – something I never want to see again.'[16]

THE REALITY OF SNUFF FILMS

Since 1975, attempts to reproduce purportedly non-fictional recordings of murder in fictional films have raised a host of intriguing legal, moral, social, but also aesthetic issues stemming from the fact that snuff films lead a paradoxical – indeed virtual – existence. These issues were first memorably raised by the snuff sequence tacked onto the unreleased 1971 Argentine movie *Slaughter*. The five-minute film-within-a-film purportedly shows a director filming an obviously staged scene in which a pregnant woman is killed. Aroused by the scene, the director proceeds to have sex on the set with a production assistant whom he ultimately (and seemingly actually) dismembers and disembowels while the cameras are still rolling. Released in 1975 with the title *Snuff*, the movie was marketed as – and apparently believed by many to be – an actual snuff film. The producer, Allan Shackleton, capitalised on rumours that such films were being made in and exported from South America, and that at least one such film had been made in the US; namely, a recording of the Tate/LaBianca murders supposedly filmed by Charles Manson and his 'family'. Despite the inept result of tacking an apparently real snuff sequence onto a tacky exploitation film about a cult of young women following a Manson-like leader named Satan, Shackleton in effect bridged the gap between realist horror and real horror. He achieved this effect not only by resorting to a more graphic depiction of violence than that shown in *Slaughter*, but by deliberately staging this violence before the camera, thereby repositioning the viewer as filmmaker (as a surrogate for the director-turned-killer) and implicating the viewer in the violence.

The movie *Snuff* inaugurated a spate of underground cult films, and eventually several mainstream Hollywood products (for example: *Hardcore* (1979), *8MM* (1999) and, most recently, John Herzfeld's *15 Minutes* (2001)), in which apparently real snuff recordings are incorporated into fictional films. As Julian Petley remarks, 'the notion of the "snuff" movie was [soon] working its way into actual cinematic narratives, typically in the form of apparently "documentary" episodes inserted into the fictional story.'[17] The technique of following an obviously staged murder with a snuff sequence is a way of making the snuff sequence seem all the more realistic. And even if, as Schneider has observed, everyone watching these films 'knows that *even the "real" murder is faked (fictional)*' – a phenomenon he calls the 'aesthetic dilemma' in snuff films[18] – viewers of films like *Henry: Portrait of a Serial Killer* may be led through a willful suspension of disbelief to be momentarily troubled and tantalised by the possibility that they are witnessing the visual record of an actual murder. Viewers can even become disoriented to the point that they can no longer be certain of ontological distinctions, and have the truly troubling sensation of what it is *like* to watch snuff *despite* their knowledge that what they are seeing is not – and indeed cannot be – real. Not only do fictional horror films in the tradition of *Snuff* incorporate staged snuff sequences to make themselves appear shockingly real, but these fictional films also *give reality* to snuff films. In making use of snuff sequences to arouse terror in viewers and to produce the horror effect, horror films and thrillers also play on people's suspicions that an underground subculture exists in which snuff films are made and marketed.

It is one thing to note that the snuff sequences in most thrillers and horror films are not so graphic that viewers mistake them for the real thing. But the artificiality of these sequences, all of which can be traced back to the hokey history of the movie *Snuff*, has led skeptical critics to flatly deny the existence of such films, and to dismiss snuff as a modern myth. Thus Petley calls snuff movies 'entirely mythical', and repeatedly refers to 'the stubborn absence of any real evidence' of such films.[19] The problem with such an assertion is that it fails to distinguish between snuff films *per se* and snuff 'as a commercial commodity', a concept that Kerekes and Slater (in a line cited by Petley) call 'fascinating, but illogical.'[20] While the existence of a commercial underground market in snuff films is open to question, there is no doubt that sexually sadistic killers *do* make visual records of their deeds. Besides the Charles Ng/Leonard Lake tapes I have already cited, there is the case of Melvin Henry Ignatow, who in 1988 forced his girlfriend Mary Ann Shore to photograph him sexually abusing and torturing his fiancée Brenda Schaefer, who died during the ordeal of chloroform inhalation. As former US Attorney Scott Cox described the more than 100 photographs that eventually were found: 'They're just gruesome. It's like looking at a snuff film. At the beginning you can tell she's mortified and she's being ordered to disrobe and so forth. And then it depicts her being sexually assaulted.'[21]

Perhaps the most notorious recent murder case involving video recordings is that of the Canadian couple Paul Bernardo and Karla Homolka. Technically the videotapes they made of their victims Leslie Mahaffy and Kristen French were not snuff films because, as in the photos of Schaefer's ordeal, they only recorded the sexual abuse leading up to the girls' deaths and not the killings themselves – and in the case of Mahaffy, her dismemberment. In this respect, the content of the real-life Bernardo tapes inverts the camcorder sequence in the fictional feature *Henry: Portrait of a Serial Killer*: whereas the latter sequence shows Henry and Otis slaughtering a suburban family but breaks off when Otis begins to molest the corpse of his female victim, the Bernardo tapes depict his sexual degradation and violation of his victims, but breaks off before the actual killings. As might be expected, staged depictions of murderous violence are acceptable in mainstream movies while explicitly sexual scenes are taboo. (Sexual scenes are acceptable as long as it is clear that, like murder scenes, they are simulated and not real.) For a real-life sexual sadist like Bernardo, in contrast, the object is to preserve a visual record of sexual violence; recorded documentation of murderous violence remains taboo.

The absence of any visual record of the murders became a key issue in Bernardo's 1995 trial, in which Bernardo and Homolka each accused the other of doing the actual killing. (Bernardo maintained that the murders of both Mahaffey and French were carried out by Homolka in his absence.) However, the prior death of Homolka's younger sister Tammy Lyn appears to have been inadvertently recorded, since the anaesthetised girl expired at some point during her abuse. While it can be argued that this was not a snuff film because Tammy Lyn was unconscious during the filming, and because her death was accidental and not intentional, such technicalities only serve to point up the absurdities entailed in identifying and categorising snuff films: if the actual death of the victim must be shown and the victim must be conscious, then the various tapes made by Bernardo and Homolka meet only some of the requirements of the snuff film, and none of them satisfied all the requirements.

Far from supporting the view that snuff films do not exist because no one would be foolish enough to record evidence of the crime of murder (Kerekes and Slater, for example, claim that 'sexuality aside, it is unlikely that ... *any* figure ... would allow themselves to be filmed committing the act of murder'),[22] the Bernardo tapes lend credibility to the view that such films *do* exist. After

69

all, the reason Mahaffy and French were killed in the first place was to eliminate them as witnesses of their own molestation; in effect they were killed to keep them from revealing what the tapes *themselves* revealed. (Indeed, after Tammy Lyn's inadvertent death while she was unconscious, there was little to keep Bernardo and Homolka's crimes from escalating to intentional killings of conscious victims.) So even if the tapes did not record the girls' actual deaths, they recorded the sexual violence to which they were subjected that culminated in their deaths. Eventually the tapes were used as evidence that Bernardo had not only kidnapped and raped but also killed Leslie Mahaffy and Kristen French. In effect, the tapes recorded the *reason* – and indeed were *themselves* the reason – why the girls were killed.

We know in any case how important it is for the sadistic killer to keep a visual record of his sexual violence that may culminate in murder; indeed, *this visual record is itself the reason why the victim must die*. When the photographs that Mary Ann Shore admitted taking of Melvin Ignatow torturing Brenda Schaefer could not be found, FBI profiler Roy Hazelwood urged police to continue their search, claiming that Ignatow would not have destroyed them. 'That was his record,' Hazelwood maintained. 'That was his trophy. That was the most important part of the entire crime that was still left to be examined.'[23]

If no one seems to have seen snuff films it is not because they do not exist, but either because they cannot be found or they cannot be shown. The only people who get to see snuff films (besides the people who make them) are law enforcement officers, prosecutors and the defendants' lawyers. At Bernardo's trial, the infamous sex tapes were strictly barred from the general public. Only 69 people, most of them prosecutors, were authorised to see them. When true-crime author Stephen Williams offered a detailed description of the taped scenes in his bestselling 1996 book *Invisible Darkness*, he was charged with two counts of disobeying the judge's order restricting their viewing. Williams denied seeing the tapes, saying he had got almost all the details from material available to the public, but he refused to say where he had come by the rest – an offence for which he risked prosecution in Canada.[24]

While Williams managed to gain unauthorised access to the incriminating videotapes, the prosecutors who *were* authorised to see the tapes had at first been prevented from doing so because Bernardo's attorney Kenneth D. Murray concealed them for 16 months. (During this time, Homolka cut a deal with the prosecutors and was charged only with manslaughter because she had agreed to testify against her former husband. Similarly, in Ignatow's case the photographs which his girlfriend confessed she had taken of him torturing his fiancée were not found until after his acquittal. Unable to stand trial for murder under double indemnity laws, Ignatow could only be given a five-year sentence for perjury.) In 1997, professional misconduct complaints were issued against Murray, who was charged with becoming 'the tool or dupe of his unscrupulous client'. In the case against him, the Ontario courts and the Law Society of Upper Canada had to decide whether to 'interpret the videotapes as communications from Bernardo or, as one lawyer said, the crime itself'.[25]

Given the temptation on the part of defence lawyers to conceal graphic evidence of their clients' crimes, and the tight security surrounding (and, at least in Canada, the heavy penalties awaiting authors and journalists who disclose) such evidence once it is seized by the police and impounded by the courts, it is no wonder that snuff films seem to some a purely mythic phenomenon. On the one hand, such films lead an elusive, phantom existence that cannot be verified; on the other hand, supposing that they *do* exist, they depict a reality so horrific that it cannot be shown except in cinematic simulations like those in *Snuff* and *Henry*. Snuff films present us with a paradoxical singularity in cinema: a glimpse of ultimate reality shorn of any and all special effects, and yet a subgenre whose own elusiveness makes it seem the stuff of myth – the ultimate special effect.

PASSING SNUFF OFF AS FICTION

The mythic status of snuff films has spurred underground and, increasingly, mainstream filmmakers to incorporate simulated snuff scenes in their movies, employing all manner of special effects – prostheses, camera angles, et cetera – to produce the illusion of reality. Sometimes, however, these movies about snuff films deal with the opposite problem: a character who produces a snuff film tries to find a way to exhibit and distribute it by making it seem fake. Thus in Larry Cohen's *Special Effects*, film director Chris Neville (Eric Bogosian) inadvertently kills a girl on camera, and then decides to use the footage of the actual murder in a fictional feature that will appear 'totally real'. In the course of the film, however, Neville switches from his original goal of making his movie 'as real, as totally real as I can get it', to 'taking reality and making it look make-believe. That's a special effect too.'[26]

An even more striking example of the same ploy to pass actual snuff films off as fake horror cinema is Doug Ulrich's *Screen Kill* (1997), which concerns a goth-rock musician named Ralis who invites a horror film enthusiast named Doug to make a slasher movie with him. Doug soon discovers, however, that his partner Ralis is actually making snuff films, and that he, Doug, has been filming Ralis in the act of killing victims who also thought until the last moment that they were merely playing a role. Thus Ulrich exploits the familiar formula used in numerous other films such as *F/X* (1986), *Body Double* (1984), *Mute Witness* and *The End of Violence* (1997), in which a character in the business of making horror movies suddenly finds that he or she is involved in a real-life horror show.

As it turns out, Ralis is not content merely to make snuff films; he is determined to market them commercially, and has come up with a plan to do it. 'I know a way of setting up a distributor,' he tells Doug, who cannot believe he is serious and who worries that 'We'll have the fucking FBI all over us for making snuff movies!' Ralis then calmly explains his plan:

> You see, that's the thing. We don't put it out as a snuff movie. Snuff movies show one long
> take of someone getting killed, which makes it obvious that it's the real thing. Now what we

can do is we can insert different cut-aways with the actual kill, which will give the audience the illusion that they're watching a very realistic special effect.

The snuff filmmaker Ralis simply plans to employ the opposite technique of realist horror films such as *Screen Kill* itself (which the actor playing Ralis, Al Darago, happens to co-direct). Whereas *realist* horror incorporates seemingly 'documentary' episodes of violence as (real) footage within the main (fictional) film, thereby adding authenticity to the fictional production, the *real*-horror filmmaker Ralis inserts fictional 'cut-aways' in the actual snuff sequence, thereby making the real murder scene seem fictional. After all, an obvious giveaway that a snuff film is not authentic are the cut-aways and the multiple camera set-ups and editing they entail. (As Petley points out, the murder sequence in the film *Snuff* seemed fake precisely because of the presence of such cut-aways: 'the "murder" is filmed in classical "Hollywood" style, complete with alternating point-of-view shots and so on, which would have meant that the unfortunate "victim" would have had to have remained in place throughout the course of various camera set-ups!')[27] In contrast, it is precisely the *absence* of such cut-aways and 'visual angles' that makes a snuff sequence in a film look like it is documenting an actual murder. By inserting cut-aways into the sequence shots of his murders, the snuff filmmaker Ralis in *Screen Kill* simultaneously solves both the problem of how to make staged movie violence seem real, and the problem of how to make his snuff films available to a mass audience.

This crafty mixing of documentary and fictional footage to create an indeterminate, virtual murder scene is of course nothing new. Citing the 'huge vogue' of Gualtiero Jacopetti's *Mondo Cane* series of documentary films in the 1960s, the British novelist J. G. Ballard has noted how they 'cunningly mixed genuine film of atrocities, religious cults, and "Believe-it-or-not" examples of human oddity with carefully faked footage'. Yet, as Ballard points out, it is not just these cult shockumentaries that play havoc with reality and fiction, but the genre of the war newsreel, most of which 'are faked to some extent, usually filmed on manoeuvres'.[28] Nowhere is this confusion of the real and the fake more evident than in Ruggero Deodato's *Cannibal Holocaust* (1979), in which actual newsreel footage of a military death squad at work is included as a film within the film. Far from reinforcing the distinction between fiction and reality, the inclusion of this archival material thoroughly blurs any such distinction because the fictional deaths in the film are presented as being more real than the documentary footage of actual killings, the latter of which are dismissed by characters within the film as 'fake'.[29] Yet while the *effect* of incorporating documentary footage in fictional films may be to subvert the distinction between fiction and reality, the *purpose* of this ploy is typically to make the fictional frame story seem more convincing and real, even if – as in *Cannibal Holocaust* – this means branding actual documentary footage as fake.

Once snuff films began making their way into commercial cinema, first as cult films and later as mainstream movies, a paradoxical situation arose. Audiences enter a theatre to see a horror movie

FIGURE 7 Fiction as death film: *Cannibal Holocaust*

or thriller with the express understanding that they will witness graphic spectacles and simulacra of death, but that real death itself can never be shown. But is this really so? Oliver Stone's graphic use of the Zapruder film in *JFK* (1991) is, in fact, an instance of a type of snuff film being introduced – at once surreptitiously and flagrantly – into a mainstream Hollywood movie. Technically, of course, the Zapruder footage is not a snuff film because it was inadvertently filmed by a bystander at a public event who was not in any way involved in the murder. Yet its form is typical of snuff films. As described by Pasolini, it is the 'most typical' of sequence shots: 'the spectator-cameraman … did not choose any visual angles; he simply filmed from where he was, framing what his eye saw – better than the lens.'[30] Yet when Stone introduces the Zapruder footage as a film-within-his-film in the courtroom scene in *JFK* to give his movie added credibility, he does not present it simply as the straightforward documentary footage that it is. Instead, Stone works his own artistic fakery on the footage so that it begins to take on a unreal or surreal fictional quality of its own. 'In Stone's *JFK*', as Ken Morrison observes,

> the Kennedy head shot is lifted out of the Zapruder film and exploited by techniques of close-up, replay, and optical enhancements. Moreover, it is strategically held until the end of the courtroom scene to maximize its impact in an entertainment medium. In this way, frames 313 and 314 are placed within a Hollywood homicide technique.[31]

Here we have the inverse effect as that in the underground cult film *Snuff*. Whereas the snuff sequence tacked on at the end of that film was a staged sequence that was made to seem real, Stone incorporates footage of an actual murder in his film in a way that makes it seem unreal and staged, much in the manner that Ralis presented his snuff films in *Screen Kill* or that Deodato introduced archival execution footage in *Cannibal Holocaust*. By adding cut-aways, close-ups and optical enhancements, Stone transforms Zapruder's minimalist sequence shot into a polyvalent artifact in which any and all interpretations and conspiracy theories are equally tenable. Through its incorporation of Zapruder's filmed record of a real murder, Stone's *JFK* is actually more graphically violent and horrifyingly real than his 1994 film *Natural Born Killers*, despite all of the controversy sparked by the latter film's simulated violence.

SNUFF AND SURVEILLANCE

It is worth noting, finally, how public space has changed altogether since 1963, particularly with respect to the deployment of surveillance cameras in most major public places. These days, when cameras are everywhere, an assassination attempt in broad daylight in an open public place like Dealey Plaza, Dallas (site of the Kennedy shooting) is likely to be documented by an array of cameras, both manned and unmanned. In fact, visual records of murder today are less likely to be made by the killer himself than by surveillance cameras that happen to record – and in some cases even incite – a violent act. Thus, in 'techno-artist' Natalie Jeremijenko's piece 'Suicide Box' (1996), a motion-detection video system programmed to capture vertical motion was set up for a hundred days by the Golden Gate Bridge in San Francisco. The camera 'watched' the structure constantly and recorded people leaping to their deaths, some of whom may have been impelled to jump by the presence of the camera. As justification for her apparatus, Jeremijenko claimed it generated 'information about a tragic social phenomenon that is otherwise not seen'. Jeremijenko has since been working on a project called 'Bang-Bang', which she describes as 'a set of low-power automated video camera triggered by ammunition fire. Whenever there's an explosive event, it collects two seconds of video. They're being deployed in places where one would anticipate ammunition activity: East Timor, Kosovo, L.A.'[32] A case can be made that such automated documentaries that conflate art, snuff and surveillance represent one direction that underground films may be heading in the future.

In effect, there has been a new high-tech twist in the relation between snuff and surveillance since the 1970s and 1980s when, as Julian Petley has described, the British police's quest for a 'chimerical snuff film' led them to launch a 'surveillance campaign of horror and cult film enthusiasts, as well as individuals with sado-masochistic proclivities. In effect, the police ended up making the very films they were looking for.'[33] With the proliferation of surveillance cameras today, from satellites in outer space, to stoplights at busy traffic intersections, to the motion- and sound-sensitive video-cameras of techno-artists, it is only to be expected that the authorities will once again create the very snuff films they claim to be looking for – a paranoiac possibility explored by Wim Wenders in his film *The End of Violence*.[34] Even if filmmakers heed the call of critics to renounce fictional violence in their pictures, they will have little effect on reducing violent crime in real life. This is because the filmmakers who have the greatest interest in and closest relation to actual violence are not movie directors or producers, but the 'undercover' secret police and security agencies that have appropriated the most advanced film-recording technology for 'security'/surveillance purposes. In a postmodern cyber-society like our own, the underground is no longer 'under ground', and 'realist horror' films are being superseded by visual records of real horror whose reality, however, may go entirely unrecognised.

CHAPTER 6
A REPORT ON BRUCE CONNER'S 'REPORT'

Martin F. Norden

Hailed as one of his generation's most influential artists, Bruce Conner nevertheless has been a rather elusive figure in the world of American underground film. Overshadowed by such peers as Andy Warhol, Stan Brakhage, Kenneth Anger and Maya Deren, Conner has shunned the spotlight for decades, preferring instead to let his work in a wide range of media – printmaking, drawing, sculpture, collage, photography and film – speak for itself. Happily, a major retrospective titled *2000 BC: The Bruce Conner Story Part II*, launched by Minneapolis' Walker Art Center in 1999, finally gave him the attention he so richly deserved (even if there was no 'Part I' – a typical Connerian twist). This essay builds on the momentum generated by *2000 BC* by focusing on the defining achievement of Conner's career as an underground filmmaker: *Report* (1964–67), his highly personal meditation on the John F. Kennedy assassination. By providing a close textual reading of *Report* and finding its place within its historical and cultural context, I hope to show that Conner captured and critiqued the complexities of the time in a powerful and uniquely filmic way.

EARLY HISTORY AND EMERGING STYLE

Born in McPherson, Kansas in 1933 and raised in Wichita, about sixty miles away, Conner began thinking 'outside the box' at a very young age. His earliest teachers admired his imaginative artistic expressions, but by the time he had reached the third or fourth grade, a deadening conformity had all but enveloped his school and threatened to vitiate the youthful artist's emergent talents.[1] Chafing against the conservative values that permeated the American Midwest during World War Two and the postwar years, Conner found himself a social outcast for much of his pre-adolescence and young adulthood. 'When I was in Wichita, if you were even interested in poetry, classical music, art, you were called a queer, a commie, or just a jerk,' he told interviewer Peter Boswell.[2] After desultory stints as an art student at the Universities of Wichita, Nebraska, and Colorado, Conner decided on a new course of action; frustrated by the general conformist spirit of the times and the escalating rhetoric of the Cold War, he moved to San Francisco in 1957 in the hope of linking up with peers who shared his views on art and politics.

It proved a momentous decision, for Conner almost immediately became associated with that city's celebrated art and literary scene, a renaissance dominated by such avant-garde figures as Lawrence Ferlinghetti, Robert Duncan, Jack Kerouac and Allen Ginsberg. Conner's artistic career quickly attracted serious attention, with his earliest successes taking the form of intricate sculptural assemblages consisting of 'found' items such as bicycle parts, broken toys and women's undergarments. When he branched out into filmmaking in 1958 (beginning with the singularly titled *A Movie*), Conner discovered that his ideas about assemblage could cross media lines with relative ease. He had established the conceptual foundation for a decidedly different kind of film.

FILMIC FRAGMENTATION

Conner has proven to have few equals when it comes to creating films that intentionally destroy the illusion of reality commonly found in mainstream movies. His signature style, developed over a period of about forty years, is an extension of his sculptural techniques; he combines 'found' or 'discovered' fragments of other people's films (sometimes with his own original footage mixed in, sometimes not) to create new cinematic entities. The juxtapositions created in these compilation films are frequently unexpected and startling, often leading to what critic Carl Belz has called 'a combination of grim satire and morbid irony'.[3]

In the process of reworking footage from such items as cartoons, television commercials, old Hollywood movies and newsreels, Conner has gone out of his way to include recognisable emotive or associative concepts, which he then isolates from any former frames of reference. When these concepts are edited together as a montage and exhibited on the screen in his trademark rapid fashion, a new structural relationship emerges and offers many interesting effects. As Brian O'Doherty has pointed out, these re-edited images often engage the spectator's imagination in an unusual and provocative manner; they 'send the mind pinwheeling out of the movie on a tangent while the next sequence is also demanding attention – a very new kind of split-level effect the way Conner does it.'[4]

In addition to altering the values of his found imagery, Conner has used such unusual material as Academy leader (the '10-9-8-7…' that begins every film but is usually for the projectionist's benefit only) and sequences of solid black or solid white frames in which the screen appears to go blank. He has also frequently employed the process of 'looping' (i.e. repeating) the same shots until they seem more film than reality. By incorporating all of these special images and techniques, Conner effectively exposes film (if you pardon the pun) for what it is: a medium, not reality. We, the audience, are constantly reminded that we are watching a movie: a representation of reality, rather than a window on it. Under Conner's skilful editing, the various items and devices are unified in purposeful and concentrated efforts.

A PRODUCTION HISTORY OF 'REPORT'

Report is an outstanding example of this general approach, but ironically Conner, who threw himself into the project within days of Kennedy's death, originally wanted the film to be an extended piece of fairly straightforward reportage. At the time of the assassination, Conner happened to be living in Brookline, Massachusetts – JFK's birthplace – and intended to make a documentary about the impact of the assassination on the presidential hometown. 'I lived seven blocks from where he was born,' he said. 'I decided then that I would dedicate myself to recording what had happened and what would happen in Brookline because he was going to be buried there and I would live there for the next two or three years to work on that film and make a pilgrimage to the grave every day with my camera and show what had happened.'[5] The Kennedy family decided to bury JFK in Arlington National Cemetery instead of Brookline, however, forcing the filmmaker to change his plans.

Conner received an experimental-film grant from the Ford Foundation in 1964 and, reconceiving his film, decided to use part of the Ford money to acquire the rights to assassination-related television imagery. He had to rethink *Report* yet again, though, after the networks refused to cooperate. As he told interviewer Robert Haller:

> I went to CBS and NBC and tried to get footage out of the day he was shot, and they didn't want to give anything to me. They wanted to have a script first (this was the material from the four minutes after he was killed). They were very up-tight and paranoiac. They wanted a script and they kept shoving me from office to office until I finally figured out they just didn't want to have me using the film, or seeing it, or having anything to do with it. … So, I ended up making *Report* [by] getting parts of films that were available to the public, a year later.[6]

What resulted was no less than eight different versions of *Report*, which, in Conner's words, came out 'one after the other. I would take a print and then I would take the footage and change it and I would make another print.' Confessing that he was 'obsessed' with the project and did not want to let go for fear that Kennedy would truly be 'dead' for him once he finished, the filmmaker produced the eight *Report*s from 1964 until 1967, eventually settling on the eighth version as his final and disposing of the other copies. For Conner, completing the film meant finally coming to terms with Kennedy's death: 'When *Report* was finished then he was dead, so it took two and a half years for me to acknowledge that he was dead.'[7]

The final version of *Report*, which built on the others and runs 13 minutes, emerged as a strange hybrid of Conner's creative impulses; the film was and is partly a documentary, but it also follows the lead of his earlier films by relying heavily on re-edited excerpts from newsreels, old Hollywood movies and television ads to provide poignant commentary on the JFK assassination and US society in general. It is a documentary with a difference, as Roy Huss and Norman Silverstein observed shortly after the film's release:

> Documentarists always engage in such manipulation (i.e. juxtaposition), but Conner here creates a new kind of documentary by means of rapid cutting and crosscutting, nonsynchronous sound, disrupted time order, repeated segments of action, and reversed motion. The assassination of President Kennedy is, to be sure, 'reported', through authentic footage of the motorcade and a tape of the radio coverage of those confused events. However, Conner entirely reshapes this material to bring out its essence.[8]

Conner has rejected surrealism as a label for his work – 'I don't think I'm a surrealist; I'm a realist,' he told Mark Caywood in a 2000 interview[9] – but nevertheless *Report* is somewhat of a surrealistic documentary in that it deals partially with actual newsreel footage and radio commentary of the event yet often jumbles the chronological order and relative synchrony of these items in a dreamlike fashion. In fact, the film on first viewing may appear to have been put together rather casually; Conner not only fractures the time order with apparent randomness but also intersperses with the JFK motorcade footage a wide variety of concepts which seem to have nothing to do with the assassination at all. On further examination, however, we find that many of these supposedly unrelated concepts either become instantly analogous to the assassination or serve as ironic statements on American society during the early 1960s.

A CLOSER LOOK

Report wastes little time getting to the actual moment of JFK's murder. The film's first sequence begins with a medium shot of President and Mrs Kennedy taken by a newsreel camera as their open-top limousine passes through Dallas' Dealey Plaza. Mrs Kennedy is the nearest of the two to the camera, and her face is directly angled at it. She smiles and waves as the camera follows the limousine.

She partially blocks President Kennedy from our view near the end of the shot as a result of the movements of both the car and the camera, but we can clearly see him brush his forehead – a simple gesture that soon takes on a foreboding quality in Conner's hands.

At this point, the soundtrack comes alive with ambient motorcade noise and the voice of a radio reporter commenting on the presidential visit. This shot of the Kennedys is repeated ('looped') several times and the off-screen reporter says, 'It appears as if something has happened in the motorcade route.' A moment later, after Conner has reversed the shot in mirror-image fashion, the reporter notes that 'there has been a shooting'.

This combination of sound and image is the first of *Report*'s many abrupt and contradictory juxtapositions; we see pre-assassination images but hear post-assassination commentary. *Report* gives us precious little time to process this aural-visual conflict, however, since it then goes off in an entirely unanticipated direction. Though the soundtrack continues to provide the radio coverage of those confused moments immediately following the shooting, Conner replaced the newsreel imagery with several minutes' worth of 'flicker' footage – footage consisting entirely of frames of pure black and pure white, alternating at a stroboscopic rate to create, in Boswell's words, 'a rhythmic sequence that evokes the dying President's slip from consciousness. During this sequence, the entire room in which the film is being projected becomes a flickering black-and-white environment.'[10] It is a stunning segment, with its intentional ambiguity inviting a variety of responses. As Carl Belz has suggested:

> The section of 'blank' footage occurs … just after 'something has happened' to the motorcade and during the chaotic and foggy moments which followed. In other words, as the 'live' action vanished into a veil of unknowable disorder, the visual material likewise blanks out. The newscaster's words 'something has happened' then take on multiple implications. As the flashing greys persist upon the screen, people in the audience actually begin to wonder if 'something has happened', not only to the President, but to the film itself.[11]

The flickering slows and stops after a few minutes, rendering the screen opaque. The radio commentary, which up to this point has covered the unfolding events at Dealey Plaza and Parkland Hospital, switches to the Texas School Book Depository and the blankness of the screen is replaced by a looped image of an officer holding Lee Harvey Oswald's rifle aloft. The commentary returns to the hospital, and we are shown the looped image of Mrs Kennedy unable to open the locked door of the ambulance that holds the body of her husband.

Report repeats the earlier newsreel footage of President and Mrs Kennedy in their limousine just moments before the shooting, and the accompanying soundtrack consists of various eyewitness accounts of the assassination. In yet another unanticipated strategy, Conner then inserted snippets of Academy leader to offer a seemingly endless repetition of a countdown in one-second increments that begins with the number 10 and ends at 3. Though the leader's general image – a frame-filling circle that has both a horizontal and a vertical line intersecting it – very much resembles the crosshair pattern of a rifle's scope, it functions mainly as a clock ticking away the seconds of the President's life; indeed, the official death announcement on the soundtrack occurs during the Academy-leader sequence.

Though Conner has been dismissive of this first section of *Report* – 'There's no real film there,'[12] he suggested – it powerfully captures the turmoil and uncertainty of the moments immediately following the assassination. Its effectiveness depends heavily, though, on the audience's prior knowledge of the events of that day in Dallas. For example, we see JFK repeatedly brush his forehead through the looping effect, and, as we hear the assassination commentary, we begin to wonder if Conner had access to previously unscreened footage and will actually show the moment of JFK's death from a perspective other than the one we know all too well: the one represented in the famous amateur film shot at Dealey Plaza by Zapruder. (He does, actually, but not in a traditional sense.) Similarly, Conner looped a shot of the presidential limousine as it approaches the camera, an effect that causes the vehicle to appear to snap back after it moves forward a little. The limo does make progress but only slowly and in a highly fragmented way. By looping the shot numerous times but allowing it to run a little bit longer each time (thereby enabling the vehicle to move forward but gradually and fitfully), Conner gave form to the audience's desperate, and futile, wish to pull the President back from impending doom.

Despite this section's highly provocative qualities, it is the second section that truly demonstrates Conner's virtuosity as an image manipulator. It abounds with puns and ironic and satiric statements, which Conner created by editing a diverse range of appropriated images – some less than a second in length – to the banalities of the pre-assassination radio commentary. In other words, Conner cut the visual images, many of which would be meaningless outside of the context of *Report*, so that they would link up closely with certain phrases uttered by the announcer on the soundtrack. Indeed, the major ironies of *Report* arise from the juxtaposition of the announcer's pre-assassination remarks (which have an innocently positive tone, since he is obviously unaware of what is to happen) with the harsh visual realities of the events surrounding the assassination – such as the moment when Jack Ruby shoots Oswald, a television image that was seared into the American public's collective memory – and various outside concepts. With the awareness that the announcer's running commentary reproduced below is about such items as President and Mrs Kennedy's arrival at Love Field, the crowds who showed up to greet the couple, the weather at Dallas, and the security precautions taken for the presidential visit, here is a partial list of *Report*'s contrapuntal puns, offered in no particular order:

Audio	Visual
'…Air Force Jet 1…'	A title that reads 'END PART 1'; 'Jets' breakfast cereal commercial
'…placards held high…'	Marching pickets

'…the doors fly open…'	Refrigerator doors opening; close-up of a 'Ry-Krisp' cracker being broken
'…a split-second timed operation…'	A bull gores a matador
'…nothing left to chance…'	Texas School Book Depository
'…a bright sun, the weather couldn't be better…'	Atomic bomb 'mushrooms'
'…to witness the arrival of the President and his First Lady…'	JFK's caisson pulled by horses
'…Just to be sure you find yourself in the proper location, we'll give it to you once again…'	Jack Ruby shoots Lee Harvey Oswald
'…Mrs Kennedy has just been presented with a bouquet of beautiful red roses…'	Bouquet of roses on the floor of the empty presidential limousine; the word 'TRAGEDY' is superimposed
'…when the President stops moving, that's when we become concerned…'	President's flag-draped casket
'…the President's steak [dinner]…'	A scene from a bullfight
'…tight security…'	WWI battle scene from *All Quiet on the Western Front*
'…children trying to get over the fence…'	WWI soldiers machine-gunned while trying to cross barbed wire (from *All Quiet*)
'…so [the Kennedys] can make their way downtown…'	JFK's horse-drawn caisson moving through Washington DC
'…gunmetal-grey limousine…'	Oswald's rifle held aloft
'…if there's any trouble…'	Woman holding box of 'S.O.S.' pads
'…one of those impromptu moments for which the President has become known…'	JFK's horse-drawn caisson moves from the Capitol

Some of the puns are mere parodies and plays on words; others, however, are more resonant and give indications of Conner's attitudes and opinions on the assassination and US society in general. For example, wars, weaponry and destruction, and America's fascination with them, collectively form a key motif in *Report*. The film is absolutely loaded with such images, with many but by no means all appearing in the puns noted above. Among the more prominent are World War One battle scenes from the classic 1930 Hollywood movie *All Quiet on the Western Front*, atomic bomb 'mushrooms', a bullet penetrating a light bulb in extreme slow motion, armed policemen and, perhaps most conspicuously, the looped (and thereby forcefully transformed) image of an officer holding Oswald's rifle high above his head. According to critic David Mosen, the film reflects a major American preoccupation:

> In Conner's eyes society thrives on violence, destruction, and death no matter how hard we try to hide it with immaculately clean offices, the worship of modern science, or the creation of instant martyrs. From the bullfight arena to the nuclear arena we clamor for the spectacle of destruction. The crucial link in *Report* is that JFK with his great PT 109 was just as much a part of the destruction game as anyone else. Losing is a big part of playing games.[13]

In addition to the puns, many of which seem to be transmitted at an almost subliminal rate, *Report*'s second section contains at least one extended ironic statement: a 'mad doctor' sequence. Conner lifted the scenes for this sequence from the 1935 Hollywood film *Bride of Frankenstein*, in which Dr Henry Frankenstein (played by the British actor Colin Clive) attempts to instill life into his latest charnel-house creation. The shots that Conner inserted into *Report* show the doctor throwing the switch that activates his electrical life-giving apparatuses. Significantly, Conner did not include any footage that shows the monster actually coming to life. Conner intercut still shots of JFK's casket lying in state with these 'mad doctor' scenes. An important piece of commentary during this sequence is 'When the President stops moving, that's when we become concerned'. Moments before the sequence begins, we see the brief flash of a cartoon star with the word 'WISH' on it.

This last item conceivably represents a strong wish on the part of the audience to find a way to instill life back into the late President; however, the only 'solution' that Conner offers his audience in this dreamlike movie is the stereotypical mad doctor routine. Dr Frankenstein's electrifying attempts at inducing life into a corpse have become clichéd after all these years and, out of the context of *Report*, would be funny, yet the film forces its audience to turn to the mad doctor's techniques as its only hope. Conner shows this desire to be futile, as he did earlier with the attempt to hold back the presidential limousine through the looping process.

Several analogies emerge from the mélange of images offered by *Report*. Surprisingly, Conner deals with the obvious Kennedy-Lincoln comparison only briefly. (He references Abraham Lincoln in just two scenes: one of the Lincoln Memorial, and the other of a house with a large sign in front of it reading 'House Where Lincoln Died'.) The strongest analogy within the film presents itself in a rather unusual form: a bullfight.

The bullfight sequence, a major part of *Report*'s second section, intriguingly matches the JFK assassination on a number of levels. Both events are preceded by scenes of huge cheering crowds. Both the bullfight and the motorcade are heavily stage-managed events, scheduled and planned out well in advance. There is the pomp of a parade in each. Both the matador and Kennedy obviously appreciate the jubilant cheers from the respective crowds that have turned out to see them (Conner reinforced this notion by inserting a shot of the matador grinning broadly and strutting before the crowd, while the radio commentary at that point, referring to Kennedy, contains the line, 'He is walking and shaking hands'). Violence erupts against the main figure in each of the otherwise very controlled productions (i.e. the bull goring the matador, the President's assassination). Finally, the bull is killed just moments after it has gored the matador, which compares with Oswald's murder shortly after the assassination. Though the extended analogy ultimately breaks down (unlike the motorcade spectators, the bullfight audience expected a show that flirted with violence, and JFK certainly did not taunt Oswald the way the matador goaded the bull), the bullfight sequence is the most visually apparent comparison with the assassination in *Report*.

Scattered throughout the film are fragments of television commercials, and they collectively lead to another analogy: President Kennedy as a 'packaged commodity'. Such instances include a brief segment from a 'Jets' breakfast cereal commercial coupled with the announcer's description of JFK's arrival via Air Force Jet 1, and a shot of a refrigerator's doors magically opening (while a stylishly coiffed and dressed suburban housewife reacts in delight) combined with a further description of Kennedy's arrival, '…the doors fly open…'. This concept of the President as commodity is strongly reinforced in the final scene of *Report*, when a woman whom we have glimpsed throughout the movie presses a button on a cash register-like machine. The camera zooms in for a close-up of the machine and reveals that the button reads 'SELL'. This concluding image, combined with the radio reporter's final observation that the JFK motorcade is *en route* to 'the Trade Mart', suggests that, from the media's perspective, the President was a commodity to be sold to their audiences like anything else.

Conner's decision to juxtapose patently commercial images against those of JFK was quite conscious on his part. In the weeks and months following the shooting, he became increasingly upset by the rampant commercialisation of the Kennedy myth. He was disturbed by what he saw as 'all the grotesque and sacrilegious and immoral things that were done' and the hypocritical attitudes that guided them. 'The excuse was that it was respect for the dead and his memory and stuff,' he lamented. 'Jack Kennedy banks, and all sorts of memorabilia and nonsense documentaries and gooey posters.'[14] Fellow underground filmmaker Stan Brakhage stated flatly that 'the exploitation of President Kennedy's death' was Conner's primary concern in *Report*,[15] and Conner could not agree more: 'When I started, the big problem was that I had to show what had happened: *the exploitation of the man's death* [emphasis in original text]. That's what I had to show. That's what I wanted to show and I had to show it because nobody else was. There was tons of other information coming through the media – but this exploitation was the most obvious thing to me.'[16]

A central irony of *Report*, and one clearly not lost on Conner, is that the film could be seen as a contribution to the glut of Kennedy-inspired pop-culture artifacts that he so detested. 'The problem in making the film was that in order for me to do the film I would also have to go through the same processes that those people were using to exploit Kennedy,' he noted.[17] Unlike 'those people', however, Conner created a reflexive work, one that critiques the society responsible for the very images he used to create it. In fact, Conner painted such a bleak picture of US society in this otherwise ambiguous and open-ended film that he invites us to take a considerably darker view of the 'JFK as commodity' concept. Conner could be seen as intimating that the assassination was brought about by a conspiracy against the President, rather than by the efforts of a lone gunman. A group of influentials may have decided to get rid of, or 'sell', the President, as one would do with stock holdings. Taken in this light, *Report*'s final scene becomes the most horrifying one in the entire film; the decision to murder the nation's chief executive is now framed in terms of a business transaction.

FINAL THOUGHTS

Report is perhaps the most outstanding example of the many films, underground and otherwise, that utilise the contrapuntal arrangement of images and sounds to create sociological statements in the form of irony, metaphors and analogies. What makes the film special is Conner's ability to intertwine images of fact and fiction to such an extent that a new 'reality' takes place. Conner shows that the images are just that: images. One might argue from a Bazinian standpoint that the images of JFK are ontologically bound to the 'real' JFK, but ultimately they are flickerings of light and shadow, albeit ones heavily invested with prior associations and thus ripe for artistic manipulation. Bruce Jenkins put it well when he wrote:

> In Conner's world of heroes and villains, distinctions between the real and the fictional … become inextricably merged. Cognizant that the cinema (and television) is already once-removed from reality, Conner is able to endow his icons, whether historical or imaginary, with the same force and the same substance. … The complex ideographic language he forges from bits and pieces of reality and fiction forms the basis for a [representation] about our media-bound culture that neither fiction nor reportage alone can render sufficiently.[18]

In so doing, Conner has bent the culture back upon itself in a highly compelling and thought-provoking way. Though the results have proven quite unsettling for some viewers,[19] *Report*, like any exceptional work of art, has enabled others to see an aspect of their world in a totally unexpected way and, perhaps more importantly, prompted them to question it.

CHAPTER 7
VOYEURISM, SADISM AND TRANSGRESSION: SCREEN NOTES AND OBSERVATIONS ON WARHOL'S 'BLOW JOB' AND 'I, A MAN'

Jack Sargeant

UNDERGROUND/OVERGROUND: WAYS INTO WARHOL

The films of Andy Warhol are possibly some of the best known yet paradoxically the least viewed of underground movies. The bulk of the films remain largely unseen, rarely broadcast on television, and only the last three titles have been officially released on video. Only the most famous ones – notably *My Hustler* (1965), *Chelsea Girls* (1966) and *Lonesome Cowboys* (1968) – are exhibited at cinemas or galleries with anything approaching regularity.

Warhol's career as a filmmaker has traditionally been divided into four stages by film historians such as Sheldon Renan and Richard Dyer.[1] The first-period films, such as *Kiss* (1963), *Sleep* (1963), *Haircut* (1963), *Eat* (1963), *Blow Job* (1963), *Couch* (1964) and *Empire* (1964), were produced between 1963 and 1964. These films are characterised by the use of a singular long take, shot from a stationary camera angle, and their emphasis is on the celluloid's plasticity as much as the subject matter presented.

Warhol's second period, roughly running from 1964 to 1965, was produced largely with the assistance of Ronald Tavel (who would go on to form the Theater of the Ridiculous). These movies still use the fixed camera perspective but introduce sound as an element of the diegetic cinematic experience, with Tavel feeding lines to, or engaging with, the 'cast' from behind the camera. These films include *Harlot* (1964), *Suicide* (1965), *Horse* (1965) and *The 14-Year-Old-Girl* (aka *Hedy, the Shoplifter*, aka *The Most Beautiful Women In The World*, 1966). Warhol's third period of filmmaking – from 1965 to 1966 – relies on quasi-vérité scenarios written by Chuck Wein, and includes *Beauty #2* (1965) and *My Hustler*.

Both Renan and Dyer have suggested that Warhol's fourth period is characterised by his use of expanded cinema, beginning with the double projection feature *Chelsea Girls*, which opened in New York in the Autumn of 1966. However, the first-period films were also screened in expanded cinema scenarios as early as January 1966, and such multiple projections formed part of Warhol's 'Up Tight' events at the Cinematheque on 41st Street, several months before the shooting and cinematic release of *Chelsea Girls* (see below).

Further, given that the previous periods are defined by the collaborators involved, this distinction between the third- and forth-period films seems somewhat false. I would therefore suggest that Warhol's last period of film production, for the sake of discussion, is better described as beginning in 1967 with films such as *I, A Man* (1967), *Bike Boy* (1967) and *Lonesome Cowboys*, and reaches its apex with cult films such as *Heat* (1972). In these films, the narrative emphasis gains greater importance.

Equally, this final period sees a more widespread focus on the concept of the superstar, the Factory's own version of the Hollywood star system and a greater use of colour film stock. The last of these fourth-wave films were the most famous of Warhol's output – *Flesh* (1968), *Trash* (1970) and *Heat* – and were produced in collaboration with Paul Morrissey, a protégé/collaborator who directed all three pictures (and who, it has been suggested, also directed most of the Warhol movies post-1967).[2] These final few productions are better described as midnight movies than as underground films and *Flesh*, *Trash* and *Heat* have been released on video.

Identifying four broadly temporal stages within Warhol's cinema represents an approach based purely on a move from avant-garde film through to a more immediately recognisable mode of narrative cinema. However, it would be just as viable to suggest that Warhol's films also progressed through a series of stages based on the ways in which they were presented to an audience. Thus, while early productions were screened at the Factory or at underground cinema functions at venues such as the Filmmakers Co-op, some films were also presented in multiple screenings as a backdrop to the 'Up Tight' events. Here, screenings were merely one part of a larger affair that included pulsating music and performance/dance displays.

FIGURE 8 Trash goes respectable: Nico and Gerard Malanga in *Chelsea Girls*

Later films differed again merely because they were screened at more 'respectable' cinemas, beginning with *Chelsea Girls*, which, after a brief and very successful run downtown, moved to the midtown Cinema Rendezvous on West 57th Street. This move uptown garnered a *New York Times* review that condemned Warhol for screening his movies beyond the confines of Greenwich Village.

Warhol's realisation that audiences wanted to see this work was the first clear step towards his making more commercially viable films and a move away from the supposedly difficult early movies. In *POPism*, Warhol acknowledges that by December of the following year, 'We began to think mainly about ideas for feature-length movies that regular theatres would want to show.'[3]

IT IS ALL ABOUT IMAGE, ABOUT SURFACE, WATCHING

I guess I can't put off talking about it any longer.

Okay, let's get it over with. Wednesday. The biggest nightmare came true. ... I'd been signing America books for an hour or so when this girl in line handed me hers to sign and then she did – did what she did. The Diary can write itself here.

[She pulled Andy's wig off and threw it over the balcony to a male who ran out of the store with it...][4]

For a few minutes, Warhol's worst fear became actualised. Already the victim of exceptional and brutal violence, having been shot and nearly killed by SCUM manifesto author Valerie Solanis, Warhol was understandably upset. But this is not the fear of an assassination attempt; rather, in 1985, Warhol is upset that the surface has cracked. And, perhaps more than anything else, Warhol was interested in the creation and deconstruction of spectacle.

The Empire State Building is the supreme icon of New York City, of Deco architecture, of collective memories of cinematic experience; who can forget Kong's final confrontation with the Air Force whilst hanging from the building's spire? The Empire State Building was – as Warhol would later note – the first of his superstars:

Suddenly B said, 'There's your first Superstar.'

'Who? Ingrid?'

'The Empire State Building.'

We had just turned onto 34th Street.[5]

Possibly the most notorious of Warhol's observation movies, *Empire* consists of eight hours of film of the Empire State Building – an icon of modernity celebrated as pure spectacle. This represents the cinematic equivalent to Warhol's paintings and screen prints of tins of Campbell's Soup or of Brillo Boxes. The commonplace rendered as art because of the way Warhol perceived it, reproduced it and demanded the viewer engage with it.

But if *Empire* was the most infamous of these films, it is only because it exists in the popular imagination as the supreme trial of patience. Like the excesses of modern art it becomes in the mind of the audience a conceptual joke – do you need to watch all of the film to have seen it, or is a casual five-minute section of *Empire* as good as viewing the whole movie? It should, of course, be noted that Warhol did not stand and film the whole movie; assistants and friends all supervised the shoot (including poet, writer, filmmaker, underground legend and independent film prothelyser Jonas Mekas). But this is only one aspect of pop iconography. Playing with our collected impressions of the totems of our culture, recognising them as signifiers for modern life, *Empire* is about the response of the audience as much as the icon itself. It raises the question of how we look at art and the world around us. Like the variations in the silk-screening process leading to fluctuations and nuances in colour and tone, each individual frame in *Empire* is slightly different in tone, in texture, as the light changes. One aspect of Warhol's 1960s work is the recurring theme of repetition and non-identical repetition, that is, the repetition of the same thing only differently.

PEOPLE WATCHING

But Warhol was also concerned with people. The stars of his portraits (Elvis Presley, Elizabeth Taylor, Marilyn Monroe, et cetera) found their echoes in the various personalities that made their way to Warhol's studio. Thus, those who came to the silver-painted Factory would often be asked to sit for a screen test. Three minutes of 16mm film capturing the faces of everybody from personalities such as Lou Reed or Allen Ginsberg, through to the faces of young hustlers and aspiring models. Some of these tests were collated into groupings that became the basis for films such as *The Thirteen Most Beautiful Boys* (1964–65) and *The Thirteen Most Beautiful Women* (1964). The entire series is best known to contemporary audiences under the collective title *Screen Tests* (1964–66).

> As for Andy, I wondered if he really liked people, or did he just like being fascinated by people? [6]

In these unremittingly sadistic films, individuals undergo the gruelling screen test ordeal in whatever way they choose. Almost inevitably the individuals try and look cool, but posing for three minutes invariably becomes impossible and the projected veneer of image begins to collapse almost immediately. In some cases the subjects begin to crack, smiling nervously and glancing from side to side, as if searching for help from behind the cold, unblinking eye of the Factory's camera. Only the most self-assured individual can remain focused enough to carry off their image for the length of an unedited shoot.

Warhol's fascination with spectacle is thus concerned not merely with the creation of the icon, manifested by the subjects of the screen tests as cool and composed, but also in the simultaneous deconstruction of the icon. When their image collapses and the person underneath emerges in minute flickers of anxiety, then the self-designed spectacle collapses and a new form of spectacle emerges. This is not the emergence of an essence, but a manifestation of immanence. Nothing is revealed; certainly any truth of the subject remains under erasure. The brief displays of nervousness – quickly hidden behind a new pose, or a drag on a cigarette (the ultimate cinematic signifier of cool) – enables the subject to re-immerse themselves in the spectacle, thereby allowing the viewer to catch a glimpse of the constructed nature of the spectacle of the public self.

The Warhol screen test must rank as one of the harshest initiation ceremonies yet devised. The subjects hope to appear suitable to join the Factory crowd and even Warhol's inner clique. (Whether or not this clique actually existed is largely unimportant, those individuals filmed sitting in front of the clattering camera, be they queer street hustlers or wealthy uptown socialites, collectively believed that there was something unique in the Warhol entourage that should be aspired to.)

FIGURE 9 Cinematic sadism? The screen tests of Andy Warhol

Like a medieval inquisition, we proclaimed them tests of the soul and we rated everybody. A lot of people failed. We could all see they didn't have any soul. ... But what appealed most of all to us – the Factory devotees, a group I quickly became a part of – was the game, the cruelty of trapping the ego in a little 15-minute cage for scrutiny. ... Of course, the person who loved watching these films the most – and did so over and over, while the rest of us ran to the other end of the Factory – was Warhol.[7]

Other films made by Warhol betray a similar scopophilia, in which the pleasure of looking at somebody's emergent discomfort is equally apparent. Thus *Screen Test #2* (1965) betrays a sadistic glee when actress Mario Montez, whilst being interviewed by Ronald Tavel, is harangued until she breaks down and reveals to her inquisitor that she is actually male. In his account of screening *The 14-Year-Old-Girl* in *POPism*, Warhol reveals a similar event: 'When he [Montez] saw that I'd zoomed in and gotten a close-up of his arm with all the thick, dark masculine hair and veins showing, he got very upset and hurt.'[8]

While Mary Woronov's autobiography recounts that her role in various Warhol movies – including what is probably his most famous work, *Chelsea Girls* – consisted of exorcising her demons, the director and writer encouraged her to give full vent to her dark side regardless of the effects. Indeed, if other members of the cast became agitated or upset then so much the better. Although to accuse Warhol of misogyny would be too simplistic and crass, it is nevertheless pertinent to observe that competition between the females in the film is brutal.

> The Factory was like a court, the old court of King Louis or something like that – and people were always fawning after his favour, and at times he did toy with them. And one of the many ways that he'd toy with them is these girls would fight over whether they were going to be in a movie, or not in a movie, and whether they were a superstar or not, and whether they were sitting next to him or not. And the queens who also were there, would thrive on a bit of fighting amongst the girls.[9]

> A girl always looked more beautiful and fragile when she was about to have a nervous breakdown.[10]

Warhol's interest in cruelty and S&M may not have necessarily reflected his own personal tastes. These were merely aspects of his surroundings – both spatial and temporal – that fascinated him, just as he was fascinated with the drug and sex habits of those who entered his zone. However, the distance he enjoyed from the events around him suggests a certain coldness that in part must be seen as sadistic:

> I still care about people but it would be so much easier not to care … it's too hard to care … I don't want to get too involved in other people's lives … I don't want to get too close … I don't like to touch things … that's why my work is so distant from myself.[11]

It was not for nothing that he was referred to as Drella – a fusion of Dracula and Cinderella – surreptitiously (and less so) by many amongst his amphetamine-fuelled entourage. He wanted to live vicariously through the experiences of those he filmed, people who performed their personalities and paraded their dysfunctions for his lens and ultimately for his voyeuristic pleasure.

SEX AND SILKSCREEN SUICIDES

Between 1962 and 1968 Warhol created a series of shocking silkscreen prints – 'The Disaster Series' – replete with images of gangsters, Bellevue Hospital, electric chairs, race riots, car crashes, suicides and newspaper headlines heralding numerous apocalyptic events. Even the artist's most enduring image, that of Marilyn Monroe, must be seen as belonging to this series. She was, after all, the world's most famous suicide, and it was this act that inspired the series of Monroe screen prints. These

92

powerful images betray a fascination with various manifestations of violence: from the results of the grisly car crashes, through to the violence about to be realised in the brightly (electrically) coloured electric chairs.

These silkscreen prints reveal something that is both universal and forbidden: death. Death emerges in the images as both an actualised event (realised in the prints of a car crash or of a body plummeting from a building) and as an iconographical representation (for example, in a newspaper headline or a currently empty electric chair).

This engagement with the taboo, and with showing the forbidden, is also present within Warhol's films of the same period. Most obviously it appears in his representations of all manifestations of sexuality and, to a lesser extent, drugs (see, for example, *Couch*, *Blow Job*, *Chelsea Girls*, *My Hustler*, *Bike Boy*). Warhol was obsessed with observing the chaos of the urban world around him. The excesses of his friends, associates and the numerous people who made the Factory their home, was a source of detached fascination for Warhol in the same way that society's momentary excesses – manifested in events such as riots, violent death and stardom – were a source of interest. In this work, the forbidden and the hidden are exposed and dissected under the artist/filmmaker's gaze, just as his earlier works (c. 1961–63) had engaged with an examination of the banal commonplace manifested through objects-as-icons such as the cans of Campbell's soup or Coke bottles. But Warhol's art – whether depicting images of consumerism, capitalism or execution – was never expressly political, the dissection neither offering, nor even so much as suggesting, an analysis of the mechanisms of power inherent within the electric chair or a drug deal or a sex act. Instead, the dissection is about fascination (be it Warhol's, the media's, society's or, more commonly, all three) and the nature of the reproduced image itself.

> I don't really feel all these people with me every day at the Factory are just hanging around me, I'm more hanging around them.[12]

In *Blow Job*, one of Warhol's earliest movies, a young man with a greasy quiff receives the infamous blow job for an estimated 45 minutes. Shot so that only the man's head is visible, the oral sex occurs off-camera. The man leans back against a wall. The scratched celluloid is silent, nothing but projector hum. The young man, face in partial shadow, looks down. His head rolls back, presumably adjusting his pose so as to facilitate oral copulation. He looks down; again his head rolls back. At one point his mouth moves. The film burns to white. Next reel. Leader. More of the same. Head lolls. Eyes flutter. At the close of the film the protagonist lights a cigarette. End.

Warhol shot this 16mm film in 1963. According to *POPism*, the film was cast with 'a good-looking kid who happened to be hanging around the factory that day.'[13] He received a steady stream of blow jobs from the 'five different boys [that] would come in and keep blowing him until he came.'[14] *Blow Job* premiered in 1964 and was screened at various performances by the Velvet Underground. The film emphasises the act of oral copulation, but as the projected image focuses entirely on the head of the youth on the receiving end, the gender of those giving the blow job is concealed. Warhol's statement that those giving head to the boy were male is irrelevant: to audiences watching the film, the youth could be blown by anybody. The point of the movie is to pay witness to the ecstasy on the man's face – not to the image of his penis ejaculating.

The nature of *Blow Job* is ambiguous. Do we watch it as avant-garde text, documentary or underground art film? Repeated viewings suggest that *Blow Job* may be seen as a documentary, but rather than employing the traditional conventions of the documentary form the film is a liminal hymn. Like all of Warhol's early productions, some members of the audience are forced to wonder if the film is an endurance test: should they watch the whole picture from beginning to end, or should they engage in another activity simultaneously and view it as something resembling moving wallpaper?

Blow Job works as a neo-documentary which follows the process of giving/receiving head through 45 minutes of sucking, and culminates (the audience is led to presume) in an off-screen ejaculation and (somewhat ironic) post-coital cigarette. Yet at the same time, *Blow Job* may be viewed as an *anti-*documentary, since the audience does not 'learn' anything. The audience is not given any specific information. (This raises the question, does that matter? Is that a function of documentaries anyway?) Instead they experience their own spectral appellation. Watching the flickering images of a blow job, should they be aroused? Appalled? Bored? Whilst the film functions as a voyeuristic glimpse of a sexual exchange, Warhol also emphasises surface, and engages literally with the texture of the celluloid – the scratches, the flickers and the play of shadow and light within the image are all crucially important to him. There is no editing because Warhol wants the audience to see everything – every inch of celluloid, every frame. The non-identical repetition of the projected image is what fascinates as much as the act that is transpiring on screen. This is a film about film as much as it is a film about oral sex or New York queer culture. Warhol wants the viewer to see the action but he also wants the viewer to engage with the medium as he or she is watching it.

Stylistically different from *Blow Job* is Warhol's *I, A Man*, which was produced as a collaboration with the filmmaker Paul Morrissey. *I, A Man* – which takes its title from the erotic movie *I, A Woman* (1966), which was playing in New York at the same time the Warhol/Morrissey film was produced – locates its action in a series of encounters between a hustler-stud (Tom Baker) and six women (Ivy Nicholson, Ingrid Superstar, Valerie Solanis, Cynthia May, Bettina Coffin, Ultra Violet and Nico).

In *I, A Man*, the static camera and single-take shots that dictated the aesthetic of the early films is replaced by a greater variety of camera angles. (However, the film is still remarkably slow by contemporary standards, and the introduction of in-camera editing creates occasionally disjoined moments, loops of repetition and flashes of apparently random images.) Moreover, the silence that characterised *Blow Job* is replaced with a diegetic soundtrack. *I, A Man* is less film-as-art, film-as-installation or film-as-backdrop as it is simple, very loose narrative cinema. This is in direct contrast to Warhol's previous films, which were engaged predominantly with the act of watching (even *Chelsea Girls* emphasised the experience of watching the double-projection images more than the experience of listening to the dialogue).

Like *Blow Job*, *I, A Man* retains an air of authenticity, as the audience can imagine the events in question actually transpiring. But while *Blow Job* records events as documentary evidence, as phenomenological experience played before the camera, *I, A Man* presents a series of sexual encounters with which the cast engage as a form of naturalistic melodrama. Each encounter is punctuated with a rambling conversation on topics that range from killing cockroaches to astrological symbols to lesbianism and so on. These conversations echo the rambling engagements presented in Warhol's previous cinematic collaborations, but without the camp ferocity of Tavel's dialogue or the dry irony of Wein's scripts.

The 'acting' that occurs in the film is less about taking on a role than it is about putting specific people (Factory regulars, superstars, wannabe superstars) together and allowing their personalities to emerge and engage with one another. Like the earliest Warhol films, *I, A Man* also exists as phenomenological evidence, in this case of the meetings between the various individuals within the film. Where *I, A Man* differs from Warhol's earlier works is in its emphasis on the star personas of the people involved rather than on the activities in which they engage. In earlier films the activity of stardom and the potential collapse of image (as in *Screen Tests*) was emphasised, whilst in *I, A Man* the star personas are maintained throughout.

Although more narrative than *Blow Job*, *I, A Man* still maintains a degree of engagement with the plasticity of film. In its editing, the cuts create momentary flashes of images, and the audio track cracks and spits like a sadist's whip. These effects continually remind the audience that they are watching a film and so are engaged in a mutually complicit voyeuristic experience with the director and producer.

Throughout all of his movies, Warhol and his numerous collaborators attempted to engage with the notion of cinema from a uniquely personal perspective. One of Warhol's main interests – most clearly envisioned in the earliest productions – is the act of voyeurism, in how an audience engages with the process of watching film. This interest is still apparent in his later works, the central difference being the way in which the audience is seduced via the process of narrative.

Like the Disaster series, films such as *Blow Job* and *I, A Man*, despite their stylistic differences, both seek to illuminate the 'obscene' and forbidden, framing that which society excludes despite the fact it is actually the everyday. Warhol is showing the audience something that is traditionally concealed because to see that which is hidden fascinates, and to see something completely, to succumb to a visual seduction, is ultimately what fascinates Warhol, and what seduces the audience of the Warholian cinema.

CHAPTER 8
'YOU BLED MY MOTHER, YOU BLED MY FATHER, BUT YOU WON'T BLEED ME': THE UNDERGROUND TRIO OF MELVIN VAN PEEBLES

Garrett Chaffin-Quiray

Only as a group do the first three 'underground' feature films of Melvin Van Peebles fully express his artistic development and independence from conventional moviemaking. By focusing on *The Story of a Three-Day Pass* (1968), *Watermelon Man* (1970) and *Sweet Sweetback's Baadasssss Song* (1971) there is opportunity to consider his contribution to film history and assess his cultural importance. Indeed this frame supports the idea of him being a filmmaking pioneer by allowing an examination of the counter-hegemonic tendencies in his work along with exploring his relationship to blaxploitation cinema.

BLACK BACKGROUNDS AND FRENCH PURSUITS

Born on 21 August 1932, Melvin Van Peebles attended Township High School in the Chicago suburb of Phoenix, Illinois, where he graduated in 1949. Transferring to Ohio Wesleyan University after one year at West Virginia State College, he graduated in 1953 with a Bachelor of Arts in English before enlisting in the US Air Force.

After starting a family and ending his military career, he spent time in Mexico where he dabbled as a painter before moving to San Francisco and employment as a cable car operator. Following the sale of his car he produced a few short films to gain a foothold in Hollywood, including *Three Pickup Men for Herrick* (1957) and *Sunlight* (1957), although an agent reportedly told him, 'If you can tap dance, I might find you some work. But that's about all.'[1]

Shoring up his disappointment and capitalising on the GI Bill, he moved his family to Holland where he enrolled at the University of Amsterdam to study astronomy. While there he divorced his wife, joined a theatre troupe and started acting. To make ends meet he worked as a street performer and depended on his lady friends for support and a place to live.

Henry Langlois, founder of the Cinematheque Française, eventually saw his short films and invited Van Peebles to Paris where he spent the next nine years singing, dancing, acting and writing the novels *A Bear for the FBI*, *The Chinamen of the 14th District*, *The True American*, *The Party in Harlem* and *La Permission*. He also produced the Francophone short film *Cinq cent balles* (1963) and began seeking entry into the French feature-film market.

When he learned he could adapt one of his novels into film with a $70,000 grant from the French Cinema Centre if he could find a producer with matching funds, he partnered with OPERA, a production team consisting of Michel Zemer, Guy Pefond and Christian Shivat, and adapted *La Permission* for the screen. The resulting feature was shot in six weeks for a cost of $200,000 and was given the new title *The Story of a Three-Day Pass*.[2] The film depicts the story of an army man named Turner (Harry Baird) who receives a promotion and a three-day pass. While on leave he visits a Parisian club and meets a woman named Miriam (Nicole Berger). During their weekend together the couple explore the countryside and confront the complexities of their romantic ideals along with the bias of people around them. Once spotted by a group of his army cohorts who report what they see to their Captain (Hal Brav), Turner is demoted and confined to barracks where he remains disconnected from his lost love as the film ends.

Following the narrative pattern of a tragic love story, *The Story of a Three-Day Pass* departs from generic convention by centring itself on a black man. This difference is emphasised in the early remarks of Turner's Captain, who explains that a three-day pass is being offered to him because he is 'obedient, cheerful and frightened', 'a good Negro', towards whom the Captain feels a protective connection. Delivered in direct address as Turner demurs in crosscut reaction shots, the Captain's remarks speak to Turner's status as an army cog in collusion with the white-dominated American racial hierarchy. The sequence also demonstrates his relative position at the bottom of that hierarchy.

Once released from this orderly and paternalistic world, Turner roams through the streets of Paris wearing his sunglasses with a sense of freedom in the camera's depiction of his liberty and youth. Among his experiences he sees a puppet show about slavery and civilisation's development that emphasises his role in France as an African-descended American soldier upholding United Nations peace treaties circa 1967.

When he later enters the nightclub where he meets Miriam, Turner is positioned as the lone black figure among the lily-white dancers and club-goers who surround him. He is repeatedly refused a dancing partner until he finally asks Miriam, with whom he shares an immediate simpatico. Despite their initial attraction, however, other club-goers jostle them along with remarks on the colour of his skin, causing Turner to storm off saying, 'I'm not a nigger. I'm a person.'

Forced to explain how he is under constant attack from racially weighted words like 'black' and 'nigger', Miriam is shocked for having been ignorant of such signifiers but is quickly forgiven because of their French context. As Van Peebles would later comment, 'I had to keep things simple. It was intended for a French public, and they would never understand the fine points of white-negro bias in this country [the United States].'[3] Speaking at the same point within the film, Turner asks, 'how can anyone think that 'black' is a compliment?' thereby developing one of the film's more remarkable departures from narrative moviemaking.

With an alternation between diegetic and non-diegetic music and occasional reliance on freeze frames, Van Peebles inserts a pair of dream states into the unravelling romance, one from each of his lead characters' point-of-view. The first concerns a plantation-like world where Miriam is set upon and ravished by Turner as a black slave. The second exists in a tribal environment where Miriam is sacrificed to a black mob and symbolically raped. Inserted in parallel to the film's action, neither of these two powerful fantasies exactly describes the lovers' situation, although it is clear theirs is not a purely innocent love story. The sequences also provides a glimpse of Van Peebles' use of folklore, racial stereotype and historical myth to enliven his story and develop layers of meaning aside from the basic aesthetic achievements of his craftsmanship.

Another powerful, though less fanciful, illustration of clashing racial identities in the film is the scene where Turner and Miriam bump into three of his fellow soldiers from the army base. Wordlessly, the tension lurking beneath their affair rises to the surface like a jack-in-the-box being sprung. Very quickly Miriam's easy acceptance of their affection is demonstrated as being ignorant of unstated social codes concerning racial segregation. Just as quickly, Turner's inability to accept his attraction to Miriam shows the ingrained effect of his assimilation into racist American institutions and attitudes.

When Turner's Captain finally demotes him in another direct address sequence, his words express the urgency of separating the black and white races. More remarkable still is the way his reprimand takes the form of a war allegory when he says:

I don't see why, just because you were on a three-day pass, you thought that you could go further than the normal two-day weekend travelling distance from the base. What would you do on the battlefield? I'm very disappointed in you and you have to learn, to learn a lesson, all of you. Now if the only way you can learn is by the rod, then it will be by the rod. I am also restricting you to your barracks until further notice.

With jump cuts, freeze frames and dream states cross cut into the narrative action, photo montage including the use of newsreel footage and a loosely contained conceit about sexual predation between the races, *The Story of a Three-Day Pass* contains the seeds of Van Peebles' later pursuits. Though these techniques are employed throughout the film, and though they disrupt the continuity of its forward action, Van Peebles serves up a very palatable romantic tale complete with attractive lead actors.

The attributes of location shooting serve as a counterpoint to the simmering racial tensions then laying waste to American urban centres and they are a strong aesthetic achievement. Unfortunately, such abstraction is also a limitation in that *The Story of a Three-Day Pass* was considered a French production and remains strangely disconnected from the American landscape it remarks on, however lightly. Still, this debut feature allowed Van Peebles to adapt one of his novels, direct the resulting film and ultimately find his way into the Hollywood fold.

VAN PEEBLES COMES TO HOLLYWOOD

At a time when divestiture and divestment of theatrical distribution channels was tearing apart the vertically integrated studio system, Hollywood executives looked for solutions to secure steady business remembered from the industry's high point in 1946. Simultaneously, other forms of leisure entertainment were competing for the discretionary income of movie patrons, perhaps most notably television, causing both the timbre and subjects of movie entertainment to change.

Unable to find an edge or formula to attract audiences, some movie producers went so far as to let their companies slide into bankruptcy. Larger conglomerates eager to make use of studio resources acquired still other movie companies to make use of their film libraries. Riding the success of his first feature, Van Peebles was invited to Hollywood to supply a dose of outsider creativity. He found himself, 'in a difficult spot as an inexperienced director who's been pressed into service by an industry that has suddenly decided, after decades of racism in its ranks, that it needs black directors.'[4] Columbia Pictures signed him to shoot a farcical drama involving timely, contemporary issues and thus he followed in the late 1960s career paths of several black male directors like Gordon Parks with *The Learning Tree* (1969) and Ozzie Davis with *Cotton Comes to Harlem* (1970) before him.

Based on a script by Herman Raucher with the working title *The Night the Sun Came Out*, Van Peebles scored and directed the film, this time in colour, and eventually released it under the title *Watermelon Man*. Shot in 22 days and released with a budget just under $1 million,[5] it tells the story of a bigoted, white insurance executive named Jeff Gerber (Godfrey Cambridge), who lords over his liberal-leaning wife Althea (Estelle Parsons). One day he wakes up a black man. Misadventures ensue before Jeff finally takes consolation and strength in his new identity, although he ends up separated from his family and participating in a black, pseudo-military organisation.

Basically a fable of role reversal, *Watermelon Man* is also a finely crafted tale that mixes its bawdy comic ruptures with the tragic potential of its topical material. As the film opens to Jeff's morning habits as he exercises, bathes and darkens his pale white skin under the lamp of a home-tanning bed, the Gerber family resembles millions of other white families of the period. The patriarch is an extrovert who earns his living among the white-collar class while the matriarch stays at home looking after the affairs of family, hearth and home.

Among the very first conflicts in the film is a disagreement between Jeff and Althea. Captured in long shot as they watch the evening news featuring riotous blacks, Jeff is roundly intolerant while Althea expresses her sympathy for civil rights struggles. Their peace is maintained by keeping conflicts buried in the symbolic bedroom. As a result, their relationship is a metaphor for the wider American system that limits cultural conflicts through institutions of control and censorship. That the footage they watch is newsreel imagery of race riots only underscores the systemic controls in America as defined by a police force struggling to control protesting black others. This sequence also makes a point of characterising Jeff as being purposefully ignorant of the social changes going on around him. Likewise, Althea is superficially aware of these struggles yet unable to experience the levels of change, safely ensconced, as she is, behind her home's closed front door.

The moment Jeff wakes up a black man to the confluence of personal conflicts and social upheavals testifies to how personal problems become highly charged and political. Because Jeff's blackness is often played off as a gag, his transformation into the watermelon man invites audience identification with the film's lead character, especially since he participates in virtually every scene of the movie. It is also no accident that his change to being a frustrated, black revolutionary from a loudmouthed, white bigot takes place through real world experience once he leaves his domestic haven.

Still believing himself to be white Jeff faces the world and learns of racial profiling in the police force, the sex play of white women looking for big black bucks, the segregation of social clubs that no longer accept his credentials and the eventual defection of his wife and neighbours. Memorably, this last set of defections happen all at once when Jeff returns home from a day on the job at a garbage dump only to face an empty house with his family absconded to visit a far-off relative. At the same time, he is approached by a group of his white male neighbours who are interested in buying him out of their neighbourhood so they can recover lost property value.

His failed reintegration into society forces him to reconsider notions about himself, his family and his professional pursuits. Initilly filled with anger, he learns to productively identify with his new racial group to become an independent insurance salesman exclusively targeting the needs of the black population. He also ends up being involved with a group of black men that resembles a revolutionary troupe of urban guerrillas.

FIGURE 10 A 'black' comedy of role reversal: *Watermelon Man*

Before this transformation is complete, however, Jeff goes through stages of shock and denial in reaction to his changing skin colour. Unable to accept the surreal switch in his material reality, Jeff assumes his home-tanning bed is to blame for the darkening of his skin. Even as he seeks satisfaction from the manufacturer with a replacement device, the bed's deliveryman mistakes him as a house thief and incites a fight before Althea intervenes to clarify the confusion. Jeff also bathes overnight in a bathtub filled with milk to no change in colour. This results in him explaining away his condition as being an incredibly deep tan that will take time to heal.

Naturally this explanation is unbelievable, but it is the launching point for Jeff's introduction into the world of racial assumptions used to denigrate black people. He finds himself associated with watermelon, fried chicken, thievery, riotous behaviour, laziness, jive talking, rape, murder, drunkenness, sexual wildness and consignment to the margins of conventional white society. Painfully he learns to accept these new rules for conduct, though with an ironic sensibility.

That Jeff was born white and was inexplicably turned black positions his understanding of the world as being both artificial and arbitrary. It is artificial because no innate law or principle lies behind the white-dominated socio-cultural hierarchy, and it is arbitrary because the viciousness of prejudice as practiced against the black race runs counter to the basic principles of American society. As Kathleen Carroll wrote in a review of the film, 'There is nothing laughable about these situations and the film becomes only more and more irritating. The one thing one can say for it is that it doesn't compromise. Cambridge ends by accepting his new role as a black.'[6]

It is this relationship between the film's star and his diegetic world that racialises a viewer's identification as being white to feel outrage at Jeff's treatment when he becomes a black man. Society's racist unfairness only becomes convincing in light of his basic whiteness, one that exposes core racial assumptions at the heart of America since Godfrey Cambridge is, after all, a black man.

Because Cambridge's Jeff Gerber is first introduced in white make-up and because another black man directed the film, there is a basic rupture at the centre of the text. This rupture exists between the white-washed sentiment of Hollywood executives hoping to achieve box-office success from potentially divisive topic material in contrast to Van Peebles' counter-hegemonic vision suggested by aspects of the film and its central performance. Indeed, part-way through production Van Peebles was nearly forced to film an alternative ending where Jeff wakes up to realise that his racial reversal was merely fantasy. Unconvinced of this false sentiment, Van Peebles refused to shoot the alternate ending in favour of a final, more militant address that supports the examination of racial role reversals enacted by the film.

In this way, some of the stylistic choices of Van Peebles' first feature show up again in *Watermelon Man*. Among them is the use of jump cuts, cutaways during dialogue as visual counter-points to the action, repeated shots and coloured filters to heighten the melodramatic impact of the film's themes. Together these stylistic choices point in the direction of an alternative, non-Hollywood form for Van Peebles' first feature film, but these same devices also serve to heighten the excitement of this film too, the most mainstream and, perhaps, the most entertaining of his body of work. As Cynthia Gillespie commented at the time of the film's release, 'One should appreciate the Van Peebles style – energetic, militant and a little rough around the edges.'[7]

Using such devices as contrapuntal sound, direct address and found footage within the narrative itself, Van Peebles delivers on the promise of difference from the industry's stock-in-trade that was requested by his studio masters. Offering small reversals of form and substance in the way his second feature continues to grapple with racial themes that were then current, his movie succeeds in spicing up the tired content of the domestic melodrama. This excitement also helped to extend the movie's audience by exposing audiences to black actors like Godfrey Cambridge as well as in casting historically important actors like D'Urville Martin and Mantan Moreland in supporting roles.

By first experimenting with form and content in *The Story of a Three-Day Pass* and then extending his technical craft to target a wider audience in *Watermelon Man*, Van Peebles' effort paid off in rewarding his outsider's dilemma of acquiring the material advantages of Hollywood while also carving space to explore a more independent vision. With the culmination of his cinematic style liberated from the usual production circumstances on his third feature film, Van Peebles once again focused on questions of racial identity and cultural conflict to produce his most famous work.

RATED 'X' BY AN ALL-WHITE JURY: SWEETBACK'S REVOLT

Dedicated 'to all the Brothers and Sisters who had enough of the man', Melvin Van Peebles used his director's salary from *Watermelon Man* to fund 19 days of production for *Sweet Sweetback's Baadasssss Song* in late 1970. Budgeted at $500,000 and, at one point, infused with a $50,000 loan from Bill Cosby, Van Peebles wrote, directed, co-produced, scored, edited and starred in his most unconventional film to date.

To keep costs low he hired non-union labour, labelled the film a porn production and took on much of the marketing responsibilities himself using the production company 'Yeah, Inc.' He also released the film through Cinemation, an exploitation movie distributor, to eschew traditional distribution channels by pumping money into radio advertisements targeting black audiences to merchandise both the film and its soundtrack album.[8]

After five and half months of editing and an X-rating from the Motion Picture Association of America, Van Peebles threatened lawsuits against Jack Valenti and the MPAA but used their reaction for his own ends. Employing the catchphrase, 'rated X by an all-white jury', he tagged the film's posters and advertisements and printed T-shirts for an added boost to the film's ancillary markets. He also manufactured nightgowns, sweatshirts emblazoned with the phrase 'I am Sweetback', a paperback book and the Mama's Tub Red and Mama's Tub White table wines.[9]

Released to acclaim and disdain in the black community and the white mainstream, *Sweet Sweetback's Baadasssss Song* took the top box-office position from Arthur Hiller's *Love Story* (1970) for two full weeks. Depending on the estimates, it also went on to earn between $4.1 and $11 million in theatrical rentals,[10] along with producing certain symbols, scenes and stock characters that would prove central to mainstream Hollywood for the rest of the 1970s.

The film opens with a medieval truth claim that reads, 'Sire, these lines are not an homage to brutality that the artist has invented, but a hymn from the mouth of reality.' Continuing on to detail Sweetback's background as a feral child raised among prostitutes, the action jumps forward to see him performing as a stud in a kind of backroom minstrel show. When he witnesses police brutality practised against a young black revolutionary named Mu-Mu (Hubert Scales), Sweetback defends the younger man and is forced to flee from the authorities for his outrageous conduct. Through the rest of the film he races towards Mexico and is helped along the way by members of the black community.

After finally making good his escape, viewers are warned, 'Watch Out. A baadasssss nigger is coming back to collect some dues.'

According to Donald Bogle, Thomas Cripps, Ed Guerrero and Mark Reid among others,[11] *Sweet Sweetback's Baadasssss Song* is generally listed as the pivot film for blaxploitation cinema. Writing contemporaneously to the film's release, Penelope Gilliatt suggested in 1971:

> *Sweetback* is presumably the first of a line of films. The next ones will get gentler, with luck, and better characterised, and signed with a clearer authorship than this, but they can never be anything like *Guess Who's Coming To Dinner*, or lose the tongue they have found here, which is a shock in the cinema.[12]

However, this perspective ignores other influential mainstream films released during the same period, not least of which was *Shaft* (Gordon Parks, 1971). Therefore, to claim *Sweet Sweetback's Baadasssss Song* as the foundation for blaxploitation and its high points in such fare as *Superfly* (Gordon Parks, Jr., 1972) and *Willie Dynamite* (Gilbert Moses, 1974) is too simplistic. What Van Peebles' film did manage to convey was the interest and viability of black cultural products independently produced by, and for, a primarily black audience. Among Hollywood producers and financiers alike, this notion was percolating with an understanding that, 'given the right film … the black audience can be the biggest movie-going public in America'.[13]

In 1971, Melvin Van Peebles managed to tune his filmmaking to the pulse of his times with an uncanny sense of how to affirm his sense of black community while entertaining that audience with images and sounds largely marginalised in the mainstream cinema. As he was later quoted on the subject, 'the first move for a disenfranchised people is a sense of self.'[14]

By acquiring the necessary skills for renovating genre structures and playing with social satire in his first two feature films, Van Peebles was freer to revolt against conventional form and content. Foremost among his goals in this effort was not adhering mainstream standards about how black people were being represented. He also wanted to ensure that *Sweet Sweetback's Baadasssss Song* would look and sound as good as industry standards required. Plus he wanted to provoke and entertain his primary audience of other black Americans, his 'constituency' as he called them,[15] and he wanted his film to be a standard-bearer for making theatrical films outside Hollywood. Expanding on this final point, Van Peebles wrote:

> The recognition of the correlation between image and destiny is not new, what is new for black third world and disenfranchised people is the means for putting their realities before the mass audience. But now more and more brothers and sisters are snatching this power and the job of reclaiming the minds of people, especially black people has begun. Anyway that's why I'm into images and mirrors.[16]

Pursuit of these four goals departs from mainstream cinematic practices and means the resulting movie satisfies a different set of critical reactions. Lacking the polish of a well-made plot, the expertise of highly trained actors, actresses and production staff, and the reach of an homogenising marketing team to shape the overall product, *Sweet Sweetback's Baadasssss Song* is a challenging and difficult picture.

The film's success lay in its ghetto view of black American experience put front and centre for cinematic entertainment without isolating such experiences along the margins of plot and action. Sweetback's flight from the police into the seams of illegitimate commerce, including backroom sex showcases, whorehouses, gambling dens, voodoo churches and halfway houses for political revolutionaries is treated seriously, as are the people he encounters along the way. Emphasising this typically overlooked segment of the black community also positively valued this subculture by affirming the connections between social transgression and forms of criminal conduct.

With just over ninety minutes running time, *Sweet Sweetback's Baadasssss Song* lays out the main points of its plot within the film's first third. Through the second third that roughly details Sweetback's adventures in Los Angeles, he visits his nominal boss, an old girlfriend, a community church, a gambling den and a forested hideaway and ends his adventures, in the final third of the film, running from the law. As a sexual man raised in a whorehouse and able to wield his libido as the tool of his stud's life, having sex with various women helps him avoid conversation and forces a relentless quality of movement into his quest for freedom. Not to be forgotten, his sexuality also gives rise to an objectifying sexism layered throughout the film.

As a cinematic rebel, Sweetback is a stoic black hero. He takes action unlike his forebears, Jeff Gerber and Turner, who struggled to communicate through the difficulties of prejudice running rampant in their world. Sweetback is a man born at the bottom rung of society yet he is able to understand injustice by recognising how a politically active militant like Mu-Mu is the future of his race and culture. Unfortunately, Van Peebles' talents as an actor undercut the impact of this one-note hero and make him out to be less a man than a somewhat laughable masculine prototype.

Because his character was rendered one-dimensional, his image along with the more commercially viable John Shaft (Richard Roundtree) became instantly synonymous with black machismo in 1971. The use of such cinematic devices as contrapuntal sound, reversed negatives, animation, freeze frames, split frames, superimposition, direct address, photo montage, location shooting and scene repetition further enhanced the look of this new black man and how he was framed on-screen. Importantly these visual and aural motifs became a sign of the times.

Where these same devices were used to explore inter-racial romance in *The Story of a Three-Day Pass* and then exploded to look at the social reversals of *Watermelon Man*, *Sweet Sweetback's Baadasssss Song* uses them to define a new style substituted for mainstream conventions. Its collection of technical idiosyncrasies and stylistic flourishes imbue it with an alternative experience as much through the chance encounters of its independent production circumstances as by the planned values

FIGURE 11 The director as black rebel: *Sweet Sweetback's Baadasssss Song*

of any consistent set of themes. This departure helped substantiate an already existing bond between political representations in fiction films and the needs of an under-represented movie-going audience to watch and connect with on-screen characters and their struggles.

Thinking critically of the film in its release, however, Vincent Canby surmised, 'Instead of dramatising injustice, Van Peebles merchandises it.'[17] His point was that Van Peebles readily performed the steps of exploiting a truly revolutionary, and independent, vision of blackness by rendering the most obvious white stereotypes about black people as the continuing basis for commercial cinema. Clayton Riley agreed with Canby's sentiment in that, 'black people had been stung by the movie's relentless vulgarity and Van Peebles' apparent obsession with the ruined landscapes of black life. And the outrage has a solid point, there is little positive black imagery in *Sweet Sweetback*'.[18]

Implicit in these dissenting opinions from the celebratory remarks promoted during the film's release and its subsequent glorification in later film histories is the importance of black popular films for carrying the burden of reversing white dominated racial hierarchies. *Sweet Sweetback's Baadasssss Song* does engage this kind of reversal by emphasising a sovereign black cinematic voice. However, Van Peebles was actually most successful in recognising the economic lessons of the movie industry and then using these lessons to his advantage by producing one of the most notorious films of the 1970s.

Thus, the film is open to being considered the one movie that targeted black spectatorship as never before in the popular cinema. One can accept this proposition while also subjecting it to the scrutiny of a wider critical reaction. Lerone Bennett, Jr. took up such a position (or which his efforts are laudable) when he wrote a cautionary article about the film's impact and popularity:

> *Sweet Sweetback* ... is a trivial and tasteless negative classic: trivial and tasteless because of the banality of conception and execution; a negative classic, because it is an obligatory step for anyone who wants to go further and make the first black revolutionary film.[19]

That Hollywood paid attention to the period's black cultural products and influences lends credence to the commonly held belief about how the mainstream immediately ransacked *Sweet Sweetback's Baadasssss Song*. It exported his stoic black male lead, the use of popular music, underworld surroundings and the inclusion of sexually explicit and violent sequences. The idea is given further weight through the sheer repetition of Sweetback's adventures that later became cliché-ridden in the blaxploitation cycle, but this commonly held belief is coincident, rather than causal, in nature.

It is true that Hollywood did Van Peebles one better by conventionalising his story about an urban outlaw through film after film after film. It is also true that Hollywood was already releasing such work when Van Peebles was producing his third feature. Therefore, *Sweet Sweetback's Baadasssss Song* is not primarily important for having turned the film industry on its ear. Instead, the film's legacy is the demonstration of artistic ingenuity, including the development of alternative distribution channels and marketing practices. Van Peebles' reversal of the dominant system was in pitching the terms of movie financing to his advantage even while his films responded to similar cues and influences then affecting mainstream products along with works outside the commercial fold. By accepting these influences and refocusing them Van Peebles also managed to imbue his film with an increased sensitivity that was exceptionally appealing to black moviegoers.

CONCLUSION

With a body of work that includes novels, stage musicals, plays and soundtrack albums, Melvin Van Peebles' first three feature films centre on the subjects of racial identity and the cultural clash of blackness within a white-dominated American system. This twinned thematic fuels his work and develops alternative appeals running in parallel to the mainstream culture that proved immediately translatable into action-adventure formulae for the newly fomenting commercial purpose in blaxploitation cinema.

That Van Peebles' counter-hegemonic efforts were popular in their own right is a matter for the historical record. The very fact of how cinema history remembers *Sweet Sweetback's Baadasssss Song*, though, and to the exclusion of very much regard for his earlier features, suggests two peculiar tendencies. On the one hand, there is the promotion of a great man theory that lacks historical context or a discussion of artistic development across a body of work. On the other hand, there is an on-going historical effort to emphasise his third film as the birthplace for blaxploitation, an effort that simplifies the complexity of independent and mainstream cinemas in the 1960s and 1970s while also minimising this important work and the cycle of films generally, though improperly, considered to be its result.

In part this tendency is due to the controversy surrounding *Sweet Sweetback's Baadasssss Song* and films of its ilk that capitalised on a paucity of images appealing to an under-represented black American population. It is also due to the backlash against Melvin Van Peebles for having the audacity to write, direct, co-produce, score, edit and star in a film that so directly inflames its viewers but was never eclipsed in force of popularity or influence by any of his subsequent cinematic work.

The elevation of *Sweet Sweetback's Baadasssss Song* recognises the commercial importance of black film representations in the late 1960s and early 1970s but it also disregards the political and cultural importance of other films from the period. Regardless, Van Peebles' politics, aesthetics and context remain for us as the incendiary images and sounds of his recorded body of work. Likewise his first three feature films have an amateurish quality that intentionally interrupted the dominant forms for representing cinematic subjects, but most especially black American cinematic subjects.

The persistent attraction of *The Story of a Three-Day Pass*, *Watermelon Man* and *Sweet Sweetback's Baadasssss Song* to new audiences through time invites continued investigation and on-going re-evaluation. This persistence of influence is also an indication of how films, and their filmmakers, can be formed and re-formed by their changing historical contexts.

CHAPTER 9
DORIS WISHMAN MEETS THE AVANT-GARDE

Michael J. Bowen

SEXING UP THE UNDERGROUND

Although exploitation film studies are only in their infancy, it has already become evident that historians and theorists have begun to identify certain resonances between low-culture sex and horror films and the work of the culturally accredited, cinematic avant-garde. Both exploitation and avant-garde cinemas are generally credited with an ability to shock, a concept now associated importantly with the cinema in its 'primitive' form – spectacular, non-narrative, focused around the body. Exploitation films would normally seem to shock audiences by recourse to the obscene – through the representation of things that are visible but which are usually proscribed from emerging into sight. The cinematic avant-garde, on the other hand, seems to shock audiences by manipulating visual experience itself, by playing with tolerances of vision in such a way that the act of seeing becomes a shockingly aberrant phenomenon. Both avant-garde and exploitation cinemas, therefore, comment equally upon the cultural organisation of visuality, on the spectator's encoded experience of seeing.

It is not the general case, however, that the operation and effects of the avant-garde and exploitation cinemas are granted equal significance by most film scholars. The avant-garde cinema maintains a place within critical discourse far more privileged than that of the exploitation sub-genres. Exploitation films are, after all, widely held to be inarticulate and aesthetically regressive; authorless and derivative, they pander to the worst impulses in human nature – violence and unregulated sexuality. Avant-garde films, on the other hand, experiment consciously with the boundaries of experience, both personal and aesthetic; although often controversial, they strive for formal originality and deal with questions of widely recognised intellectual worth.

That said, most scholars would also agree that during the 1960s a certain number of attributions did begin to manifest themselves linking the cinematic 'underground' – the term used during the period to describe the filmic avant-garde – with the dominant strain of 1960s low-budget exploitation – the so-called 'sex-exploitation' genres. These links, in fact, were a subject of interest to numerous contemporary commentators:

> A particularly curious aspect [of the recent, non-conventional cinema] has been the almost inevitable confusion between the Underground and the commercial, sex-oriented cinema. This confusion is compounded by the fact that most of the Underground newspapers in America carry advertisements for sexploitation sagas which are placed side by side with advertising displays for the works of Warhol … Kenneth Anger, etc.[1]

This 'almost inevitable confusion', however, apparently rested upon a basis more complex than media misalliance alone. There were structural, even thematic links between the two cinemas. As the same writer observes:

> [Both sexploitation and avant-garde films] share the same insistence on portraying sexual activity and deviations; the same desire to abolish all censor control; they have in common low budgets, the use of amateur or semi-professional actors and a disdain or disregard for the gloss and polish of Hollywood film techniques. … Leaving aside the large proportion of Underground films which aren't concerned with sex at all, it's fair to say that the most commercially successful [underground] artists … have been those who featured sex prominently in their works.[2]

This essay will seek to examine in greater detail the relationship between certain elements of the intellectually accredited underground movement of the 1960s and the work of one 'sexploitation'

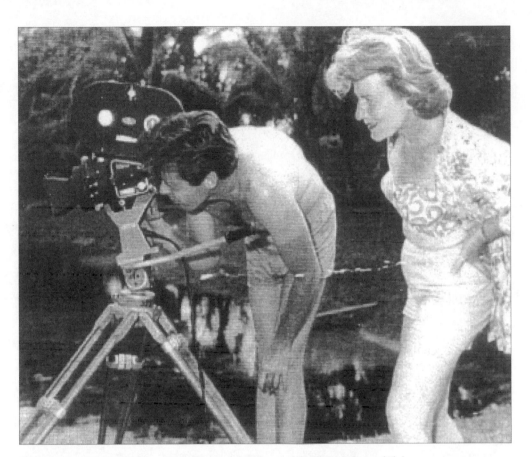

FIGURE 12 Doris Wishman working at Sunny Palms Lodge nudist camp with cameraman Raymond Phelan

auteur active during the same period. Doris Wishman's cinema has been the subject of only limited critical analysis,[3] but has in recent years gained a certain notoriety among aficionados of the abject, no-budget film world of the 1960s and 1970s.[4] The director proved herself to be a by-product of the anomalous circumstances under which independent production was able to operate during these tumultuous decades. With at least 27 feature titles to her credit, Wishman is probably the most prolific American woman filmmaker of the sound era as well as a self-taught cinematic stylist whose work has been deemed by one critic 'easier to recognise than Orson Welles's'.[5]

Wishman's definition exclusively as an exploitation filmmaker, however, is highly problematic. Her own stated commercial orientation, seeming adherence to recognised exploitation formulas and association with New York's low-budget 9th Avenue film world seem to mark her efforts as those of an 'exploiter'. Her marginalisation within this sphere (her films were among the least known and least successful in the exploitation genres), her explicitly recognisable and unconventional style as well as her recent recuperation within avant-garde retrospective/exhibition circles, however, indicate that Wishman has a certain role in the discourse on film art.

IRONY ... OR NOT IRONY

With only a modest background in film distribution and no formal training in production, Doris Wishman's arrival as an independent filmmaker was actually the product of a confluence of forces that I intend to examine in more detail. Her knowledge of independent distribution gave Wishman a good sense for the idiosyncrasies of the 'state's-rights' film market – a loose association of regional distributors who had lived in the shadow of studio-controlled distribution networks since the 1920s. Wishman's lack of training in film production (almost impossible for a woman to acquire formally in this period) – dictated that she rely upon the technical support of various assistants. However, the dynamic industry for film and television production in New York during the early 1960s put her in an excellent position to access talent and services necessary to her efforts.[6]

Except for her reliance upon camera and editing personnel, however, Wishman tended to work with few collaborators, usually writing, producing, directing and overseeing the editing of her own films. It also seems significant that Wishman rarely attracted investors. Her first feature – *Hideout in the Sun* (1960) – was financed primarily by family loans, while subsequent financing originated substantially from distribution advances and Wishman's own reinvested profits. In this way, Wishman managed to retain a high degree of control over her own filmmaking efforts.

It was typical of Wishman's work, however, to correspond to the general outlines of certain recognised genres within the rapidly transforming sex-exploitation world of the 1960s and 1970s. Inspired by the legal and commercial success of *Garden of Eden* (1954) – a film that offered a fictional account of daily life in a Florida nudist camp – Wishman launched her production career in the colourful nudist genre. With the demise of the nudist market in the mid-1960s, however, she switched allegiance to the then-ascendant, black and white, sex and scandal genre known as the 'roughie'. With the advent of 'soft-core' in the late 1960s, however, Wishman began a graduated manoeuvre to distance herself from the burgeoning 'hard-core' market and seek out an alternative filmic language.

In command of a system of production and assisted by her familiarity with outlets dedicated to marketing low-budget sex-exploitation features, Wishman had established herself by the early 1960s as one of the most active independent producer-directors working in the sex-exploitation *milieu*. Economically self-sufficient and dedicated to her craft, she claims to have cared little for the fact that she received no critical recognition for her efforts as a filmmaker. This may seem especially odd during a time when cinephile culture was rapidly proliferating and the discourse on 'auteurism' had been galvanised by both European and American 'underground' innovators.

Curiously, however, Wishman's work did not go completely unnoticed by the film critical culture of the early 1960s. In a somewhat accidental review in the Summer 1962 issue of *Vision*, a columnist reported his response to a randomly-encountered double-bill featuring a dated Eva Gabor jungle romance (*Love Island* (1952)) and, at the top of the marquee, Wishman's *Hideout in the Sun*.[7]

While the author goes on to critique in detail the tedious, 'sexless' quality of the nudist genre as a whole, it is noteworthy that his low esteem for the 'salacious elements' in Wishman's work does not extend to the film's plot. Defrocked of its dull but exploitable nudist trappings, he finds the film's story, in fact, to be worthy of a backhanded compliment:

> The plot of the first film – *Hideout in the Sun* – was so ludicrous that had it been intended for a ten-minute short it would have been one of the funniest, wildest ever. ... Needless to say, the dramatic urgency ... comes to a grinding halt once we hit the nudist colony.[8]

Describing the story in detail, the film concerns a pair of bank-robbing brothers hiding out from the police in a nearby nudist resort. One of the brothers – the bad one – falls to his death in a snake pit while running from the police. The other brother, having fallen in love with his nudist accomplice, decides to turn himself in to the law, planning to return to the peaceable nudist lifestyle once he has settled his debt with society. Padded out to seventy minutes with the addition of nudist exploitation footage – the trope of the genre itself – the film was reportedly 'like slow death.' But taken for its residual narrative, the above critic seems to see the basis for an engaging short film – 'the funniest, wildest ever.'[9]

What is 'so wild' about Wishman's nudist narratives is her inclination for genre mixing. Wishman's nudist films appear to unfold on two levels. Firstly, there is the level of the nudist spectacle (the functional reason for the existence of the genre itself), while a separate level of narrative occupies a space in Wishman's work entirely on its own. One has the impression of two films, one locked inside the other, unable to achieve mutual narrative resolution. In *Hideout in the Sun*, for instance, the trope of gangsters going on the lamb is subverted by their efforts to hide out inside a nudist resort. In *Nude on the Moon* (1960), the stereotype of the science fiction film is set at odds with the discovery of a colony of topless 'moon dolls' living on the lunar surface. Equally, in *Diary of a Nudist* (1961), a girl reporter goes undercover to write an exposé, not on urban political corruption but on nude sunbathing. Naked gangsters, topless aliens, a nudist Girl Friday – all invoke a stock of cinema clichés subverted by their reorientation within the larger context of the nudist film's generic limitations.

For spectators versed in the mechanics of genre, such stark violations of generic boundaries cannot help but instigate a certain sense of absurdity. An important mode of avant-garde readership, the ironic resonance of Wishman's nudist films aligns her efforts with the 1960s underground by providing an opportunity for transgressive reading. 'It's claimed that George Kuchar had a satiric purpose in making *Colour Me Shameless*,' one 1960s critic notes facetiously, pointing out a similar tendency to mix genres within the work of one of the Underground's most widely heralded operatives. 'Most of the sex-and-deviation films are also amusing by ... slightly sophisticated standards.'[10] Films such as Wishman's could be enjoyed for their moments of irremediable hybridity as well, therefore, as the tedious spectacle of celluloid flesh giving way to the lived experience of watching a film lost in the play of its own contradictions.

This effect of irony in Wishman's cinema is complicated, however, by evidence that her transgressions were not intentionally ironic. Within Wishman's film world, the juxtaposition of incongruous elements follows a logic only obvious to the filmmaker herself. Ironically, the real rationale that is driving Wishman's system is the logic of genre alone. 'I was really only interested in the stories,' Wishman has frequently reported, 'but if the public wants nudity, you've got to give them nudity.'[11] Confronted by the opportunity to work within the confines of genre or not to work at all, Wishman chose the former. But the uncompromising manner in which she interpolated her narrative visions into the spectacle of nudist exploitation subverted genre once again. Wishman sees her nudist efforts, in fact, as dramas – not as comedies – wrapped within a commercially dictated shell. Similarly, the commentator above opines that Warhol's 'humor' in films like *My Hustler* (1964) and *Flesh* (1968) also 'seems accidental rather than intentional.' 'It becomes difficult,' he argues, 'to distinguish between the two.'[12]

AN ERUPTIVE MOBILITY

Wishman's second critical period began in late 1964 with the release of her first film in what would come to be known as the 'roughie' genre. Distinguished by its lurid subject matter – particularly emphasising illicit and sado-masochistic sexuality – as well as by its stark, minimalist production values – black and white, hand-held cinematography and gritty urban settings – the roughie substituted a violent eroticism for the naive exhibitionism and colourful locations of the upbeat nudist romance.

With her switch to roughie aesthetics, Wishman also entered immediately into her most widely recognised period of stylistic innovation. Films such as *Bad Girls Go to Hell* (1965), *My Brother's Wife* (1966) and *Indecent Desires* (1967) have attracted the attention of numerous cinephiles and counter-culture film fans able to rediscover such grind-house relics through the agency of home video. The irony implicit in this statement, of course, arises from the fact that Wishman's films were technically never 'discovered' in the first place. Flashing invisibly across the marquees of fading downtown cinemas, bundled into salacious double-bills that no newspaper would dream of reviewing and for which many would not even accept advertising, Wishman's contribution to the film art of the mid-1960s went entirely unnoticed. In the days before the advent of legal hard-core, the roughie was the equivalent of a bona fide dirty movie, and Wishman's situation within the genre virtually guaranteed her continued anonymity.

Recent interest in Wishman's roughie period, however, seems to have little to do with its sexual content – or lack thereof. Conforming to the conventions of the genre, her offerings tended to exhibit little nudity and less sex, rarely defying the still-lingering censorial standards of the mid-1960s. It may be, in fact, that this very absence of sexual content constitutes one of the cores of fascination with Wishman's 'rediscovered' cinema. In an arguably post-porn universe in which public sexual expression has been linked – perhaps insidiously – with personal liberation, the reflex to repress the spectacle of sex seems to have become a form of pornography in its own right. Wishman's roughies now appear as a nebulous meditation on our own assumptions about the effects of sexual freedom: before AIDS, before feminism, Wishman's negation of the truth of sex haunts a world in which its absence now appears to have become a sort of deviant sexual thrill.

What seems to attract most viewers to Wishman's mid-1960s film work, however, is its extraordinary mobilisation of stylistic signifiers, suggesting the operation of a unique and astonishing filmmaking intelligence. 'Only Jean-Luc Godard can match her indifference to composition and framing,' one of her early chroniclers notes with genuine admiration.[13] The fact that a poorly funded filmmaker, working for explicitly commercial purposes, should have managed to create and replicate such a recognisable lexicon of surprising cinematic images constitutes one of the central attractions – and mysteries – of her work of this period.

Wishman's style is perhaps best typified by a unique combination of eruptive mobility and unexpected stasis. The highly mobile hand-held camerawork common in her mid-1960s efforts traverses her *mise-en-scène* like an inexplicable presence, paradoxically constructing the camera operator as a virtual character in an otherwise fictionalised diegesis. Added to Wishman's resiliently real locations – kitschly appointed 1960s interiors and cracked Manhattan sidewalks – and the spectacularly unrehearsed efforts of her semi-professional actors, Wishman's work accumulates a veritable documentary sensibility. One feels that one is witnessing the actual recording of an actual event taking place in an actual space – the record of a film being made more than of a film itself. In this respect, there is a surprising 'liveness' to Wishman's mid-1960s work, a sense of a world that cannot hide the traces of its origins in reality.

At the same time, however, one is struck by a deadly *stillness* that haunts Wishman's output during this period. In spite of the immediacy of her method of registration, Wishman's 'cut-away' editing style vivisects the most dynamic elements of her *mise-en scène*, draining the image of its tendency to represent real time and space. Her persistent reliance upon post-sync dialogue recording empties the diegesis of sonic density as well: voices – no matter what the location – seem to emanate from the profound depths of a soundproof booth. The impossible stiffness of her actors; her constant recourse to static inserts of shoes, ashtrays, knickknacks, wall hangings – anything inanimate; even her decision to use her own sparsely-furnished apartment as her principle location – all reinforce a sense that time itself has been frozen in Wishman's world. This creation of a barren nowhere in which nothing happens and where there is an absence of continuous activity or motivation, begins to become one of her films' most shocking and compelling attributes.

The overall effect of Wishman's style, therefore, is a powerful sense that the integrity of reality has been wilfully and alarmingly deranged. Her films of the roughie period manifest a marked disrespect for the boundaries of the realism of her chosen medium and recording techniques, fragmenting and even falsifying the documentary element of her work through what begins to feel like an extraordinary act of narcissistic interference. In Wishman's hands, the solidity of the shot is broken like match sticks; her style of montage treats the inviolable photographic image like a paper doll, imposing upon it the whim of some invisible hand. The visible sphere becomes captive to the almost sadistic manipulation of a narrative will, whose excessive exertions mark each cut as an irreparable scar, whose desires attempt to drain the image of any relationship with the world beyond that which it wishes to impose upon it.

As a result of these potent and vexing inclinations within her roughie work, Wishman has come to earn the interest of numerous later-day aesthetes, some of whom claim to see a relationship between her efforts in the exploitation demimonde and developments in various efforts associated with the avant-garde. Underground filmmaker Peggy Awesh – among the first to introduce Wishman's work to a modern film-going public – has screened *Bad Girls Go to Hell* at the Whitney Museum alongside the work of Jean-Marie Straub and Danielle Huillet. Wishman's appearance at the Harvard Film Archive in 1994 – her first public manifestation as an 'auteur' – was met with comparisons to Maya Deren and Chantal Ackerman. Screenings at the Andy Warhol Museum as well as numerous colleges and art theatres have also highlighted Wishman's counter-cultural resonance.

Wishman's penetration even into the music subculture ought not to be surprising. For instance, there is a notable affinity between her work and elements of the lingering punk underground – particularly in its feminist variants – within which the reputation of Wishman's films as 'sleazy' and her authorship of numerous 'bad girl' characters have proven to have a durable appeal. Paradoxically, however, it is Wishman herself who most frequently refuses to admit that there is anything unwholesome about her films; nor does she claim to champion the parade of call girls, lesbians, and fallen women who populate her scenarios. Greatly at variance with nihilist punk aesthetics, the director has unswervingly insisted that her films were made with 'love' and is deeply offended when anyone refers to them as 'trash'. She also insists that she is not a feminist and tends to stare blankly at cultural theorists who question her about her representation of gender. 'People always talk about Wishman's *style*,' the stymied filmmaker has confessed, 'but I just did what I had to do to get the film done.'[14]

Wishman's oft-noted lack of comprehension for the appeal of her work within cinephile circles both comments upon and reduplicates the mystery surrounding her films themselves. A trash filmmaker who insists that her movies were not 'trash', and yet who also refuses to accept their designation as 'art', the problem of Wishman's authorship becomes as complicated as her baffling stylistics. Few filmmakers welcomed into the circle of the underground elite do so without professing some kind of artistic mission; nor are such filmmakers generally spawned within the aggressively commercial context that gave birth to Doris Wishman. Yet, Wishman's stock among the avant-garde continues to rise: she has recently followed John Waters and Alejandro Jodorowsky as recipient of The Chicago Underground Film Festival's Lifetime Achievement Award.

THE ROUGHIE MYSTIQUE DECODED

As with her entry into filmmaking as a whole, the conditions under which Wishman's distinctive mid-1960s stylistics came into being ought to be examined in more detail. Wishman's situation as both a filmmaker and an auteur have much to do with the contexts within which 'Doris Wishman' came to be invented – not just as a repository of cinematic authorship, but also as a no-budget exploiter. In many respects, as a filmmaking entity Wishman does not really exist outside of certain processes of production and strategies of readership – a fact which, amazingly but refreshingly, she herself is usually the first to acknowledge.

The Doris Wishman of the mid-1960s first comes into being once again through the strictures of genre – namely, the roughie – a form which she freely confesses she elected to work in only after the collapse of the nudist market left her with no economically viable alternative. A poor-man's neo-realism – part film noir and part stag film – the roughie took its cues from cheap erotic fiction and the social hygiene exploitation sagas of an earlier generation. It claimed to take harsh reality as its subject matter, bespeaking the dangers of urban life and the failure of traditional values.

The look of the roughies, however, conformed to the economics of independent filmmaking of the period. Black and white film stock – more affordable than colour – typified the production standards of most low-budget filmmaking enterprises through the 1960s, particularly in the neo-realist and avant-garde modes. The look of *cinéma verité*, the French New Wave and newsreel photography soon made black and white synonymous with the 'realist' agendas associated with these forms. Black and white was also increasingly associated with an ideology of authenticity once colour photographs began to become a dominant mode of mass representation.

Hand-held camerawork participated in the ideology of realism as well. Increasingly the mechanism for fast-paced, documentary reportage, hand-held cameras had found their niche in neo-realist cinemas by the late 1950s. This blurred the boundaries between feature production – long subservient to the 'seamless' industrial mode of Hollywood filmmaking – and the freeform look of home movies. The noticeable reference to the photographer embedded in hand-held camerawork also augmented the overall effect of authorial presence so important to the blossoming auteurist sensibility. Someone beyond the diegesis was clearly focusing, panning and recording the filmic event. The presence of the filmmaker, therefore, entered the diegetic universe as a reflection of technology.

Wishman's oft-noted indifference to visual composition is a telling reflection upon the effects that such generic structures of registration had upon her work. The style of camerawork frequently attributed to Wishman's name – 'her singular camera technique' as one critic puts it[15] – generally had little to do with the director herself. As frequent Wishman cameraman, C. Davis Smith, has noted in an interview: 'Doris didn't get into how the scene was lit or how you should shoot it. She only wanted to know whether or not the action had been recorded.' Hand-held shooting was quick, Smith claims, and 'it worked well for that type of show.'[16] Wishman herself has also commented that the choice of black and white was as much conventional as aesthetic: 'It was just what people were using.'[17] Wishman's 'singular ... technique' therefore had its origins in the pre-existence of a largely-encoded schema of registration which aligned her mid-1960s films both with the realist ideology of black and white and the heightened sense of authorial presence implied by mobile camerawork.

Within the realm of editing – admittedly Wishman's favourite aspect of the filmmaking process – similar exigencies also need to be taken into account. Given the extremely limited budgets available to her, Wishman's ability to record multiple takes, re-shoot problematic footage and assemble adequate 'coverage' for her films was often severely limited. Not an uncommon predicament among low-budget exploiters – often referred to as 'one shot wonders' – the hurdles she had to overcome in the editing process were continual and extreme. Missed cues, bad focus, disappearing props and unfilmed plot components frequently forced Wishman to develop new story elements at the editing table itself. Continuity problems invariably arose, forcing Wishman as editor to search for an available solution.

The solution to her problems, however, came in the form of a discovery she claims to have made early in her career – the cutaway. An old editor's trick used to smooth over the transition between discontinuous shots, Wishman realised that the panacea to her editorial woes was a quick insert of some object situated within the vicinity of the scene's main action. A tabletop, a picture on the wall, somebody's feet, a quick 'reaction shot' of a person in the room – all could serve to cover a bit of bad dialogue or to smooth over the obvious elisions in a scene created at the editing bench. As elements within the diegesis, in Wishman's estimation these extra-narrative glances did not disrupt narrative continuity but served instead to bandage the ruptures that confronted her during the editing process. The technique, however, has frequently been described as cubist in its effect.

Wishman's noted 'cutaway style', therefore, had deep roots in economic necessity and in filmmaking tradition as well. In her eyes, the manipulation was little more than a corrective to the flaws endemic in her otherwise irregular registration process. In spite of the fact that avant-garde commentators often identify a stylistic effort in this highly visible element of Wishman's work,[18] the director herself acknowledges a major difference between the intentions of her own editorial efforts and the efforts of those who utilise similar techniques to achieve avant-garde ends. 'There's nothing worse than a jump cut,'[19] she has pointed out, noting that the goal of all editing should be to maintain narrative continuity.

AN OBSCENE SPLENDOUR

It is in Wishman's final period, however, that her affinity for and accessibility to avant-garde reading strategies seemed to reach its crisis point – its apotheoses, as well as its definitive rupture. Confronted by shifts in exploitation filmmaking toward increasingly explicit representations of sex and violence during the early 1970s, she faced a difficult choice. Should she continue to adapt to these changes and produce increasingly violent and sexually explicit work, or should she attempt to break with genre altogether and set out on her own?

Following the lead of the soft-core film market in the late 1960s, Wishman at first attempted to conform to the will of the new genre. Her first colour film after the roughie period, *Love Toy* (1968), signified a turn toward a more sexually central theme – a man gambles away a fortune, earning it back by offering the winner a night with his teenage daughter. It is also acknowledged that she worked on at least two hard-core films under pseudonyms during the mid-1970s as well – *Satan Was a Lady* (c. 1975) and *Come with Me My Love* (c. 1976). Dominated largely by scenes of sexual intercourse, neither Wishman's narrative irony nor her stylistic inventiveness seemed able to rise to the challenge of subverting the generic spectacle of sexual pleasure.

Gradually abandoning the standardised codes of the hard-core genre, however, Wishman's cinema of the 1970s came to be typified by a less explicit but actually somehow more *obscene* organisation of the somatic spectacle. The obscenity of Wishman's 1970s efforts arises from its depiction of the body as a profoundly disruptive and disrupted phenomenon. Her work of the period posits a body out of control, tending toward collapse, representing the instability of somatic existence itself.

Transplanted penises that drive their hosts to murder, breasts impregnated with cameras and bombs, the agony of surgical gender reassignment. These strategies were ostensibly invented to reduce the need for stronger modes of sex and violence within her work. However, the admixture of murderous sex and sexualised dismemberment that typified Wishman's work concocted a stronger, more vitally offensive play of taboos than that of her generic counterparts.

This obscenity is especially noticeable in the case of two Wishman features starring the striptease sensation Chesty Morgan. *Deadly Weapons* (1974) and *Double Agent 73* (1974) are both premised upon the gimmick of Morgan's monstrous 73-inch bust. In the first feature, *Deadly Weapons*, Morgan hunts down and smothers her lover's killers with her enormous bosom. In the second film, she is a spy who uses a secret camera implanted in one of her breasts to photograph an underworld cartel. Exceptional in Wishman's oeuvre for the attention the two films received from the press, Morgan was referred to by one critic as 'a refugee from *Freaks*', while another evaluated her pained performance as 'more pathetic than if she were to have been posed in a side-show'.[20]

Besides Morgan's sexual monstrosity, however, the central gimmick of her breast as a weapon exemplifies Wishman's strange conflation of eroticism and violence within these films. In *The Amazing Transplant* (1970), a grafted penis becomes a kind of weapon as well, urging its formerly impotent recipient to rape and murder women. *In Let Me Die a Woman* (1978) – Wishman's only foray into the 'documentary' field – violence and sexuality are monstrously joined in the testimony of actual transsexuals, who see their organic gender assignment as a form of disease. In one scene excised from currently available prints, Wishman features a distraught pre-op who is shown removing his own penis with a hammer and chisel. The film, however, does not shy from exhibiting the removal of a penis and scrotum in footage from an actual male-to-female sex change operation.

WATCH THE MOB GET BUSTED
WHEN 'CHESTY' TAKES HER REVENGE

R
COLOR

The INCREDIBLE

CHESTY MORGAN

SEEING IS BELIEVING!
73 - 32 - 36

in **"DEADLY WEAPONS"**

... THE ONLY WAY TO GO!

FIGURE 13 Chesty Morgan in *Deadly Weapons*

In addition to such sensational and disturbing subject matter, Wishman's films of this period also evince a stunning aesthetic obscenity as well. Artless, incomprehensible, for many impossible to watch – not only the film's content but the very filmmaking itself revolts aesthetic decency. Consider the agonies of *Let Me Die a Woman*, its 'documentary' integrity turned inside-out through the addition of staged soft-core sex scenes in which its authentic transsexual subjects perform simulated intercourse. Equally, the patent ugliness of *The Amazing Transplant*, whose return to colour intersects nauseatingly with the worst excesses of the 1970s palette. Then there is the inexplicable and sublime tackiness of Chesty Morgan's wardrobe – reportedly her own clothes! – mixed with the impossible vision of her haggard grimace whenever her character is called upon to smile. 'Atrociously directed and edited and invariably out of focus,' one of the previous critics scolds dejectedly.[21] '*Deadly Weapons* is an insult not only to those who view it, but also, perversely, to its uniquely endowed subject.'

It is painful to watch Wishman's output from the 1970s. This pain reflected in the face of every female viewer who momentarily imagines herself burdened with Chesty's stretch-marked endowments. This pain is also seen in the reaction of cinephiles as well. Her films of this period grate painfully against the colourful backdrop of her earlier nudist romances and the unexpected stylistic revelations of her classical roughie melodramas. Their discontinuities confound instead of astonish; their amateurism depresses instead of inspires; the only reward associated with watching them is the

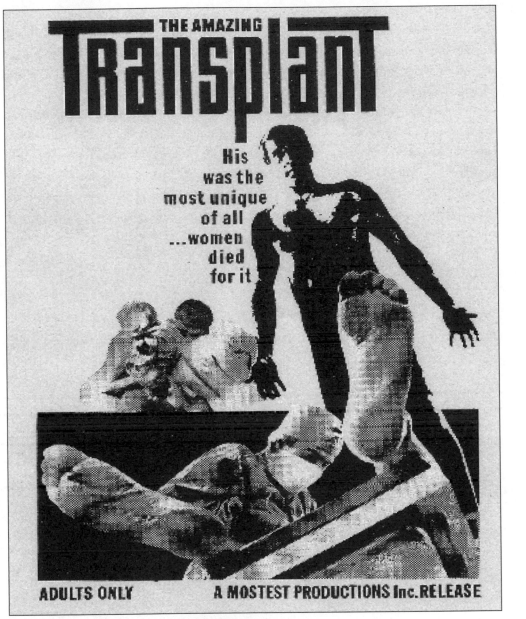

FIGURE 14 Conflating eroticism and violence in *The Amazing Transplant*

satisfaction of knowing that one has seen the last, the most wretched, the worst movie that has ever been made.

There is, therefore, an element of radical displeasure associated with watching Wishman's films of the 1970s – a displeasure that, in some ways, pushes her efforts definitively into the realm of the avant-garde. Wishman's aesthetic of obscenity goes beyond 'trash', beyond 'camp', beyond 'low-tech'.

It is a challenge to filmmaking itself. Her formal pornography works to de-fetishise the cinematic experience, exposing its cherished affectations as contrivances, ripping out the heart of its pleasurable illusions. It is not morality but vision itself that is shocked by Wishman's excesses – the shock of the avant-garde. Before Wishman, one had never known that it was possible to produce such an obscene splendour.

Wishman's romance with the filmic avant-garde, therefore, is fruitful but precarious for both parties. It is precarious for the avant-garde in the sense that in its appreciation of Wishman it might ultimately lose its faith in the cinema itself; precarious for Wishman in the sense that she might – much to the detriment of her vision – gain that faith which the avant-garde has lost. The marriage of avant-garde and exploitation remains an uneasy alliance. Film studies, however, can only profit by looking more frequently into the basement – and not just the 'underground' – of the filmmaking experience.

CHAPTER 10
FULL THROTTLE ON THE HIGHWAY TO HELL: MAVERICKS, MACHISMO AND MAYHEM IN THE AMERICAN BIKER MOVIE

Bill Osgerby

The Menace is loose again, the Hell's Angels, the hundred-carat headline, running fast and loud on the early morning freeway, low in the saddle, nobody smiles, jamming crazy through traffic and ninety miles an hour down the center stripe, missing by inches ... like Genghis Khan on an iron horse, a monster steed with fiery anus, flat out through the eye of a beer can and up your daughter's leg with no quarter asked and none given; show the squares some class, give 'em a whiff of those kicks they'll never know...

Hunter S. Thompson, *Hell's Angels: The Strange and Terrible Saga of the Outlaw Motorcycle Gangs*[1]

'SHOW THE SQUARES SOME CLASS': MASCULINITY, OTHERNESS AND REBELLION IN THE BIKER MOVIE

'Hey Johnny, what are you rebelling against?' asks a pretty college girl, an epitome of teen convention with prim dress and neatly coiffured hair. 'What've ya got?' growls back the leather-jacketed leader of the Black Rebels Motorcycle Club, played as a study in taciturn brooding by a wickedly sexy Marlon Brando. Though brief, the snatch of dialogue is pivotal to *The Wild One* (1954), the film that paved the way for a slew of biker movies churned out by Hollywood throughout the 1960s and early 1970s. Loaded with defiant nihilism, Brando's retort exemplifies the mood of renegade alienation and freewheeling machismo that pervades the film. It was this sense of undirected anger and unleashed passion that became central to the succession of movies based around the exploits of marauding motorcycle gangs – a genre whose combination of sexually charged menace and seditious nonconformity had special appeal to both the hucksters of exploitation cinema and the underground auteurs of the art-house circuit.

The biker flick traded in many themes common to the wider genre of the road movie. The restless anomie of the celluloid biker, for instance, exemplified the 'distinctly existential air' identified by Timothy Corrigan as a defining quality of the road movie.[2] Other traits Corrigan highlights as principal to the road genre were also evident in the archetypal biker film. For example, a sense of social destabilisation, with characters having little control over the course of events, was a recurring theme within the biker flick. Equally, the biker's reverence for his 'sickle' was the quintessential expression of what Corrigan sees as the road movie protagonist's spiritual investment in his vehicle – to the extent that the car or motorcycle 'becomes the only promise of self in a culture of mechanical reproduction'.[3] Most of all, the biker movie exemplified the masculine focus that Corrigan argues is central to the road movie, the genre promoting a male escapist fantasy in which masculinity is linked to technological power and the road is defined as a space free of the onerous shackles of domesticity.[4] The biker flick also shared the 'romantic alienation' of the road genre, Steven Cohan and Ina Rae Hark arguing that the archetypal road movie 'sets the liberation of the road against the oppression of hegemonic norms'.[5] Moreover, the narrative of rebellion integral to the biker genre matched what Cohan and Hark interpret as the road movie's capacity to explore the tensions and crises of particular historical moments.[6] In juxtaposing the lawless marginality of the motorcycle gang against the conservatism of small-town America, the classic biker flick explored the shifting contours of contemporary cultural life, epitomising what David Laderman sees as the road movie's characteristic positioning of conservative values and rebellious desires in an unsettling dialectic that encompasses both utopian fantasy and dystopic nightmare.[7] But while the biker movie engaged with themes common to the road movie genre, the 'chrome opera' put a distinctive spin on the 'road' formula by giving exaggerated (and often grotesque) form to the road movie's mythologies of masculine power and existential freedom.

FIGURE 15 The archetypal bike rebel: Marlon Brando in *The Wild One*

The daring independence and cocksure cool that pervade the iconography of the motorcycle represent an exceptionally phallocentric form of symbolic power. The sexual connotations to straddling the massive cylinder blocks of a Harley are unmistakable – an avatar of macho sexual power that the biker flick exploited to the full, extending and intensifying the road movie's paean to masculine bravado. The figure of the 'bad boy' biker was also fundamental to the genre's aura of virulent machismo. In its depiction of snarling, maverick outsiders, the biker movie conjured a form of masculinity predicated on aggressive individualism and difference. Based around the salacious exploits of 'outlaw' motorcycle gangs such as the Hell's Angels, the lurid biker films of the late 1960s and early 1970s were especially notable for their themes of an uncontrolled, macho 'otherness'. Primitive and barbarous, the outlaw biker was cast as existing beyond the margins of the 'normal', his unrestrained lusts and sneering disaffection setting him beyond the pale of mainstream culture.

Yet the biker movie's treatment of these themes was avowedly ambivalent. In the biker genre the anarchic excesses of the motorcycle gang were constructed as a spectacle that was both appalling and beguiling, the biker flick mixing horror and fascination in equal measure. On one level, the later biker films of the 1960s and 1970s presented the bestial depravity of outlaw motorcycle gangs as chilling evidence of a societal order in a state of collapse. But in other respects the biker movies themselves flouted mainstream tastes and conventions. Revelling in their anti-heroes' wanton displays of savagery and violence, biker flicks themselves sought to 'show the squares some class' – their emphasis on transgressive difference effectively blurring the boundary between exploitation and experimental cinema.

'A WHIFF OF THOSE KICKS THEY'LL NEVER KNOW': WILD ONES, ANGER AND MOTOR-PSYCHOS

The biker movie's origins lie in the teen exploitation films of the 1950s. Facing a decline in adult cinema audiences, Hollywood increasingly appealed to the lucrative youth market, the 'teenpic' industry coming of age in the 1950s with a glut of quickly made, low-budget features aimed at the young. Films such as *Rock Around the Clock* (1956) and *Shake Rattle and Rock!* (1956) capitalised on the rock 'n' roll boom, while *Hot Rod Gang* (1958) and *Ghost of Dragstrip Hollow* (1959) exploited the latest adolescent crazes. Juvenile delinquency was also a recurring theme, with a flood of 'J.D. flicks' – for example *Untamed Youth* (1957) and *High School Confidential* (1958) – which purported to sermonise against the 'evils' of juvenile crime, yet simultaneously provided young audiences with the vicarious thrills of delinquent rebellion.

Released in 1954, *The Wild One* was an early entry in the 'J.D.' film canon. The story of a motor-cycle gang's invasion of a sleepy rural town, the movie was loosely based on actual events. Returning from the stresses of war, many former servicemen struggled to settle back into the routines of civilian life. Some, searching for camaraderie and excitement, were drawn to the world of the motorcycle, and fraternities of rootless bikers began to take shape. It was one such group whose weekend of drunken carousing in the Californian town of Hollister in 1947 became the basis for *The Wild One*. Fictionalised in 'Cyclists' Raid', a short story by Frank Rooney published in *Harper's Magazine* in 1951, the Hollister incident was taken to the big screen by director Laslo Benedek.

The film was produced for Columbia Pictures by Stanley Kramer, whose earlier success with *Home of the Brave* (1949) and *High Noon* (1952) had marked him out as a pillar of liberal moral-ity at a time when the major studios were cowed by McCarthyite witch-hunts. However, while *The Wild One*'s narrative of conflict between a nomadic biker gang and conservative townsfolk had been originally conceived as an indictment of middle America's greed and prejudice, this was an angle too radical for industry censors. Kramer's intended ending had seen the town's merchants refusing to press charges against the bikers because of the dollars the gang had pumped into their coffers, but this portrayal of capitalist hypocrisy was considered too contentious and was scrapped in favour of an enigmatic romantic pairing between gang leader Johnny (Brando) and archetypal goodgirl Cathy (Mary Murphy). Nevertheless, while the liberal moralising of *The Wild One* was watered-down, the film's portrayal of swaggering delinquents courted controversy and a mystique of alluring danger developed around both the film and the bikers it depicted.

In *The Wild One*, Benedek and Kramer had sought to create an air of gritty authenticity. In pre-production, hours were spent interviewing Californian bikers, snatches of their conversation appearing verbatim in the movie as the filmmakers reproduced the lore and culture of maverick motorcycle gangs. To mainstream eyes the results often seemed outrageous. Harry Cohn, directorial head of Columbia, reputedly hated the picture and grudgingly released it only on the basis of the track records of Kramer and Brando. Others were equally hostile. Amid a wider climate of unease about the course of postwar cultural change, many national newspapers and magazines slammed the film as a celebration of anti-social delinquents. In Europe, too, *The Wild One* was a target for moral crusaders and in Britain the film was banned until the late 1960s through fear it would incite juvenile crime. But despite being abhorred by officialdom (indeed, partly *because* it was abhorred by officialdom), the movie was a hit with young cinemagoers – Brando and his bikers cheered on by audiences seduced by images of seditious cool.

The Wild One established many of the conventions that became the stock-in-trade of the biker movie – the simmering tension around the bike gang and their violation of social taboos; the provincial 'squares' terrorised by subcultural Others; the fascination with polished chrome, black leather, and other markers of menacing machismo; and the synthesis of moody introspection and crude belligerence that constructed the biker gang leader as an unthinking man's Beat Poet. For most of the 1950s, however, major studios were wary of venturing into the territory of delinquent rebellion. In 1953 a Senate subcommittee had begun investigating the causes of juvenile crime, and the following decade saw its hearings give special attention to the possible influence of the media. Amid the climate of hand-wringing and suspicion, therefore, the Hollywood majors were cautious in their treatment of wayward youth.

It was, though, a domain in which the majors' lower-budget competitors felt at home. Leading the way were American-International Pictures (AIP). Founded in 1954 by James Nicholson and Samuel Arkoff, AIP specialised in courting the youth audience. The company built its reputation on films like *Reform School Girl* (1957) and *I Was a Teenage Werewolf* (1957) – movies that set autonomous and sexually aggressive teenagers against conformist and inhibited authority figures. In *Motorcycle Gang* (1957), AIP sought to reproduce the charisma of *The Wild One*. Its screenplay partially ripped-off from an earlier AIP exploitation flick (*Dragstrip Girl* (1957)), *Motorcycle Gang*'s narrative focused on the struggle between reformed delinquent Randy (Steve Terrell) and biker hothead Nick (John

Ashey) for the affections of tomboyish sex-kitten Terry (Ann Nyland). However, filmed in bright sunshine and interspersed with slapstick and wisecracks, *Motorcycle Gang* was bereft of the *noir*-esque elements that gave *The Wild One* its edge, one critic reflecting that sitting through *Motorcycle Gang* was 'seldom more disturbing than being stuck in the slow line at Disneyland.'[8] The deviant biker gang put in a further (less desultory) appearance in another AIP release, *Dragstrip Riot* (1958), but it was experimental and independent filmmakers that best capitalised on the biker's image of dark intensity and sexual danger.

Almost inevitably, Kenneth Anger – occultist, perverse visionary and premier figure of American avant-garde cinema – was drawn to the myths and rituals of the biker. Anger's reputation as incendiary auteur was established early. While still only seventeen he had completed *Fireworks* (1947), an overtly homoerotic and sadomasochistic psychodrama which showcased his trademark hallucinogenic visual style. Relocating to Paris, Anger spent the next decade working on a variety of projects, including several short films and *Hollywood Babylon*, his notorious biography of Tinsel Town's sordid underbelly. Returning to New York in 1963, Anger continued his exploration of the seamy eroticism repressed beneath the staid inhibitions of modern culture. Running across a motorcycle gang hanging out by the rollercoaster at Coney Island, Anger was inspired to make the film that won him recognition as America's foremost independent filmmaker. Premiered at the Gramercy Arts Theatre in New York in October 1963, *Scorpio Rising* was later described by Anger as 'a death mirror held up to American Culture'.[9]

Stylised and iconoclastic, *Scorpio Rising* makes explicit the edgy homoeroticism of biker culture, the film's hyperbolic symbolism invoking the macho world of chrome and leather in a sardonic commentary on American mythologies of glamour, power and masculinity. In an 'Eisensteinian' montage, *Scorpio Rising* intercuts visceral images of motorcycle subculture with a catalogue of media allusions, a jarring collision that climaxes with the blasphemous juxtaposing of Hitler and Christ. Throughout, the film's sense of knowing irony is underpinned by its kitsch Top Forty soundtrack – Bobby Vinton crooning 'Blue Velvet' as a lithe stud buttons his bursting jeans, the Crystals bawling 'He's a Rebel' as muscled bikers strike fetishistic poses in boots, buckles and studded leather.

In *Scorpio Rising* the implied homoerotic charge of *The Wild One* becomes overt. Brimming with the semiotics of moral and sexual transgression, *Scorpio Rising* gives full play to the mythologies that formulate the biker as a symbol of unsettling Otherness. A similar iconography of violation and disruptive excess also figures in the work of another leading light of American underground cinema – Russ Meyer. And, again, the biker made an early appearance in Meyer's oeuvre. A professional photographer turned independent filmmaker, Meyer had enjoyed moderate success in the late 1950s with tongue-in-cheek, soft-core sexploitation flicks such as *The Immoral Mr. Teas* (1959) and *Eve and the Handyman* (1959), before perfecting his distinctively boisterous and sardonic style in *Lorna* (1964), *Mudhoney* (1965) and *Motorpsycho!* (1965). In *Motorpsycho!* Meyer draws on media stereotypes of biker savagery to present a garish parody of mainstream culture's voyeuristic fascination with illicit desire. An exercise in sleazy excess, the movie deals with the trail of rape and murder left by a trio of malevolent bikers, the gang ultimately self-destructing after being stalked by their vengeful victims. Again, then, the biker figures as a disconcerting challenge to 'square' taboos, though in Meyer's hands the theme is given satirical inflection. *Motorpsycho!* is an exaggerated celebration of exploitation cinema, its larger-than-life clichés serving to lampoon the shrill anxieties and inhibited obsessions of middle America.

The sinister volatility of *Scorpio Rising* and *Motorpsycho!* contrasts starkly with AIP's treatment of the biker mythology during the early 1960s. Beginning with *Beach Party* in 1963, AIP's cycle of beach movies were a bubbly blend of music and comedy centred on a vivacious group of Californian teens. The surfside antics of adolescent funsters Frankie Avalon, Annette Funicello and co. were the focus for the *Beach Party* series, but a gang of bumbling bikers also made regular appearances. Led by the patently middle-aged Eric Von Zipper (comedian Harvey Lembeck mercilessly sending-up Brando's smoldering angst), the 'Rats and Mice' biker gang of AIP's beach movies existed as a comic foil to the surfers' frothy hijinx. A jokey caricature of the 1950s wild ones, the inept *Beach Party* bikers were a motif for outdated rebellion – a symbol of generational revolt configured as laughably old-fashioned against the cheerful hedonism of the surf set.

The good-time exuberance of the *Beach Party* cycle was, as Gary Morris argues, part of AIP's attempt to leave behind its schlock-horror origins in favour of films that could achieve wider commercial success.[10] But the beach movies' representation of sun-kissed, teenage fun can also be seen as constituent in broader shifts in the symbolic connotations of youth in American culture. Throughout the 1950s, notions of 'youth' had been surrounded by largely negative social meanings – fears of juvenile depravity serving as a vehicle for wider concerns in the face of rapid and disorienting socio-economic change. By the beginning of the 1960s, however, the intensity of the 'J.D.' panic was dissipating.

During the early 1960s a more positive set of youth stereotypes came to the fore, young people portrayed (celebrated even) as an excitingly new and uplifting social force. This was an iconography powerfully marshaled by John F. Kennedy in both his public persona and political rhetoric, youth coming to represent the confident optimism of America's New Frontier. Commercial interests, AIP for instance, also figured in this upbeat 're-branding' of youth. With the growing profitability of the youth market, consumer industries fêted young people as never before and 'youth' became enshrined as a signifier for a newly prosperous age of fun, freedom and social harmony. This was a discourse embodied in the beach movies' eulogy to 'fun in the sun' ebullience – an idealised teenage lifestyle in which the biker's surly estrangement looked sadly anachronistic.

The ambience of national wellbeing, however, was transient. By the mid-1960s the American economy was stumbling, while liberal optimism crumbled in the face of racial violence, urban disorder and a spiraling sense of social discontent. Against this backdrop, the beach movies' innocent high spirits looked increasingly incongruous. But it was a mood of uncertainty that gave the biker flick a new lease of life.

A 'STRANGE AND TERRIBLE SAGA': THE HELL'S ANGELS, THE COUNTERCULTURE AND EXPOITATION CINEMA

During the mid-1960s, the winged death's-head emblem of the Hell's Angels Motorcycle Club became synonymous with the murkiest fears of mainstream America. Amid the social turmoil of race riots, countercultral radicalism and escalating opposition to the Vietnam War, a new wave of moral panics gave focus to broader anxieties – particular alarm surrounding the spectre of outlaw biker gangs. The Hell's Angels, especially, were reviled as the heinous *bête noir* of civilised society. As in the 1950s, however, it was precisely this aura of fearful Otherness that guaranteed the biker subculture a special place in the hearts of both the artistic avant-garde and exploitation sleaze-merchants. Indeed, it was often difficult to tell the two camps apart, both scurrying to take advantage of 'square' society's repulsed fascination in the Hell's Angels.

The Angels had originally formed among California's loose packs of renegade bikers during the late 1940s. In 1954 a merger with a San Francisco bike gang, the Market Street Commandos, swelled the Angels' ranks and local divisions sprang up along the west coast. With the formation of the Oakland Chapter under the presidency of Ralph 'Sonny' Barger – a 6-foot, 170-pound warehouseman – the Hell's Angels developed greater structure and organisation. Under Barger's aegis the gang hammered out its own bylaws, codes of conduct, hierarchy and insignia. Against this style of biker brotherhood, Brando's leather-jacketed hoodlums looked almost quaint. By the 1960s the Hell's Angels had taken the aesthetics of liminal dissent to new extremes – with long hair, Nazi motifs, crusty Levis and customised motorcycles ('chopped hogs') whose low-slung frames, raked front forks and cattle-horn handlebars were a symbolic expression of defiant nonconformity.

The Hell's Angels were still just one among a motley assortment of outlaw motorcycle gangs – for example, the Gypsy Jokers, the Commancheros and Satan's Slaves. In 1964, however, the Angels were plunged into the media spotlight. Following a biker party in the Oceanside town of Monterey, several Angels were arrested for the gang rape of two local teenagers. The charges were later dropped, but sensational newspaper headlines transformed the Hell's Angels into America's public enemy number one. A report hurriedly published by California's Attorney General painted a lurid picture of outrages committed by assorted biker gangs, and throughout 1965 stories in the *New York Times*, *Time*, *Newsweek* and *Esquire* highlighted the Hell's Angels as the most deplorable of the bunch.

The Angels' mounting notoriety made them the bane of conventional society, but within the developing counterculture they were eulogised as rebellious outsiders who refused to be pushed around by 'The Man'. The truth was rather different. The outlaw biker culture of the 1960s exemplified reactionary chauvinism. Violent, racist, homophobic misogynists, the Hell's Angels held the civil rights movement in contempt and brutally attacked anti-war activists. Nevertheless, many among the avant-garde cognoscenti revered the Hell's Angel as a romantic 'Noble Savage', fondly imagining the outlaw biker as an icon of raw, spiritual freedom. Hence, bikers were regular houseguests of psychedelic emissary Ken Kesey, while countercultural luminaries such as Allen Ginsberg and the Grateful Dead's Jerry Garcia struck up friendships with many Angels. Hunter S. Thompson also established his reputation as literary gunslinger through his account of the gang. Originally dispatched by *The Nation* magazine to write a story on the Angels, Thompson rode with them for a year as he researched *Hell's Angels: The Strange and Terrible Saga of the Outlaw Motorcycle Gang* – his 1966 bestseller, which further heightened the gang's demonic mystique.

Countercultural luminaries were not alone in being captivated by the Hell's Angels' infamy. A *Life* magazine feature on the gang also caught the eye of Roger Corman, AIP's exploitation-meister *par excellence*. Corman had directed an array of horror and western flicks for AIP and, sensing the potential of a film based around the exploits of outlaw bikers, rushed *The Wild Angels* into pre-production. Aiming for graphic realism, Corman and scriptwriter Charles Griffith undertook background research by drinking and hanging out with Californian bikers – and, for extra *frisson*, even hired several Hell's Angels as film extras. Released in 1966, *The Wild Angels* established the template for the welter of biker movies that followed. As 'Heavenly Blues', Peter Fonda plays the leader of an unsavoury biker gang hunting down a stolen motorcycle. After a confrontation in Mexico, gang member 'Loser' (Bruce Dern) is fatally wounded and his fellow Angels resolve to return his body to his hometown – the film climaxing with an orgy of rape and destruction in the local church, the gang ultimately routed by the parochial townsfolk.

Billed as 'the most terrifying film of our time', *The Wild Angels* gave ambivalent treatment to the biker mythology. 'The picture you are about to see will shock you, perhaps anger you!' warned the movie's precredits, but the ensuing flick was far from a straightforward denunciation of the Angels' misdeeds. As Blues, Fonda cuts a quixotic figure. In a role that would become formulaic in biker movies, the gang leader is distanced from the violent extremes of his fellow Angels, but remains an uncontainable rebel. Blues is the biker constructed as romantic hero. Amid the violence and mayhem, his key speech with its demand for the Angels 'To be free, to ride our machines without being hassled by The Man. And to get loaded,' marks him out as a free spirit kicking back against the stifling conventions of the mainstream.

Here there are obvious parallels with the counterculture's rose-tinted celebration of the outlaw biker. But Corman was no Ginsberg. Where the counterculture had naively championed the Hell's Angel as an icon of resistance to the establishment, exploitation filmmakers were more calculating in their caricature of his lore and lifestyle. Rather than putting the Angels on a pedestal, the biker flick took advantage of their shock value. In *The Wild Angels* and the films that followed, the Hell's Angel was turned into an outlandish bogeyman – jarring the audience's sensibilities, manipulating their obsessions and laughing at their mores in a mischievous pageant of excess.

With a spartan plot and minimalist script (120 lines at most), the real centre of *The Wild Angels* is its salacious parade of transgression. Shots of open kissing between male gang members are calculated to offend conventional morals, while everyday norms dissolve in the portrayal of the Angels' wild partying and constant brawling, their sexual violence and their invasion of small-town America (the bastion of conservative morality). Moreover, interspersed with the frequent sequences of 'sickle action' (backed by Davie Allen and the Arrows' pulsating fuzz guitar soundtrack), the film privileges spectacle over narrative, action over intellect. This carnivalesque exhibition of the world-turned-upside-down was a theme common to AIP films during this period. As studio head Arkoff recalls, during the late 1960s outrage and misrule were the hallmarks of AIP's audience appeal:

> We started looking for our audience by removing the element of authority in our films. We saw the rebellion coming, but we couldn't predict the extent of it so we made a rule: no parents, no church or authorities in our films.[11]

The relish for reckless thrills also featured in AIP's psychedelic exploitation vehicles – *The Trip* (1967), *Psych-Out* (1968) and *Wild in the Streets* (1968). But the 'chopper opera' was AIP's finest hour. Shot in two weeks, *The Wild Angels* was panned by critics at the 1966 Venice Film Festival, but (like *The Wild One* a decade earlier) the movie was a massive hit with young audiences. AIP even had trouble keeping up with demand for prints of the film as it grossed $5 million in its opening month. The Hell's Angels themselves, however, were not impressed. Feeling they had been misrepresented and short-changed by the film, the San Bernardino Angels sued AIP for $2 million, claiming (somewhat improbably) that the movie had defamed their good character. But the gang were soon placated with a $200,000 settlement, and Angels' President 'Sonny' Barger even signed up to work on several of AIP's biker sequels.

In all, AIP went on to produce around a dozen biker flicks. In 1967, while *The Wild Angels* was still screening, the studio quickly completed *Devil's Angels*. Directed by Daniel Haller and starring John Cassavetes, this was another tale of small-town locals terrorised by depraved bikers. Again, the sparse script and storyline gave way to an emphasis on visuals, with panoramic shots of cruising motorcycles and a succession of 'set pieces' used to show off the gang's lifestyle of beer-swilling, punch-ups and rape. But it was US Films, an AIP rival, that produced the most successful biker movie of the year in *Hell's Angels on Wheels*. Directed by exploitation veteran Richard Rush, the film starred Jack Nicholson as an introspective loner, Poet, whose spell on the road with outlaw bikers ends in a violent confrontation with the gang leader over the latter's neglected and abused 'old lady'. Here, the usual exaggerated coverage is given to the wild depravity of biker subculture, though with the added spice that the Hell's Angels actually endorsed the film (the entire Oakland Chapter appearing in the opening sequence). Nicholson also appeared in a second biker flick that year, the actor assuming a more sadistic persona in *Rebel Rousers*, a lacklustre tale of biker mayhem completed in 1967 though not released until 1970.

Other independent producers also competed in the field. William Greffe came up with *The Wild Rebels* (1967), and Titus Moody released *Outlaw Motorcycles* (1967) and *Hell's Chosen Few*

FIGURE 16 Bikers, counter-culture and transgression: *The Wild Angels*

(1968), while K. Gordan Murray offered *Savages From Hell* (aka *Big Enough and Old Enough*, 1968). But AIP was still leader of the pack. Throughout the late 1960s, biker films steadily rolled off the AIP production line, the studio often recycling props and using the same actors and crew from one movie to the next. In 1967, AIP followed *Devil's Angels* with *Born Losers*, the first film to feature writer/director/actor Tom Laughlin in the role of half-Indian activist Billy Jack, who stands up against a predictably obnoxious biker gang.[12] The same year also saw AIP release *The Glory Stompers*, with Dennis Hopper making his biker flick debut as the unhinged leader of the Black Souls Motorcycle Club. Subsequent years saw further AIP biker fare with the release of *Angels From Hell* (1968), *The Savage Seven* (1968), *Hell's Angels '69* (1969, featuring cameos from 'Sonny' Barger and other Oakland Angels), *The Cycle Savages* (1969) and *Hell's Belles* (aka *Girl in the Leather Suit*, 1969). Garish, low-budget exploitation movies, they were all true to the AIP formula, revelling in wild thrills and outrageous shocks. The next celluloid motorcycle epic, however, marked a revival of avant-garde models of the biker as bohemian rebel.

'LIKE GENGHIS KHAN ON AN IRON HORSE': MYTHOLOGY, NATIONHOOD AND GENDER IN THE BIKER MOVIE

Easy Rider (1969) was very nearly an AIP production. The film that kicked the road movie genre into gear had been offered to Samuel Arkoff by the writer/producer/director team of Peter Fonda and Dennis Hopper, but the AIP studio boss demanded the right to impose his own director if production fell behind schedule. Instead, Fonda and Hopper took their brainchild to producers Bert Schneider and Bob Rafelson, who secured big league financial backing from Columbia. And from the outset the major studio ensured *Easy Rider* would be distanced from AIP's leather and chrome stable. Promotional strategies marked out *Easy Rider* as a more intellectual, highbrow affair – with the wistful tag-line 'A man went looking for America. And couldn't find it anywhere.' Further underscoring *Easy Rider*'s artistic pretension was the film's entry in the Cannes Film Festival, where it picked up an award for Best Film by a New Director.

Easy Rider is a landmark film, signalling the impact of exploitation and avant-garde filmmaking on the mindset and working practices of mainstream cinema. As Richard Martin argues, *Easy Rider* was a trailblazer of 'the fusion of mainstream and art cinema filmmaking techniques in the *nouvelle vague*-influenced Hollywood renaissance cinema of the late sixties and early seventies'.[13] The film's innovative visual style, quick-paced editing, improvised dialogue and fierce rock soundtrack gave it a sense of spontaneity and energy that resonated with audiences, *Easy Rider* grossing over $50 million on first release from a budget of $375,000. The movie's ideological positioning also gave it kudos as a hip incarnation of the cultural moment. On the proceeds of a lucrative drug deal the film's protagonists, Wyatt (Fonda) and Billy (Hopper), leave California on a motorcycle odyssey through the American Southwest. Reaching New Orleans they drop acid with two prostitutes and freak out through the Mardi Gras celebrations, then return to the road – where they are gunned down by shotgun-wielding rednecks. The characters' haphazard travelogue can be read as a cynical commentary on US society and politics. Beginning with the optimism of the open road and ending in the disillusionment of a shotgun blast, *Easy Rider* is an allegory for liberal America's collapsing ideals as the US was traumatised by burning inner-city ghettos and the mire of the Vietnam War. 'We blew it,' reflects Wyatt in one of the film's most poignant lines.

But *Easy Rider* is not simply a disconsolate critique of a society gone sour. As Barbara Klinger observes, rather than being 'a clear-cut counter-cultural message about the state of the nation', *Easy Rider* is a text of 'conflicted historical and ideological identity.'[14] Alongside the film's images of countercultural rebellion, the 'affirmative patriotisms of Americana'[15] are also heavily referenced, connecting *Easy Rider* with many of the myths and ideals of dominant American culture – in particular the mythic figure of the pioneering frontiersman. Since the nineteenth century, dominant ideological discourse has configured the frontier experience as the crucible of American independence and democracy. Here, the frontier pioneer is constructed as a rugged individualist – sturdy, autonomous and resourceful. A core theme in the imagery and narratives of the western, this mythology of individualism and freedom is also central to *Easy Rider*. Indeed, allusions to the western punctuate the film. The main characters' names (Billy and Wyatt) are reminiscent of cowboy gunfighters, while Billy's buckskin coat and Stetson are an obvious western touch. And, as Alistair Daniel observes, their journey across the vastness of the American landscape further invokes the pioneering spirit of the early settlers and the innumerable westerns that mythologise them.[16] More widely, the whole biker movie genre can be read (at least in part) as a celebration of the 'last American hero', essentially a generic revision of the western. In fact AIP effectively retooled its western assembly line for biker films, with a wholesale shift of its western production crews and actors into the creation of 'iron horse' sagas. Moreover, many biker plots were actually lifted from classic westerns. For example, the narrative of *Chrome and Hot Leather* (1968) is indebted to the *Magnificent Seven* (1960), while *Hell's Belles* (1969) borrows heavily from *Winchester '73* (1950).

This immersion in western myth explains why the biker flick is a peculiarly American phenomenon. It also locates the genre within distinctly masculine themes and discourses. Like the subculture they depicted, the 1960s biker flicks invariably marginalised women, consigning them to the pillion seat as submissive 'old ladies' or sexually compliant 'mamas'. More broadly, the biker genre shared the road movie's decidedly masculine connotations of individualism, aggression, independence and control. As Shari Roberts contends, both the classic western and the road movie are genres 'propelled by masculinity', informed by 'a residual, American, masculinist ideal' which links masculine superiority with racial hierarchies, manifest destiny and closure'.[17] Nevertheless, Roberts argues that this does not add up to a monolithic formula, the 'more fluid' character of the road movie offering potential space 'for protagonists of any nationality, gender, sexual orientation, or race'.[18]

Hence the 1990s saw the road genre recodified – its masculine, heterosexual codes reconfigured by films such as *Thelma and Louise* (1991) and *My Own Private Idaho* (1991).

The biker flick was also 'propelled by masculinity'. Indeed, the casual regularity with which biker films featured the rape and molestation of women marked them out as appallingly misogynistic. But, even here, there were spaces for recodification. Of course, there are many 'motorcycle' films that focus on women, these invariably oriented around an eroticised pairing of femininity with the phallic connotations of the powerful motorbike – from artsy erotica like *The Girl on the Motorcycle* (aka *Naked Under Leather*, 1968), to contemporary soft-core offerings such as *Hollywood Biker Chicks* (1998) or the more robust *Butt-Banged Cycle Sluts* (1995). Yet there also exists another, more transgressive, tradition in which the macho creed of the biker is inverted and women appear as dangerous and hard-hitting predators. AIP's *Mini Skirt Mob* (1968), for instance, features a group of tough biker women, while *The Hellcats* (1968), *Sisters in Leather* (1969) and *Angels' Wild Women* (1972) all focus on violent female bikers who terrorise those men who dare to cross their path.

The most incredible example of the subgenre, however, is *She-Devils on Wheels* (1968). Independently produced by Herschell Gordon Lewis (who had earlier crafted the shlock-horror classics *Blood Feast* (1963) and *2000 Maniacs* (1964)), *She-Devils on Wheels* centres on 'The Maneaters' – a sadistic, all-girl biker gang who select their sexual playthings from a 'stud line', later dragging the discarded lover behind their speeding motorcycles.

None but the most delusional would try to redeem the likes of *Angels' Wild Women*, *The Hellcats* or *She-Devils on Wheels* as 'feminist' texts. Nevertheless, in their carnivalesque inversion it is possible to identify elements of disruption. Like the oversized and domineering female characters distinctive of Russ Meyer's films, the 'She-Devils' of the biker flick can be interpreted as 'a revel in gendered excess',[19] an exercise in exaggerated caricature that sends up and usurps the conventions of respectable filmmaking. Indeed, this appetite for the grotesque and scorn for mainstream taboos is a trait central to the celluloid biker canon – and to exploitation cinema more generally. Ribald and bawdy, these are films that delight in tweaking the tail of conformist sensibilities through their love of all that is shocking, liminal and 'unacceptable'. As such, *Easy Rider* sits uneasily in the genre. Cerebral and reflective, *Easy Rider* is not really a biker flick at all. The classic biker movie rode roughshod over intellectual subtleties, the root of the genre's appeal lying in its full throttle, blood-and-thunder sensationalism.

'THE MENACE IS LOOSE AGAIN': THE BIKER MOVIE'S LAST STAND

With the box-office success of *Easy Rider*, more biker movies followed. *Wild Wheels* (1969) saw bikers battle a dune-buggy gang, while Roger Corman returned to the saddle with *Naked Angels* (1969). Even to devoted fans, however, the genre was beginning to pale and producers looked for new spins on the formula

FIGURE 17 Phalic power: female bikers in *The Hellcats*

to refuel their engines. Al Adamson (who earlier masterminded *Angels' Wild Women*) came up with a biker/blaxploitation crossover in *The Black Angels* (1970). Director Lawrence Brown, meanwhile, proffered

FIGURE 18 Contemporary biker imagery: *Chopper Chicks in Zombietown*

the even more unlikely concept of transvestite bikers in *The Pink Angels* (1971). The biker/horror hybrid also appeared with the release of *Werewolves on Wheels* (1971) and (from Britain) *Psychomania* (1971). Throughout the early 1970s the biker movie spluttered on, though releases became increasingly sporadic.

Audience fatigue played a big part in the genre's decline – the market could bare only so many two-wheel spectaculars. But other factors also contributed to the biker flick's demise.

Jim Morton suggests that the popularity of biker movies declined after the true viciousness of the Hell's Angels was exposed at Altamont in 1969.[20] Hired as security for a Rolling Stones concert, the Angels proceeded to intimidate and beat both the audience and performers, stabbing to death black spectator Meredith Hunter in front of the stage as Mick Jagger nervously sang 'Sympathy for the Devil'. After Altamont, Morton argues, the Hell's Angels were 'no longer funny symbols of rebellion', but were revealed as being 'really as dangerous as everyone said they were.'[21] However, while events at Altamont certainly blew apart the counterculture's veneration of the Hell's Angels, the outrage was actually a gift for exploitation filmmakers. Their murderous reputation confirmed, outlaw bikers featured in a new burst of exploitation shockers, with *Satan's Sadists* (1970), *Angels Die Hard* (1970), *Hell's Bloody Devils* (1970), *The Hard Ride* (1971) and *Under Hot Leather* (aka *The Jesus Trip*, 1971) – the latter seeing a convent overrun by outlaw bikers. The biker flick even gleefully capitalised on the Altamont furore, the hippy commune replacing the small-town community as the target of biker carnage in *Angel Unchained* (1970) and the ultra-violent *Angels, Hard as They Come* (1971).

After this brief and bloody renaissance, however, the biker flick finally ran out of road. This was not due to public disenchantment with biker violence, nor simply to audience boredom. More important was the fact that the image of the outlaw biker became (hushed voice) *acceptable*. By the mid-1970s the biker archetype had been rehabilitated as a stock image of Americana. Taking his place alongside Mom and apple pie, the biker became an abiding signifier for the sturdy egalitarianism and healthy independence of the 'American Way'. Indeed, this process of incorporation was detectable in the tail end of the biker genre itself. In 1969 the National Football League actually encouraged Joe Namath (star quarterback of the New York Jets) to take the lead in *C.C. and Company*, Namath starring as an all-American 'good guy' biker. In *The Losers* (1970), meanwhile, outlaw bikers join forces with 'The Man' – a biker gang helping the CIA bust out American POWs from a communist prison camp in Cambodia.

During the 1980s and 1990s the success of Arnold Schwarzenegger's character in *The Terminator* (1984) and *Terminator 2* (1991) testified to the continued Hollywood appeal of the outlaw biker as an image of dark menace. Elsewhere, the biker gang also figured in postmodern nostalgia movies such as *Rumble Fish* (1983) and *The Loveless* (1983), as well as ironic pastiches like *Killer Klowns From Outer Space* (1988) and *Chopper Chicks in Zombietown* (1991). For the masters of exploitation cinema, however, the biker flick was an exhausted genre. Co-opted into mainstream culture, the semiotics of outlaw bikerdom were no longer a dependable source of outrageous excess. Instead, the deranged serial killer and the chainsaw-wielding maniac increasingly replaced the savage biker as a symbol of terrifying Otherness as exploitation filmmakers sought new ways to 'show the squares some class' and 'give 'em a whiff of those kicks they'll never know…'

CHAPTER 11
THE IDEAL CINEMA OF HARRY SMITH

Jonathan L. Crane

Underground film is an epitaph. It describes what no longer is. And while it may be impossible to exactly date the time of death, the underground film is long departed. By the 1970s, as P. Adams Sitney notes in his history of underground and experimental film, underground filmmakers have entered the establishment. Now academy fellows and grant recipients, underground filmmakers no longer work at the margins.[1] Vanished too is the cultural milieu that engendered underground film. Today, amidst the vertically integrated regime of multiplex theatre chains, professional film schools, streaming web sites, home recording and editing gear, media megaliths, video galleries, Sundance Film fetes, Blockbuster Video and 'independent' film production, there is no autonomous space for underground films to be created, screened or imagined. Habitat *and* species are both extinct.

This is not to say that all latter-day film productions now reflect only those values that provoke no dissent from the mammoth corporations and prestigious cultural institutions that organise the mature film industry. Plenty of productions rightfully make studio heads, curators and rating boards squirm. Resistant films and videos marshalling oppositional messages are not uncommon. The limits of the envelope, the brittle lines that define the good, the right and the permissible are all still open to contention and revision.

What has closed is the bohemian film frontier. Once, singular cineastes were free to explore the nascent possibilities in a relatively unfettered and unknown medium. Today, in marked contrast, film production, distribution and exhibition are now so well-integrated and so well-regulated that there is no realm beyond the pall of the mainstream. Case in point: two years after MTV premiered in the United States, they called upon Picture Start for access to their film collection. A well-established and now defunct distributor of underground film, Picture Start had an enormous thirty-year archive of difficult, aesthetically rigorous film. MTV wanted to cut up the collection of several thousand films and use the disassembled bits for wild bumpers between outré rock videos. Within months, MTV ran through Picture Start's entire archive of outsider film; subsequently, many of Picture Start's most original artists found work in the burgeoning rock video industry. There are countless variations of this tale. All versions share the same conclusion: the redoubt between the mainstream and the recondite hinterlands has been breached. Where there were once two distinct classes of production, with very little shared intercourse bridging the two worlds of mainstream and underground filmmaking, film work today operates across major and minor leagues that are in incessant communication.

A CLEMENT FREEBOOTER

One of the signal American pioneers of underground film, Harry Smith (1923–91) produced work that can be best understood as a cryptic tutorial from a fallen world. An archetypal bohemian, Smith led an astoundingly varied and productive life that he consistently embroidered with not entirely improbable fancies (among his fabulous asseverations: he was the son of famed English necromancer Aleister Crowley, and his mother was the fabled Anastasia – last of the vanquished Romanovs). Born in Portland, Oregon to parents versed in Theosophy, Smith would spend most of his early years in rural Washington on an island north of Seattle. Living close to a Lummi Indian reservation, Smith developed a lifelong interest in anthropology and cultural production. After a few semesters at Washington State, he abandoned his formal education and embarked to California in 1945. There, a prototypical Beat, he became a member of the Berkeley demimonde.

Smith would spend most of his life in and around New York City. A genuine polymath, he would paint epic paintings of seminal bop composition, pursue filmmaking, become adept in the Occult and the Cabala, document the peyote rituals of the Kiowa, produce The Fugs and, among countless other projects, amass important and impossibly varied collections of cultural artifacts. These heterodox collections, many of which ended up in museums, include Seminole textiles, paper airplanes, Ukrainian Easter Eggs, string figures and a mammoth, awe-inspiring collection of 78s. In his final years, Smith was the resident shaman at the Naropa Institute in Boulder, Colorado.[2]

Smith's most well-known production is his *Anthology of American Folk Music*. First issued on Folkways Records in 1952, the three-volume *Anthology* sparked the American folk revival. (Smithsonian/Folkways Recording has reissued the *Anthology* with new critical essays and an expanded CD that includes clips of Smith's films, paintings and a look at some of his collections. Smith planned a fourth volume that was released posthumously in 2000 on Revenant Records.) Culled from his enormous collection of musical Americana, Smith authored a sweeping survey of distant folk and blues recordings that, as Greil Marcus put it, 'made the familiar strange, the never known into the forgotten, and the forgotten into a collective memory that teased any single listener's conscious mind'.[3] The *Anthology* did for sound what his films would do for vision: Smith remade perception.

Smith challenged his audience to hear anew. For example, the set alternated performances by white and black artists. In his detailed notes Smith does not, however, make any mention of a performer's race. In so doing, Smith erases the colour line and leaves his audience unable to apply one of the fundamental organising principles of American culture. Instead of documenting black and white music, the anthology sounded American music.

In addition, decades before the DJ was recognised as a fluid composer in his or her own right, Smith was an aural *bricoleur* of the first order. The *Anthology* is a marvelously inventive soundscape in which every musician voices their own unique plight and sings as part of an incredibly rowdy and raucous chorus. Echoing one another in harmony and discord, with fellow feeling and rancor, Smith's singers are commonly afflicted with hot blood, shared sorrows and aching hearts. In league and embattled, the characters of Smith's great, quilted composition welcome us to an America that could not otherwise be known.

This work, along with his films, also provides an even more fundamental and counter-intuitive insight. Smith demonstrates that perception is a malleable instrument. Sounds have no necessary meaning. Believing is not seeing and Smith is an anti-empiricist. His projects treat sense data, what comes in through the eyes and ears, as raw material that has value only after it has been run through the mind. As the *Anthology* so clearly demonstrates, change the rigging of the mind, make race an unimportant variable, and hearing is reborn.

In the same fashion, Smith's films rework vision. Absent are all the familiar conventions of mainstream cinema, as if there were no Hollywood and no film history prior to his highly idiosyncratic engagement with celluloid; his films absolve viewers from the sin of cinematic knowledge. Shorn of all the familiar guideposts that make watching film an act of déjà vu, Smith's productions are vertiginous constructs. In leading us astray, they offer a fresh start to viewers who might reasonably assume, having been subject to so many well-ordered and well-policed films, that films are obliged to obey soporific convention.

Smith's immaculate conceptions will likely return first-time viewers to their primal encounter(s) with the moving image. This merger, the moment when moving images make their first indelible impression on the unlettered viewer, is the time when both audience and image become contractually bound. Out of these first momentous unions comes the foreknowledge of what the moving image will bring as audience expectations for the future are made fast. Offering both a delicious, pregnant promise, this is what you can expect, and a firm contract, this is what you will receive; these formative engagements plot out the course audiences and films will share into the foreseen future. In this regard, learning to look at the screen is always a great bargain because the spectacle of the cinema has never, at any moment in its history, proffered anything less than resplendent temptation. Learning to see is also a terrible exercise in collusion; too many strange byways are foreclosed in fealty to the tyranny of audience expectation nurtured by a woefully rational mode of industrial production.

Since no one is ushered into the world of moving images by Harry Smith (Charizard, Winky, Pooh or the Mouse will clinch that distinction), a first encounter with a Smith construction occurs long after film literacy is mastered. As such, Smith's films come as a shock to the system. Seeing his films for the first time is analogous to taking a routine eye test, reading the letters on the top line and finding that all the familiar marks belong to an unknown system of signification. We should be able to read them as our perceptual apparatus is intact, we can make out what is onscreen, but these images are not readily processed. Looking nothing like anything produced by commercial and independent filmmakers, exposure to Smith's images will discomfort amblyopic viewers as they reveal a world that cannot be handily envisioned.

Compounding the effect of Smith's novel and enigmatic imagery, these films are not structured like the work of his distant compatriots. Telling no tales, as Smith ignores narrative from his first to last film, these compositions are free to explore dimensions of the cinema that are off-limits when filmmakers assume the burdensome mantle of storyteller. And while the practice of releasing cinema from narrative is not remarkable in experimental and underground film – Takehisa Kosugi screened movies without bothering to thread a film through the projector, Stan Brakhage cultivated variegated molds on film, while Ernie Gehr made *History* (1970) by exposing film through black cheesecloth without benefit of a lens – Smith still manages to produce non-narrative work that is unmistakably his own.

In fabricating unprecedented imagery and leaving story to others, Smith's work presents a formidable challenge. Some films, like *Number 14* (aka *Late Super-Impositions*, 1964), may not even seem viewable upon first exposure. *Number 14* is a half hour of super-imposed home movies. Tedious even when we are the star, home movies can become very demanding when they document the anonymous lives of rank strangers. Imagine then a double layer of unknown home movies, one nameless amateur production atop another, run for just over thirty minutes. Not, for many, an inviting prospect.

Perhaps even more disconcerting, many of his earliest efforts are not really films at all. Available collectively as *Early Abstractions*, *Nos. 1–5* (1946–51), these are hand-painted compositions on celluloid. Film that is not filmed is about as contrary a step to the medium that one can take. In painting, sprinkling, spraying, dribbling and wiping colours directly on film, Smith dispenses with the camera and demonstrates that a seemingly vital piece of equipment for cinematic production is, in fact, an altogether unnecessary accessory. In so doing, Smith creates compositions that are raggedly assembled and very beautiful. Smith would not permanently abandon the camera, but even his optically-printed images come to the screen as through a lens darkly.

Smith's images have no analogues in commercial modes of production. Nothing in the mainstream, from the 1940s to the present, looks like these early designs. Both clumsy and magical, they are unparalled creations. Like an unholy fusion of a gifted toddler's craft project and a Platonic dream – with the world rendered in pure Form – these films are a testament to Smith's dogged ingenuity and his shambolic vision. Taking an incredible amount of exacting labour to produce, without ever looking remotely polished, these early films document a sparkling naivety. Smith's innocent vision, his freedom from cinematic order, graces the audience with a new mode of cinematic production and a magical passage into curious modes of perception.

There are, along with the challenges elaborated above, additional impositions made on Smith's audience. Until the film runs out, his earliest works depict nothing but the ceaseless transformation of simple forms (triangles, circles and the like) into new spheres and geometric shapes. Later, Smith would abandon drawing directly on film in favour of collage. With this new technique, Smith's imagery became grotesquely intricate. Using countless bits and pieces snipped from turn-of-the-century catalogues, alongside images wrested from Indian, Buddhist and Egyptian iconography, Smith's insanely elaborate collages dance across the screen in complex patterns that are part of ever-larger repetitive cycles. As with the earliest work there is little in the mainstream to prepare the viewer for Smith's extremely individual cinema.

In offering a provisional reading of Smith's work it would be manifestly unfair to him and his novel creations to define them as part of an oppositional cinema. 'Different from' need not be synonymous with 'opposed to'. In taking another tack, Smith's work does not protest against the limits of the medium and the hegemonic power of the film bloc. These films make no attempt, even implicitly, to suggest that they are superior to run of the mill fare. Nor is his work a protest against a quiescent audience. He did not see the audience as needing correction. Just the opposite; late in life he contemplated re-editing his films so that new audiences might find his work more inviting. Believing that young people could process information more quickly than his aging peers, Smith thought the solution to reaching a contemporary audience lay in reforming the work rather than in re-educating the public.

NO GURU, NO METHOD, NO TEACHER

Harry Smith should not be cast as a rebel. While he did live and work almost entirely outside the system, his film art is too hermetic to be read as kicking against the pricks. For the good of pitched antagonists and their enemies, agitprop must be direct and pointed in its dissent. If not didactic, then it must be very straightforward in its departure from the limits of common practice. Anything but clear-cut, Smith's work chides no one. Harbouring no covert manifesto, it is not even remotely ideological. It should not and cannot be screened for unambiguous direction. In the end, Smith's film-work is the production of a diffident Gnostic who will gladly share his vision without ever proselytising.

Smith also discouraged acolytes by creating absurdly labour-intensive work. These films took hundreds upon hundreds of hours to produce. Like many other landmarks of obsessive art, the Watts Towers and the Nek Chand Rock Gardens, this work is beyond the physical limits of all but a handful of driven visionaries. Fashioning work impossible to mimic, Smith has no method to communicate. Yet Smith's inimitable singularity is also his greatest gift, because what he inspires is not a method of practise, but a way of seeing. Unfortunately, given the private mystery of vision, the measure of Smith's success is not easily taken. There is no ready measure of influence when an interrogative optician changes something as elemental as sight.

Generally, whatever is filmed, from George Méliès' 1902 moon excursion to *Lara Croft: Tomb Raider* (2001), carries with it the inescapable feel of the real. Even the most improbable fictions appear before us with impossible clarity. Bearing delicious visual and aural feasts, film is an amazingly limpid medium. It seems to work without mediation. Nothing appears to come between the original image, whatever was filmed, and projected reality. It is perfectly transparent. Film is, in this regard, like the perfect poison. It works its dark, irreversible magic without leaving a trace. Conversely, while no medium is capable of such discrete reserve, no medium is also so well-suited for spectacle. Nothing can so fully involve, even dominate, the spectator like a film. Larger and louder than life, film immerses the audience in a near-total sensory overload. At once self-effacing and grand, invisible and over-powering, film tattoos memory with unforgettable images while managing to never call undue attention to itself.

The retiring grandiloquence of the cinema poses a particularly vexing problem for viewers. Despite its overwhelming aura of verisimilitude, cinema is incapable of presenting things as they are. Movies do not present unmediated access to things-in-themselves. And while duplicitous images *do* mimic the real with great sensuous conviction, appearing proximate to reality itself, what we see is *not* what is. Indeed, when paying rapt attention to the life of things onscreen, 'we do not perceive the thing or the image in its entirety, we always perceive less of it, we perceive only what we are interested in perceiving. … We therefore normally perceive only clichés.'[4] Not only does the cinema avoid the truth and fail to bring us things as they are, it also offers visual confirmation for our stalest truisms.

Smith manages to reverse these powerful forces and restore us to things as they are by rendering film opaque. In checking cinematic distortion, it should be clear that Smith did not reject the spectacle of film. In a series of experiments, most ill-fated, Smith made a series of complex lighting gels and frames to augment his screenings; he devised synchronised projection systems to show multiple films simultaneously; he envisioned special sensory chairs for specific films, with variable shapes, sizes and wired effects tailored to the individual personality of the filmgoer and their location in the auditorium; he invented an ultra-deep focus device that would allow a camera lens to descend through multiple planes of imagery. He also embarked on a very expensive and time-consuming attempt at remaking *The Wizard of Oz* (1939). But in expanding the possibilities for the camera and spectator, Smith always took special care never to allow the film apparatus to disappear from sight. All of his films are self-conscious film productions.

FIGMENTS OF TRUTH

Aside from never allowing the film apparatus to slink from view, an important corrective, how does Smith engineer a cinema incapable of fostering a lie and underpinning untruth? More accurately, how does Smith transcend perjury, as no film is altogether capable of telling the truth? The short answer: he returns us to the things themselves. Having admitted that this cannot be done, that the very nature of film as a mediating gauze places the real at an unbridgeable distance, how does Smith manage an impossible feat?

Having early in his career painted large canvases that could easily be taken for film stills from his later work, Smith responds to the challenge of cinema in the same fashion as besieged painters responded to the invention of photography. What could painting do when photography captures the real with far greater ease and precision than even the deftest brush-wielder could realise? In the shadow of the photograph, painters ceded reality to photography and revisioned painting as a necessarily unrealistic art form. Instead of simulating three dimensions via complex *trompe l'oeil* effects, painters opted to explore the canvas as a flat plane. Freed from simulating reality in two dimensions, painters could use the canvas as a plane upon which to test new modes of vision.

Smith will approach film in the same fashion. Instead of appropriating film as an illegitimate conduit for the real, Smith treats the medium as if it were best suited to depict only height and width. The argument that Smith is a painter on film gains currency when we take into account the absence of depth of field in almost all his films. Everything stays on the same plane. Depth and perspective are abandoned. In so doing, Smith makes moving paintings. This is not a terminological quibble because in creating films without depth of field, Smith has fashioned a cinema that gives up film's most powerful reality effect. Lifelike worlds with three spatial dimensions are worlds that we might enter. Images that fail to proffer this illusion foreclose the possibility that they can be read as potential habitations. Uncompromisingly flat, these films offer no range for movement. Absent the magnetic illusion of three dimensions, Smith creates cinematic spaces that are exclusive and uninviting. When a Smith film is projected on the screen, we are faced with a film that must be looked upon as a flat canvas and not an open space.

Defining Smith as a painterly filmmaker does not mean there is no distinction to be drawn between his work on canvas and his film compositions. Even the most robust action painting is inert. Film allows Smith to make mobile canvases and gain an important measure of control over time. A century after the introduction of photography, Smith can restore painting to three dimensions; this time, however, Smith will create animate paintings with a novel and unprecedented combination of three-dimensionality: height, width and time. Time in hand, Smith takes painting to a new realm.

Animating frozen canvas across time, Smith initially composes painterly film images from simple geometrical shapes that exist only as ideations and mathematical constructs. In so doing, he creates an animate Platonic universe in which the world of Form dances on parade. A metaphysical *Sesame Street*, the *Early Abstractions* are a phantasmagoric revel in the abstractions of the mind.

There are no empirically available coordinates for the images of the *Early Abstractions*. Circles, triangles and rectangles are not to be found in the world of the senses. These are immutable Universals and they do not exist on this plane. In the ready-to-hand arena of sense data there are only transient particulars. Instead of timeless circles, triangles and rectangles, there are only dented coffee can lids, scarred shark fins and friable concrete blocks. Any perception of circularity, triangularity or the like is the final product of mental machinations.

Instead of purporting to show the things themselves, Smith will illuminate the constructs we employ to approach the things themselves. In his hands cinema is not a recording device, it is an instrument of analysis. This then is the key to understanding how Smith avoids cinematic fraud. Instead of presenting duplicitous *a priori* assertions, Smith's cinema is open to philosophic interrogation.

His films assay perception in an attempt to divine the epistemological utility of the senses. Rejecting cinema as a transparent, realistic enterprise, Smith returns over and again to the question of what can be known of images and their worldly correlates. Holding that what we see and hear depends on the mechanisms of thought, Smith is an idealist. He abjures any direct connection between the screen and the things of the world. Insisting that there is no way of readily knowing what is real and what is a shared or individual phantasm, Smith's films beckon us to reconsider how we produce sense.

Of course, this sounds infernally dull as the subject of film. May as well plow through the writings of Berkeley, Russell or Kant. What makes Smith a filmmaker and not a philosopher with diverting visual aids is that these arguments are only the sub-text of an entirely involving synergetic experience. And while it is vital to underscore Smith's idealism, these films are more than arid philosophical ruminations. Always challenging us to rethink the foundation upon which we make sense of images, Smith never abandons the hedonistic potential of the screen.

In *Early Abstractions*, for instance, consider how Smith depicts the multiple shapes that constitute our geometric vocabulary. Taking perception back to basic forms, Smith cuts his films with exacting attention to rhythm. Most of the early films move in 4/4 time so that his arithmetic arabesques metamorphose into various permutations as part of a kinetic dance. No tweedy Don ever considered the question of appearance and reality with such slinky grace. At many later screenings, Smith would sync the *Early Abstractions* with The Beatles' *A Hard Day's Night* (1964). In tandem with a backbeat that cannot be misplaced, Smith's time signatures are unmistakable.

Smith always cut with attention to rhythm. On numerous occasions he mentioned how his films were edited in synchrony with the beat of the heart and the intake of breath. And while it is doubtful that he realised this aim – to do so would take a complex polyrhythm, as the heart and lungs do not contract with the same pulse – it is certain that Smith's films are exquisitely in time. In returning us to the elements, Smith always keeps the beat. Fashioned for the head, these films never leave the body behind.

Rhythm aligns time with the body. Absent rhythm, time is an infinite and featureless expanse of interminable duration. By dividing time into repeating cycles of varying duration, rhythm makes time manageable and meaningful. Finding the rhythm of the moment is a crucial component of human knowing. Feeling the world rushing by, as time takes flight, and feeling the world crawl, as time slows down, our perceptions of duration are dependent on refined judgement. Just as we learn to interpret the things we see, chronographic perception is not a given. We have to find the beat.

In *Number 11* (1957), Smith synchronises the images of his previous effort, *Number 10* (1956), with Thelonious Monk's 'Mysterioso'. By this time, Smith has left behind simple figures for the semiotic blizzard of wildly heteroclite collages. Seemingly impossible to fully interpret, but a lysergic mindwash to watch, *Number 11* and *Number 10* collectively demonstrate how important rhythm is when making meaning from the buzzing, blooming confusion of an enigmatic world.

Without Monk's snaky piano, *Number 10* is a fever dream involving a tireless letter carrier attempting to communicate with his beloved. Amidst grave dancers glad in wispy silks, jangling skeletons, Kali, moon mushroom, and so much more, the film is an impossible rebus. How to make sense of it all? Sided with Monk's measured stroll across the keys, the film coheres. Patterns too complex to be perceived in silence emerge as the music takes off. Soon Monk's music begins to change too. A bop classic, when paired with Smith's imagery, 'Mysterioso' is re-cut. Anyone who has heard it before will hear the tune afresh in the light of Smith's numinous imagery. Remedial synesthesia, *Numbers 10* and *11* demonstrate how understanding is an alchemical wonder fashioned from the senses, the pulse of the body and the mental constructs that underlie perception.

Smith's last readily available films take these mental and physical gymnastics to the brink. *Number 12* (1957–61), better known as *Heaven and Earth Magic*, and *Number 14* are acid tests. As mentioned above, *Number 14* is thirty minutes of super-imposed home movies accompanied by selections from Brecht and Weills's 'The Rise and Fall of the City of Mahagonny'. Edited down from a length of eight hours or more, *Number 12* is an hour-long distillation of Smith's most elaborate and abstruse collage. Imagine Rube Goldberg and Hieronymus Bosch animating the same frame in tandem with Currier and Ives. Difficult in the extreme to describe, *Number 12*, in Smith's words...

depicts the Heroine's toothache consequent to the loss of a very valuable water-melon, her dentistry and transportation to heaven … the second part depicts the return to the earth from being eaten by Max Muller on the day Edward the Seventh dedicated the Great Sewer of London.[5]

NOT, IT WOULD SEEM, A LOT TO GO ON

Surprisingly, after endless hours of research, Smith's description of *Number 12* can be distilled into something resembling a straight-ahead plot summary. Similarly, with a comprehensive Smith bio in hand, the doubled images of *Number 14* can be matched with the events of Smith's life. Critics have laboured mightily to read these films as cognitive labyrinths and Occult armories stockpiled with highly cultivated and deeply veiled Theosophical arcana.[6] And while all of these well-intentioned efforts offer meaningful insights into Smith's idiosyncratic practice, they fail to adequately address the true challenge of Smith's most difficult work.

These films represent the limit point of Smith's respect for and appreciation of the viewer. In constructing films that resist interpretation with an adamantine vengeance, Smith gives his viewers a chance to make their own way amidst an amazing scrap-heap of visual detritus and aural cacophony. Like multi-media Lego blocks, these films can be assembled howsoever you see fit. In keeping with Artaud's epigram gracing *American Magus: Harry Smith*, Smith's Ideal cinema proclaims 'Do what thou wilt shall be the whole of the law.' Fortunately, this entitlement cannot be exercised lightly. Only in the face of difficult challenges does the liberty to do as we wish have value.

A pioneer from the film frontier, Smith did not chart unexplored territory so that we might comfortably make our way to settled ground. A cartographer with an animus for maps, Smith charges us to connect the dots. Sending us packing, Smith produced a body of complex work riddled with cruel doubt. No image is to be trusted. At the same time, he saturated the screen with mobile illuminations alive with wonder and serendipitous beauty. What we make of terrible and magnificent icons is our own choosing.

CHAPTER 12
WHAT IS THE NEO-UNDERGROUND AND WHAT ISN'T:
A FIRST CONSIDERATION OF HARMONY KORINE

Benjamin Halligan

THE NEW UNDERGROUND?

A consolidation of the predominant characteristics of recent Hollywood filmmaking occurred in the success of two late 1990s box-office hits: *Titanic* (1997), the zenith of the film-as-experience strain of 'high concept' North American cinema, and *American Beauty* (1999), acclaimed for the originality of its approach to its material. The films came across as experiences for the taking, labelled as such for the multiplexes, 'must-see' talking points. In this respect, the latter was 'art as entertainment', the former 'entertainment as entertainment'; a difference of degree between the two, but the denominator is common and both trailed Academy Awards in their wake.

Walter Benjamin once observed a phenomenon that seems, from this close distance at least, especially applicable to the latter film and the 'art as entertainment' sensibility. The application is necessary since *Titanic* seems to exemplify, and perhaps anticipates, a contemporary trend in North American filmmaking:

> We are confronted with the fact ... that the bourgeois apparatus of production and publication is capable of assimilating, indeed of propagating, an astonishing amount of revolutionary themes without ever seriously putting into question its own continued existence or that of the class which owns it. In any case this remains true so long as it is supplied by hacks, albeit revolutionary hacks. ... I further maintain that an appreciable part of so-called left-wing literature had no other social function than that of continually extracting new effects or sensations from this situation for the public's entertainment.[1]

The assimilating nature of *American Beauty* occurs in the successful translation of the style and preoccupations of an 'underground' sensibility into box-office material. The originality of *American Beauty* was nothing so much as a repackaging of aspects of 1990s 'independent' American filmmaking (of the commercial fringe), as exemplified in, say, the work of David Lynch and Abel Ferrara. In this case, the bourgeois apparatus of production was the burgeoning Disney-to-be, DreamWorks SKG. The assimilation was in the nature of the 'bodysnatchers': the film became an acceptable version of the same thing.

With respect to the matter of degree (art-as-entertainment and entertainment-as-entertainment), the 'art' sensibility manifested itself in *American Beauty* through incidentals and inessentials, elevated to the level of the all-important. This is true of individual moments (the bag blowing in the wind – itself from Antonioni's *Il Deserto Rosso* (1964)) and also underlies the nature of the narrative as a whole (the generically dysfunctional family unit within the milieu of 1950s-like American suburbia, à la Lynch). The narrative's experiential aspects, which function to immerse the viewer in the pervading sense of the superficiality of the generic suburbia, gives way to a sense of a critical distance from the film – a distance filled with irony, reflexive pastiche, 'knowingness'. It creates an environment in which the expected can itself expect to be usurped and the audience is warned not to feel alienated should this occur. Thus it offers a sense of 'difference' within the familiar. This critical distance in relation to art as entertainment recalls Brecht's reading of film in the 1930s: the smokescreen of 'art' obscures that which, in this case, posits a very tight spectrum of entirely passive expressions of 'rebellion'.

The nature of the assimilation (of which the success of the film is a part) indicates the uncertainties of Hollywood filmmaking in the 1990s (an inability to understand or control their audiences or the 'digital revolution'). Arguably, this had translated into a knee-jerk plundering of left-of-field filmmaking in order to appeal to the more wayward audiences the Hollywood industry felt were endangered. This sense of endangerment had coloured Hollywood strategies since the near breakdown of the 1992 GATT trade talks with Europe, and the shift, in the late 1990s, to the majority of box-office returns from Hollywood films being reaped from outside North America. To be crude about the perceived marketing strategy, since non-Americans were noted to sometimes prefer art-as-entertainment over entertainment-as-entertainment – to desire 'difference' – then that element must also be addressed, repackaged and assimilated and so find its position within the products of Hollywood. It becomes a matter of articulating a foreign language within a familiar linguistic system, so that the foreignness becomes ultimately little more than a nuance, a quirk.

When even 'difference' becomes a commodity, then a certain equilibrium has been achieved. Like the Czech film industry under Soviet reorganisation in the early 1970s, all dissidence is annihilated; those responsible for it are either silenced or exiled, and the films and their nature either banned, appropriated or regurgitated. The North American film of the late 1990s fell into two camps: firstly, the monumental blockbuster, of which *Titanic* was the most notable, the heart of a nexus of global products. Secondly, the film of 'difference', a type of production that seemed to exist to mop up all audiences who did not buy tickets for the doomed ocean liner. All films in between were pushed towards one of the two poles, so that there was no 'in between': a film was either the same or not the same, and not to be the same was to come to still be the same; not being the same had been co-opted. This co-optation came in the way in which those 'not the same' products aspired to must-have status: bought up by subsidiaries of major studios, forcefully pushed at festivals. This constitutes the eradication of real difference through the imposition of a linguistic system. A reorganisation by stealth: the Czechs had it relatively easy, artistically speaking.

The wider impulse for (alas, desire for) assimilation can also be seen in the general trends of filmmaking of the formerly 'underground' or semi-underground American auteurs in the 1990s. At worse, they recast themselves as hacks, albeit revolutionary hacks (particularly in light of the challenging and newly re-emergent Russian, European and New Asian film scenes of the period). But this shift to the mainstream by the Coens, Soderbergh, Jarmusch, Van Sant, Larry Clark, Lynch and others was tempered by one 'slight return': Harmony Korine, who, with his films *Gummo* (1997) and *julien donkey-boy* (1999), went defiantly in the other direction.

LOW CONCEPT AND WHITE TRASH: A BACKGROUND CONSIDERATION OF KORINE

Harmony Korine (born California, 1974) is seemingly as idiosyncratic as his films. A former skateboarder, he scripted Larry Clark's controversial study of wayward youth, *Kids* (1995), before directing *Gummo* and *julien donkey-boy*. Neither film lends itself to a plot synopsis since very little 'happens' in a conventional sense and there is little or no story to develop. However, the former concerns a number of dispossessed young people who spend their time in a variety of illegal ways; the latter concerns Julien (Ewan Bremner), a mentally ill young man who works washing floors in a hospital and lives with an eccentric family. *Gummo* met with widespread criticism upon its release;

many felt that Korine exploited those he filmed, offering a questionable voyeuristic experience masquerading as an *exposé*. David Walsh termed it 'a libel against mankind'.[2]

Korine has spoken disparagingly of the influence of the more 'acceptable' contemporary American filmmakers (particularly Martin Scorsese), preferring films by Werner Herzog, Buster Keaton, Michael Powell, David Lynch, Carl Dreyer, Jean-Luc Godard, John Cassavetes, Rainer Werner Fassbinder and particularly British television director Alan Clark. Such films tend to be distinguished by cinematic 'statements' rather than strategies of political engagement. He has also written an experimental novel and created a number of mixed-media installations.

In this context, 'low-concept' would be an applicable term. *Gummo* itself inverts the norm of the nexus of global products: rather than the television spin-off from a film, it comes across as a film spin-off from television (specifically, *The Jerry Springer Show*; indeed, one of the principal characters of *Gummo* was taken from the paint-sniffing segment of a drug prevention episode of *The Sally Jesse Raphael Show*). It contains within it its own still-born marketing campaign: white trash freak show, heavy metal soundtrack, the piling up of outrage upon outrage. Barely have the words 'New Line' and 'Time Warner' first appeared on the screen than a torrent of juvenile obscenities fades in on the soundtrack. On the face of it, *Gummo* seems tailor-made for the bored browser in the video shop: a spectacle that will offend; packaged outrage as entertainment.

This difference can be understood in terms of divergent aspirations. While the semi-underground auteurs of the 1990s looked towards models of (troubled liberal) filmmaking such as neo-noir and the 'issue' film, Korine aspires towards one of the idiosyncratic auteurs of the New German Cinema: Herzog. Korine claimed to have fallen under the influence of Herzog as a Californian teenager. According to the director, Herzog represented an absolute foreignness to him (specifically in *Even Dwarfs Started Small* (1970)), a kind of cinematic 'abduction by UFO' experience, wrecking any evolving sense of what a film should or should not be. His influence was felt in *Gummo* and Herzog himself was present in *julien donkey-boy*. No spirit of Scorsese for Korine, no Coppola compositions or Penn timeliness. Rather, he looks to some of the most idiosyncratic areas of film history – the monumental statements of Herzog and the New German Cinema: unwieldy metaphors, ambiguous relevance, insane propositions. Korine's model was the lack of a model particular to Herzog's unique vision.

Herzog's 1970s–1980s work was characterised by metaphors that refused to reveal the *actualité* of which they spoke: the vague sense of man against nature, or God, as a parable for civilisation and capitalisation (*Fitzcarraldo* (1982)), of revolution as a pointless and doomed activity (*Even Dwarfs Started Small*), of characters newly adrift in an alien landscape (*The Enigma of Kaspar Hauser* (1974); *Stroszek* (1977)). For the auteurs of the New German Cinema, 'meaning' could not be found in the recent history of West Germany, and so meaning must be resisted in art that invariably reflects that recent history; a mimetic approach. The New German Cinema itself was characterised by such a problematic relationship to the problematic history of film in Germany. Herzog rejected conventional senses of history in his films, Fassbinder embraced it and its contradictions, Wenders sought the present and its contradictions. It is Herzog's 'unstuck' metaphor – the grand gesture as a grand gesture, insanity as proof of living – that informs Korine's slight return. Herzog returned the compliment too, in a suitably idiosyncratic manner. In discussing *Gummo* with Korine, he commented:

> What I like about *Gummo* are the details that one might not notice at first. There's the scene where the kid in the bathtub drops his chocolate bar into the dirty water and just behind him there's a piece of fried bacon stuck to the wall with Scotch tape. This is the entertainment of the future.[3]

To which Korine replied, revelling in his difference (now authenticated by the master of difference):

> It's the greatest entertainment. Seriously, all I want to see is pieces of fried bacon taped on walls, because most films just don't do that.[4]

The authentification of 'difference' for *julien donkey-boy* came via a Dogme 95 certificate: Korine as a member of the brotherhood of Danish film punks.

Structurally and aesthetically, the films exist beyond any familiar art-house or underground category. They present a foreign language in these respects. In terms of the expected political reading, Korine invites and then rejects a liberal agenda with his sketches of the wretched underbelly of American life. On one level he voices the Neo-Realist's question in terms of the type of imagery he presents – 'Why and how has this come to pass?' However, the crux of his vision lionises the marginal and disregarded icons of late twentieth-century culture, reinventing them into an ironic form of Poetic Realism (finding meaning in the meaningless), vastly at odds with his Neo-Realist elements. His frame of reference recalls the ironies of Jeff Koons' 'instant art' approach to the refuse of consumer culture (i.e. that there is no refuse but, rather, an endless cycle of consumption of defecation). Indeed, Korine was first encountered in the Koons milieu – art and fashion magazines – rather than brought out as a precocious festival cinéphile. Korine constantly hones in on the most superficial aspects of existence.

AGGRESSION, THE GROTESQUE AND 'GUMMO'

Korine summons up the ambience of Midwest heavy metal lifestyles in *Gummo*: the ridiculous posturing of the music overlapping with the juvenile chants of the opening credits ('Peanut-butter-mother-fucker'), reflected in the style of the on-screen credits (1970s album cover gothic). Korine bleeds the sense of authenticity from expressions of 'difference' in these, his debut moments. His characters are defined by the commercial categories of 'difference' that are on offer; they are products of the cultural assimilation of the left-of-field. In this instance, the whole recalls the 'Judas Priest suicide' of the late 1980s – nihilism authenticated by an actual desire for annihilation:

> Sparks, Nevada – After James Vance demolished his face with a sawed-off shotgun at a church playground, he rode his bicycle around town shocking people with his grotesque disfigurement. Plastic surgeons had been able to restore his ability to eat and breathe, but were not able to restore his smooth, youthful face. James's physical deformity stunned the town, but not as much as the message he later delivered: Heavy metal music drove him and his closest friend to strike a suicide pact, one that only James survived. 'I believe that alcohol and heavy metal music, such as Judas Priest, led us or even "mesmerized" us into believing that the answer to "life was death",' James wrote to his best friend's mother in 1986, quoting some of the album's lyrics. James, depressed and addicted to pain medications after the shooting, died last year in the psychiatric unit of the Washoe Medical Center from drugs and complications from his numerous surgeries.[5]

In embracing the inauthentic, difference is not so easily assimilated, since its authenticity becomes more apparent.

Korine allows the nihilistic vision of the Midwest to mesmerise him too – he 'opens himself up' to its influences, enters into the milieu, fashions an expression of (rather than *from*) it. He even engages in some 'grotesque disfigurement', since in allowing the film to be submissive to the world it seeks to present, Korine also comes to take his part in the freak show parade of white trash. This cameo has neither the flourish of the Hitchcock 'signature', nor of the Welles type, which often worked to 'centre' the film around a sense of the presences of the auteur. Korine, as 'Boy on Couch', is utterly superfluous. He presents himself as a drooling, drunken supergeek, trying to seduce a world-wise gay black person of restricted growth, 'Midget' (Bryant L. Crenshaw). His voice is whispery and cracked, he slurs his way through stories of debasement, of being sexually abused as a child, and douses himself with cheap beer. The sequence jump cuts into, seemingly, alternative takes: the sense of an improvised scene, interchangeable anecdotes. There is no suspension of belief in the sequence. It is not as if Korine is presenting a fictional character that functions in any discernible way. It is not as if Korine is not himself noted. There is, rather, a sense communicated of Korine entering into the situation of the film, that his role is equally behind and in front of the camera since the behind and the front are to be engulfed by the world, that world which becomes the world of the film. In the same exploratory manner, in an interview, he said:

> As far as production design went, it was about taking things away to make it cleaner. At times the crew would refuse to film in those conditions. We had to buy them those white

suits like people wear in a nuclear fallout. I got angry with them because I thought they were pussies. I mean, all we're talking about is bugs and a disgusting rotty smell. I couldn't understand why they had no guts. I was like, 'Think about what we have access to,' but I guess most of them didn't really give a shit. But Jean Yves Escoffier, the cinematographer, was fearless. When the others were wearing their toxic outfits, he and I wore speedos and flip-flops just to piss them off.[6]

True or otherwise, this represents the notion of a relatively unusual vantage point for the film – more that of the reportage or documentary-maker than underground filmmaker. Such a notion is not directly verified by the aesthetic – an impressionistic-equivalent – but it underlies it.

The aesthetic stylisation cannot be read as a subjective construction. Rather, the stylisation seems, by default, to 'originate in' the collective mind state of the protagonists, themselves sometimes little more than colour in the wider milieu of the film. The diegetic reason for or signifier of the nature of the stylisation is unclear. It cannot be accounted for as point-of-view subjective stylisation (in the manner Pasolini termed 'Free Indirect Subjectivity'), since the undigested mass of characters prevents the viewer from latching onto one of them as a guide through the world of *Gummo*. Nor do systems of presentation account for the approach, since Korine continually falls foul of the Neo-Realist/ethnographic methodology with his aesthetic 'lapses' into bursts of impressionism. As with the continually differing types of image quality, drawn from celluloid and video, the film has no 'constant'. Rather, the film 'enters into' the milieu and reproduces the experience in a mimetic fashion. It does not seek to present an evocation of the world in a classical way.

In terms of the opening, Korine's technique is to de-establish information rather than present the usual Establishing Shots. The implicit objectivity of the classical approach (which also allows the viewer to find a distance from the world by looking *on* at it rather than having to look *with* it) gives way to a classicism that is apparent at base but 'eroded' by elements associated with the world of the film: it speaks *of* the mind state more than it presents it. In this way, Korine allows the characters to talk in voiceover, as if to guide the viewer through the world of the film, but the voiceovers then determine the film's course. *Gummo* latches onto minds rather than characters. There are plenty of signifiers of addled mind-states throughout the film (e.g. from glue-sniffing), but when Eddie (Charles Matthew Coatney) talks, his 'attention disorder … [which] makes it hard to concentrate', seems to voice the central *raison d'être* of the films flitting, non-sequitur nature.

In the first instance, *Gummo* finds itself unable to 'concentrate' on any developed, linear narrative construction. Before Korine's appearance, the film's structure seems only to be concerned with clocking up sequences of ever greater degradation. It indicates an inability to focus on one plot line, or even to differentiate between 'actual' and 'imagined' narratives. For instance, two skinheaded brothers, body-building Jehovah Witnesses, who playfully and brutally engage in bare-knuckle boxing in their kitchen, only seem 'present' to illustrate a seemingly inconsequential voiceover anecdote which tears the film away from a sense of reality or a unity of time and space in terms of narrative development. This sequence is shot as fly-on-the-wall documentary (albeit, disconcertingly, with a fish-eye lens). There is, therefore, a stylistic 'lie' in the way the film does not codify that which seems not to exist. The characters are defiantly real and present in terms of aesthetic presentation. Other moments lapse into the codes of narrative or generic types of film. These include a coming-of-age narrative (signalled by voiceovers); Godard-like performing/improvising for the camera; a Neo-Realist-like investigation of the world of the film; abstract video art; and even, at one point, a cable dating channel (an albino waitress talks about Patrick Swayze as the ideal man and dances around her car).

Such an 'attention-deficiency' impressionism underlies the opening assault of the film: degraded video images, rhythmlessly cut together, detail 'the great tornado' hitting Xenia, Ohio. Overexposed and differing speeds of film meld with the camcorder-like footage to render the whole stylistically timeless: neither 8mm experimentation from the 1960s nor scratch video from the 1980s. This very precise event, the tornado, is decontextualised from any sense of a recent history. An unintelligible voiceover 'narrates' a bizarre commentary, fading into a series of unreal, echoed aural digressions (a ditty with the refrain 'pussy'). The furious black mass of the tornado itself is briefly glimpsed with a shot of a tattooed crucifix, suggesting the event as a kind of Biblical plague, an act of God. The tornado at the opening of the film recalls *The Wizard of Oz* (1939), another journey through an alien/familiar landscape. But such suggestions are themselves only momentarily thrown up in the miasma of the rapid bursts of montage, punctuated by glimpses of self-consciously outrageous imagery (a dog impaled on a television aerial, for example). All this, and *Supergirl* (1984) too, is touched upon in the opening narration:

> Xenia, Ohio. Xenia, Ohio. A couple of years ago, a tornado hit this place. It killed the people left and right. Houses were split open, and you could see necklaces hanging from branches of trees. Dogs died. Cats died. I saw a girl fly through the sky … and I looked up her skirt.

The film, as it begins proper (in 35mm definition), contrasts boldly with the frantic montage of the opening sequence: this is the calmness of the aftermath. The prepubescent 'Bunny Boy' (Jacob Sewell) kicks his heels on a motorway flyover. Cars and trucks shoot by below, emphasising the nowhere-ness of the location. He is topless, his torso bruised and dirty, teeth cracked, fingers tattooed, shivering in the rain. He smokes like a pro, and pisses and spits on the traffic below, all the time sporting a pair of filthy pink bunny ears. He kicks at the bridge fencing (ripped and there to deter would-be suicides). It is the full gamut of Morrissey behaviour, and the sequence has all the grimy oppressiveness of *Flesh* (1968), *Trash* (1970) and *Heat* (1972). But whereas Morrissey's elegantly wasted low-lifes seemed to follow a certain code of behaviour (as did the protagonists of the Korine-scripted *Kids*: updated Morrissey, a cut-price hedonistic odyssey of drugs and fucking, AIDS no objection), *Gummo*'s occupants only drift. Not even a punk ethos (recalled via the iconic

157

casting of Linda Manz, from Hopper's *Out of the Blue* (1980)) is apparent: the forty speaking parts in the film are united via complacency rather than rebellion, marginalisation rather than drop-out, glue rather than dope. The shammed Satanism of the snatches from Slayer videos adds another level of superficiality. No one does anything for any particular reason. And this pervades the calmness of the opening sequence.

STRUCTURAL ANARCHY: THE FILM STYLE OF 'GUMMO'

Nor does the imagery offer a sense of narrative (like, say, the Death Row photographs of Oliviero Toscani) or a dynamic or sense of action or narrative (like Nan Goldin's or Larry Clark's photographs of comparable characters and situations). Rather, the images are stripped of any sense of a socio-historical resonance and with that goes any sense of an imperative as to why Korine should show us such imagery. At times heads are optically fogged (as if those filmed had not signed release forms) and the eyes are scrubbed out from the Polaroids detailing sex parties. The whole is bathed in a urine yellow (achieved with banks of fluorescent Kino-Flos rather than standard lighting), broken by the fuzzy green globules that bubble to the surface of the distressed video images.

This approach manifests itself rapidly as the film 'moves on': cat drowning; teenage prostitution (both parties); a lump found in her breast; cat hunting with pop guns; the protagonists on a couple of *ET* (1982) BMXs. It is a vision of urban squalor akin to Godard's *Le Weekend* (1967): a refusescape, the future as built from the junk of the past. Korine invites the viewer to read the idiosyncratic nuances as absurdist (the clown-like masks; the dialogue), situationist (the tornado as a perception-altering event) and, in a way, experiential in the manner of *Titanic*: both *Gummo* and *Titanic* are spectacles of destruction, served up by major studios. Tummler (Nick Sutton) is introduced with a montage of yellowed photos. He has the look of a potential mass murderer; gaunt, prematurely thinning hair, 'downright evil' as Solomon (Jacob Reynolds) approvingly describes him. Dead eyes and Death Row ambience. Tummler and Solomon spend the few dollars they make from selling dead cats (for human consumption) on strawberry milkshakes, glue and sex with a Down's syndrome prostitute, pimped by her jock brother. Meanwhile, two platinum blonde sisters use gaffer tape to expand their nipples and Bunny Boy re-enacts a Disney cartoon in a junkyard: two small children in cowboy hats, smashing car windows, wielding toy guns, pretend to gun him down and scream 'fucking rabbit' as Bunny Boy, unmoved, lies on the filthy ground.

Korine shoots in tableau (the two sisters, jumping up and down on an attic bed, for example) and in a frontal, 'naive' way – often characters are introduced in such a fashion: approaching the camera. This composition recalls Pasolini's Neo-Realism in *Accattone* (1961), as does the ethnographic aesthetic construction of the film, a constantly changing array of faces, drawn predominantly from non-actors. However, little specific information can be read into the succession of faces; nor does the film document Xenia (it was, in fact, shot in Nashville).

Against this 'deadened' and information-free approach, which works to eliminate a sense of experience or depth to the world of the film, Korine fashions the material into moments – beats – that break through the collage, the impressionistic aesthetic and the freeform structure. They glide on the woozy, drugged-up ambience of the aesthetic: are they profound, or merely crass? It is these moments that are left once the film has finished (or, rather, 'wound down'). The collage approach alternates between image and sound: snatches of dialogue in voiceover – anecdotes, observations, incoherent drones that defy contextualisation in terms of a sense of an evolving narrative or even, sometimes, in terms of just who is speaking. It is a jigsaw: the viewer is invited to examine pieces at random as if in order to visualise the entire picture.

The technique is one long negation: an evolving denial of information for the viewer; methods of filmmaking cut off from their original political agendas. The film is even named as such: Gummo was the Marx brother who 'didn't make it' and was forgotten, negated. As the nature of Korine's own presence in the film suggests (and, in a more roundabout manner, the opening credits, or the Slayer footage), this negation is connected to the elimination of a vantage point that would allow a distance from the world of the film. In its place, a process of mimesis occurs. Korine 'writes' in a language that is not his own, one that is drawn from the space between the classical construction of the world of the film and a subjective-documentary approach to that world. A kind of mimetic visual slang evolves. The vast fragmentations of the film (in terms of narrative and the lack of a constant in the aesthetic) are the fragmentations of this language, the fragmentation of an attention-deficiency impressionism. It is an incomplete linguistic system; a foreignness that cannot be reduced to a nuance or a quirk.

In light of the negations, it is, therefore, this approach that is left: a kind of broken linguistic system of uncertain diegetic origin. It is a linguistic system that, in the manner of attention-deficiency disorder, speaks of a normality but only through disrupting it. This disruption finds filmic equivalents (the lack of narrative progression; the ensemble of characters; the lack of a constant of aesthetic; the collage) and this constitutes the film's linguistic system. In this way, it is the linguistic system and not the film itself that therefore speaks of the place, a generic 'Midwest'. The mind state is presented as evidence of the existence of the location rather than the location and milieu as reason for the mind state. In this way, Korine delivers a psycho-geographical portrait: a collective concentration that is disrupted, the inability to pull together fragments into a cohesive whole; that is, the lack of a non-befuddled perception, the lack of any ethical or indeed even motivational codes of behaviour. Korine's young protagonists may come across as latter-day equivalents of the child anti-hero of Rossellini's *Germania Anno Zero* (1947), wandering lost in a devastated landscape, but in reality Korine's vision details the psychological or spiritual devastation rather than a situation born of social problems.

This accounts for the film's structurelessness. As with Herzog, Korine works towards a moment, perhaps cathartic, perhaps 'frozen', both uppers (irrational, spontaneous acts of violence, seemingly engaged in to verify the existence of those who commit them) and downers (nostalgic-sentimental: the suggestion of a 'meaning' in imagery which does not actually manifest itself). Such scenes include the two skinheaded brothers fighting; the grandmother dying once Tummler has switched off her life-support machine; a group of bare-chested, beer-drinking men smashing a kitchen chair after a bout of arm wrestling; a wired Tummler reproducing a humorless stand-up routine; a soapy Soloman eating spaghetti and chocolate in his murky bath. These are the moments that break through the collage, that emerge from the stylistic anarchy. The film eventually lapses into a run of these: the platinum sisters make out with Bunny Boy in an outdoors swimming pool, Soloman and Tummler repeatedly shoot a dead cat, Bunny Boy holds a dead cat up to the camera, an eyebrowless girl sings 'Yes, Jesus Loves Me' in bed. The majority of these final scenes occurs in the pouring rain and are accompanied by Roy Orbinson's song 'Crying'. Again this underscores the universality of the sentiment, the way in which Korine details non-specific perception. The repeated lyric 'crying' connects to the images of water (of the swimming pool, of the pouring rain, of the soaking dead cat): it is the whole milieu that is drenched in a 'crying', not the actions of the characters.

While *Titanic* detailed the destruction of the Titanic, *Gummo* details the destruction of *Gummo*. With mimesis, the film allows the perception that it has itself been 'destroyed' (and is seen to now exist without ethical consideration and in a motivationless void: the calmness of the aftermath) so as to contaminate all norms of filmmaking. Why is the impulse for this attempt at self-annihilation a necessity? Because all that is not annihilated is being assimilated into the Neo-Underground. Korine negates his film before 'the bourgeois apparatus of production and publication' can do so, thus preserving in the face of late 1990s co-optation an innocence through the presentation of a devastated psychology. *Gummo* is Neo-Realist nuance, set in amber, and therefore distorted to those who peer into it.

CHAPTER 13
UNDERGROUND AMERICA 1999

Annalee Newitz

When we deal with underground film, the temptation is to think in binary terms. Either there *is* an underground but we have very little access to it, or there *never was* an underground, and the films called underground represent a phoney form of subversion foisted on us by hipster journalists.

Although problematic, 'underground' is a useful term, and moreover a deeply seductive idea: it suggests that despite the usual blizzard of politically cowardly and culturally unremarkable films, there is a hidden cache of daring, revolutionary and independently created movies which lurk literally just under our feet, if we would only look. I think it is clear why, from a radical perspective, this idea would be something to swoon over. And I would call it useful because even if the underground does not exist, the term itself is still a good way to designate films that break rules and remind their audiences that 'common sense' is anything but.

Two films from 1999 stick out as examples of what the US underground is doing, and where it might be headed. Sam Mendes' *American Beauty*, and *The Blair Witch Project*, directed by Daniel

Myrick and Eduardo Sánchez – seemingly as unalike as two films could be – are nevertheless both contemporary speculations about the social importance of making non-mainstream movies. And they are also fixated on death, a subject which often leads to some kind of overt political or ethical judgement in a story. Since 'judgement' is usually deemed – probably correctly – to be the opposite of entertainment, this detail in itself makes these films unusual in an industry devoted to the visually spectacular and politically safe.

It was not until the 1960s that audiences and theatre-owners started to seek out what critics dubbed 'underground films', typified by the outrageous, socially transgressive work of Andy Warhol and Kenneth Anger. At the same time, independently-owned studios like American International Films (most famous for producing the underground hit *Easy Rider*, 1969) and independently-funded directors like George Romero (*Night of the Living Dead*, 1968) were releasing movies in record numbers. By the end of the 1960s, an underground film would be loosely defined as either a subversive art film or an independently-produced movie made outside the commercial demands of Hollywood. *American Beauty* and *The Blair Witch Project* fall neatly within the categories that define 'underground': *American Beauty* offers underground artistic content, and *The Blair Witch Project* was produced and distributed by independently-owned companies.

THE WHITE PERSON'S PROBLEM

In the 1980s and 1990s, the term 'underground' was often used synonymously with 'independent' or 'alternative'. The Sundance Film Festival, famous for championing indie films, popularised the notion that independent production necessarily meant there would be liberal or alternative content in a film. Obviously, as I will explain shortly in relation to *The Blair Witch Project*, this is not true. To their credit, however, independent films of this period – unlike most underground films – often tried to deal with the lives and experiences of racial minorities in a progressive way.

With this distinction in mind, I am calling *American Beauty* and *The Blair Witch Project* underground films partly because they are about social problems and issues confronted by white people. They exhibit a monocultural underground sensibility, rather than participating in the multicultural indie tradition. Like underground movies of the 1960s, cultural differences in *American Beauty* and *The Blair Witch Project* are those of class, gender and sexuality, rather than race.

American Beauty and *The Blair Witch Project* take place in regions stereotypically associated with the privileges and horrors of being white: the suburbs in *American Beauty*; and a quiet, rural Maryland town in *The Blair Witch Project*. *American Beauty*'s suburbs, often framed in strangely beautiful overhead shots of lookalike houses and carefully landscaped trees, are full of affluent white people whose posh family lives are punctuated by moments of extreme violence, tabooed sexual desire, psychological torture, madness and profound economic anxieties. While the suburbs in *American Beauty* are figuratively haunted by dysfunction, the tiny town of Burkittsville, Maryland featured in *The Blair*

Witch Project (and on the film's high-traffic website) is supposed to be literally haunted by the ghost of a woman named Elly Kedward who was accused of witchcraft in 1785 and banished from the village, then known as Blair. After her supposed death during a harsh winter, people from the village – especially children – begin to disappear, only to turn up dead and mutilated in various symbolic ways.

The Blair Witch Project's advertising billed the film as found footage which chronicles the last days of three doomed film students making a documentary about the Blair Witch. Filmed reality-TV-style with hand-held cameras, *The Blair Witch Project*'s action is propelled forward by the slowly disintegrating relationships between Josh (Joshua Leonard), Heather (Heather Donahue) and Mike (Michael Williams) after they get lost in the 'haunted' woods and begin to find weird, menacing pieces of folk art. Because we know how it will all end – the protagonists are already dead – audiences can focus entirely on how this inevitable death came about.

On a very basic level, the film seems to suggest that Heather, the director, leads her crew astray. She is constantly getting Mike and Josh lost, and in the film's now-famous 'tearful eyeballs in close-up' monologue, Heather admits that she bears responsibility for their fate. It does not take a degree in women's studies to see that this film is more than a little uncomfortable about female authority, since a woman director leads everybody into the hands of a vengeful female witch. At the very least,

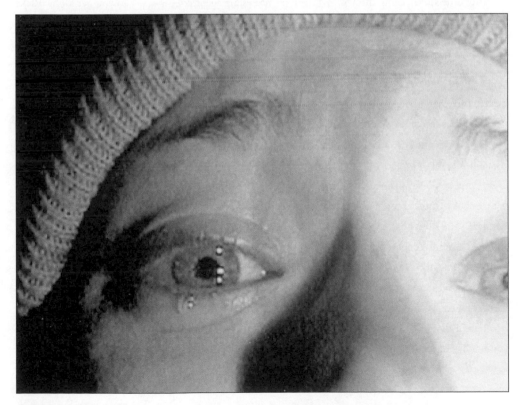

FIGURE 19 Ultimate fear in the *The Blair Witch Project*

one might say that gender difference motivates many of the film's conflicts, especially given that it is based on an invented legend about a woman accused of witchcraft.

While the characters in *The Blair Witch Project* struggle with gender, *American Beauty* is unrelentingly focused on the sexual proclivities of its characters. Our protagonist Lester Burnham (Kevin Spacey), who announces in a wry voiceover at the beginning of the film that he loves to masturbate and that he is about to die, is sexually obsessed with his daughter's surrealistically gorgeous friend Angela Hayes (Mena Suvari). His wife Carolyn (Annette Bening), whom he hates, is having an affair with an egotistical real estate agent named Buddy Kane (Peter Gallagher). And their daughter Jane (Thora Birch) is having sex with next-door neighbour Ricky Fitts (Wes Bentley), whose character is fleshed out for us in a series of scenes where his father, Colonel Fitts (Chris Cooper), beats him and discourses hotly about the evil unnaturalness of 'fags'. As the film unfolds, it becomes apparent to the audience that something about the tragically interconnected sexual lives of these people will lead to Lester's death.

FILMS WITHIN FILMS

Lester's path to death brings him into contact with Ricky, who offers Lester a pleasurable escape from a boring office party being thrown by Carolyn's real estate agent colleagues. 'Do you get high?' Ricky asks Lester, who chooses to share a joint with Ricky outside rather than endure the stifling atmosphere of 'success' that Carolyn so admires. 'Getting high' is what ultimately seems to lead Lester to quit his job in advertising, blackmail his boss into giving him a severance package and begin a second adolescence of pot smoking, listening to rock, lifting weights and pursuing sex with teenage girls.

Rather than giving us the typical Hollywood morality trip and portraying Lester's drug-induced decisions as some kind of downward spiral, *American Beauty* surprises us by representing them as a moral re-awakening. Lester's pot-dealer Ricky becomes the conscience of *American Beauty*. Using the considerable profits from his business, Ricky is able to fund his artistic obsession: videotaping everything he possibly can. As a filmmaker, Ricky is the opposite of *The Blair Witch Project*'s Heather, whose shaky camerawork and lack of direction (literally and figuratively) lead to death, ugliness and betrayal. The films that Ricky makes are about, as he says repeatedly, how beauty lurks in everyday things. He films people, dead birds and sex with equal passion; in one particularly memorable scene, he shows Jane his favourite film, a 15-minute shot of a plastic bag drifting in the wind.

What is especially remarkable about Ricky's filmmaking is that he regards his subjects with an earnest reverence and seriousness. Although *American Beauty* itself hardly suffers from a lack of irony, it is telling that one of its most sympathetic characters is portrayed as 'good' in large part because he genuinely respects the people and objects he films. The beautiful floating bag is not a snide joke. It is one of *American Beauty*'s many efforts to represent hope as something ordinary, something anyone might express without being laughed out of the room. *The Blair Witch Project*'s filmmakers are hopeless – and anything but earnest. Their Gen-X-ish ironic patter makes up most of the film's dialogue,

FIGURE 20 White heroes, white problems in *American Beauty*

and they treat the people they interview for their documentary with cynical condescension. A woman in a trailer whom they talk to about the Blair Witch causes them to giggle and roll their eyes; later, they blithely ignore warnings from two fishermen they run into on their way to the haunted forest. What they film in Burkittsville is not for beauty's sake, but rather to fulfill a class assignment in film school. Heather, Josh and Mike are also filming the haunted forest without any respect for the legends about it. Although they want to cash in on the frisson their subject will inspire in viewers, they do not believe in it themselves. Ultimately, they are making a movie in bad faith, using credulous townspeople and popular folklore for purely cynical, self-serving reasons: to generate a groovy film about a cool thing, rather than to honour the people and histories they see around them.

Despite the opposing motivations of filmmakers in *American Beauty* and *The Blair Witch Project*, the films themselves are stylistically similar. They are both works of naturalism, a term that refers to realistic stories which focus on such extremes of human behaviour that they seem practically unreal. While *American Beauty* and *The Blair Witch Project* look very different in terms of how they are photographed, both films nevertheless are careful to stick to a naturalist agenda, keeping their action within the realm of the possible and even the probable.

Certainly it is not every day that a repressed homosexual military officer murders his neighbour in a moment of sexual panic, as Colonel Fitts does Lester in *American Beauty*, but weirder things have happened. Indeed, various forms of gay bashing are fairly routine in the United States. And while *The Blair Witch Project* toys with supernatural imagery, we are also reminded at every step that there are realistic explanations for what Heather, Josh and Mike are experiencing. The menacing sounds and objects they encounter in the forest could be made by people who are 'just fucking with them', as the trio often remark to one another. And when Josh disappears, we are given ample evidence that he may have gone insane and run away. Because the camera shuts off enigmatically right before the characters die, we are left to speculate about what has really happened. No witches, ghosts or demons ever appear.

THE REAL WORLD

The importance of realism has often been at the heart of twentieth-century debates over the politics of media; the recent furor over Dutch filmmakers' 'Dogme 95' – mandating a stringently minimalist version of *cinéma vérité* as the only legitimate aesthetic for alternative film – is only the latest chapter in a complicated history of disputes over what constitutes a truly subversive artistic style.

When early twentieth-century Marxist critics Georg Lukacs and Theodor Adorno butted heads over the meaning of radical art, they spawned one of the great leftist debates in cultural studies: whether 'objective' realism or a 'subjective' modernist style were more politically progressive. Their disagreement was about whether people would be more likely to question the (oppressive) status quo if they were told stories that were realistic recreations of everyday life, or modernist meditations on our emotional and philosophical perceptions of it.

At century's end, we might couch this ongoing debate in terms of the underground. Is it 'more underground' to be realistic, or to use whatever means are at your disposal to tell your tale, no matter how fantastical it might end up seeming? What *American Beauty* and *The Blair Witch Project* teach us is that even when you take two basically realistic films in the naturalist style, they can be politically at odds with one another. Finally, if you are interested in politics, content matters more than style.

Indeed, *The Blair Witch Project*'s conservatism is part and parcel of its cynically realistic perspective on human relationships. We see our three heroes coming to believe that they are being destroyed by a supernatural force because they have such disdain for the rural and lower-class people whose legends they hope to chronicle in their documentary. At one point, when they have found yet another batch of spooky stick figures hanging from the trees, one of the characters remarks, 'Rednecks couldn't have done this', implying that Burkittsville's 'redneck' residents are simply too stupid to outwit and terrify a group of educated film students. Therefore, they are obviously dealing with the ghost of the Blair Witch. The disdain that Josh, Heather and Mike have for Burkittsville residents is matched only by their distaste for one another. In a crisis, the three of them begin to torture each other psychologically, rather than forming an alliance. Mike perniciously destroys Heather's map because he thinks she is reading it incorrectly, and the longer they remain trapped in the woods, the more the team's witty banter turns into hysterical accusations and fighting.

Led astray by a woman, tormented by what they imagine is a witch, the filmmakers in *The Blair Witch Project* are destroyed by all the things that the American Right fears most: women in positions of power, the liberal education that inspired our young documentarians and an unseeable Satanic force. We are left with the message that these filmmakers were undone not because their film disrespected the locals (who are, after all, only 'rednecks'), but because they did not have faith in the existence of an evil force that is quite literally destroying the children of America. Moreover, if we decide to go the anti-supernatural route and read the film 'realistically', then we must assume that poor, rural Americans are every bit as savage and animalistic as conservatives claim they are. Instead of getting jobs, they would rather whittle sticks all day and murder a bunch of nice, middle-class kids for fun.

While *The Blair Witch Project* occasionally breaks with realism to flesh out a fantasy of dark supernatural forces, *American Beauty* connects its characters' fantasies with agonisingly realistic sexual forces that are neither good nor bad. Like the harried filmmakers in *The Blair Witch Project*, Lester is also destroyed by a fantasy – the homosexual fantasy of his neighbour Colonel Fitts, who watches his son Ricky selling Lester drugs through a rain-soaked window and mistakenly believes that Ricky is actually giving Lester a blow job. Arriving in a weirdly zombified state at Lester's door a few minutes later, Fitts tries to kiss Lester, whom we assume is the first person privy to the secret desires Fitts has been hiding all his life. When Lester gently refuses, Fitts returns home, picks up his gun and shoots Lester in the head.

But Lester's death, as it turns out, is no tragedy. He dies with a smile on his face. Like Fitts, Lester has also finally indulged in his secret sexual fantasy – but rather than sending him into a murderous rage, his moment of sexual desublimation makes him happier than he has been in years.

When Lester acts on his potentially disturbing fantasy of sex with his daughter's friend Angela, we are given ample evidence that this 'taboo' act is precisely what both characters need. Jane and Ricky have just told the ultra-conventional Angela that they are 'freaks' and she will never understand them because she's 'so ordinary'. A weeping Angela runs downstairs and literally into Lester's arms, allowing him to confess his desire for her. During their subsequent erotic encounter, Lester's sexuality is not portrayed as monstrous, but rather a legitimate form of affection which salves Angela's hurt feelings. 'Am I ordinary?' she asks him as they kiss. 'No', he reassures her earnestly.

Implicitly, Fitts has become destructive because – unlike Lester and Angela – he associates sexual desire with horror rather than human connection. After nearly having sex, Lester and Angela demonstrate what *American Beauty* believes is the point of erotic desire when they end up having an honest conversation about their lives. Angela tells Lester about Jane falling in love with Ricky, and it is this information that inspires him to smile shortly before Fitts shoots him.

Lying in bed with Jane upstairs, Ricky hears the gunshots and is the first to find Lester's body. In a peculiarly moving scene, we watch him acknowledge the smile on Lester's dead face with his own smile. It is a moment of raw, grisly hope – even though the forces of social repression have literally murdered Lester, Ricky and Jane's self-described 'freak' romance will live on. *American Beauty* ascribes destructiveness to people who refuse to acknowledge their human urges to be sexual, and survival is for those who know how to take pleasure in things both forbidden and forgotten by status quo culture: drugs, sex and all the ordinary objects and people that populate our daily lives.

167

American Beauty's hopeful position is linked to a moral generosity and somewhat shocking honesty about human failure, as well as the ambiguity of what constitutes success. Politically, it suggests that people are destroyed by what the Right would consider admirable personal qualities: self-denial, devotion to work, sexual repression and family values. *American Beauty* indulges in its own version of *The Blair Witch Project*'s supernaturalism by featuring a narrator who is already dead (and therefore 'in heaven' or some other afterlife location), but it never uses the supernatural as an opportunity to dismiss what we have seen as possibly fantastical and therefore irrelevant to our real-life experiences.

LIFE AFTER CYNICISM

The Blair Witch Project and *American Beauty*, both slightly surreal works of naturalism, demonstrate that the underground at the close of the twentieth century may be intensely fascinated by realism, but that does not necessarily mean it is getting more politically progressive. In fact, the American underground is capable of generating independently-produced, stylistically innovative films like *The Blair Witch Project* that are politically conservative and treat the project of filmmaking itself with nothing more than clever, market-savvy cynicism.

Despite being produced and distributed by mega-media company DreamWorks SKG, *American Beauty* manages to carve out a genuinely radical and hopeful vision of both American culture and the role filmmaking might play in it. While *American Beauty* is saturated with typical Hollywood flourishes – lavish production values, high-wattage stars, achingly beautiful main characters and a white, middle-class setting – the film nevertheless comes down on the side of 'freaks', the people whose (filmed) vision of status quo America recognises that so-called deviance, lawbreaking and perversion are simply ugly labels for things that might in fact be beautiful if we could only look at them without bias. Ricky's perspective as a filmmaker is offered as one possible way to 'look closer' at social issues most people would prefer to dismiss. What separates *The Blair Witch Project* from *American Beauty*, in the end, is its realistic depiction of hope. *The Blair Witch Project* might be a hopeful sign for a flagging independent film scene, in that it has truly been a word-of-mouth sensation, but its content is just a really riveting update on the same old horror movie fears about gender, Satan and rural culture.

American Beauty suggests that we might be seeing a new trend in underground film toward social criticism which does not forget to leave some ideals standing. To the Gen-Xers who are gradually taking over our mass media, it will sound exceptionally cheesy for me to say this, but *American Beauty* makes us remember that love and the free expression of sexual desire are socially constructive forces. Everything in the world does not necessarily need to be treated with knee-jerk cynicism. Perhaps the next century will inaugurate a new kind of underground film that will not be afraid to find out what comes after irony.

This essay originally appeared in *Bad Subjects*, 46, December 1999.

CHAPTER 14
PHANTOM MENACE: KILLER FANS, CONSUMER ACTIVISM AND DIGITAL FILMMAKERS

Sara Gwenllian Jones

Since the early 1970s, film and television fans have made short films of their own, evolving a form of underground or 'guerrilla' filmmaking that draws its inspiration, characters, settings and themes from films such as *Star Wars* (1977) or television series such as *The Prisoner*, *Star Trek* or *Xena: Warrior Princess*. Sometimes these fan films involve scripted performances; more often, they consist of extracts from a source text which are re-edited to form new narratives. They are shown at private gatherings, conventions and, more commonly these days, are available online for download. Such texts occupy a liminal area between production and consumption, industry and audience; they disrupt culturally inscribed expectations about the antagonistic relation between, and mutual exclusivity of, the commercial mainstream and the underground.

In the writings of scholars such as Henry Jenkins and Constance Penley, derivative fan-produced texts are discussed as interpretive and creative reclamations of beloved cultural texts and of cultural production from the tyranny of the culture industry (which, crucially here, profits from but does not *care* about its products). But such notions of creative fan practices as modes of heroic antagonism are, I will argue, largely a construct of scholarship. As most fan websites demonstrate, fans knowingly and enthusiastically support the culture industry that produces their beloved objects. As producers of their own creative texts, fans demonstrate not the status of the radical outsider but rather a sense of involvement that refuses any absolute distinction between commercial culture and the culture of everyday social experience. Fan productions, I suggest, are less a remedy for the failings of official 'cult' culture than a reflection of the very basis of its appeal; they are neither 'resistant' nor 'oppositional' but integral to commercial culture's operations and emblematic of a commercially inflected culture of interactivity.

The flawed, unforeclosed and fantastical texts beloved of fans appeal precisely *because* they are flawed, unforeclosed and fantastical; their explicitly unfinished nature offers fans broad scope for creative intervention. Such interventions may be made for their own sake – for the sheer pleasure of creation – but they are usually also intended for an audience. In some instances, fan producers have even more pragmatic ambitions; the films and other cultural texts they produce are not creative *responses* to any official text but appropriations of its imaginary as inspiration and raw material for projects intended to catapult the fan producer into a Hollywood career. The goal is professional, mainstream filmmaking; the hijacked cult fiction is simply a resource. In this chapter, I investigate how media and scholarly constructions of fans as 'deviant' and 'resistant' consumers function to assert, police and uphold opposed categories of official and unofficial culture, production and consumption, the mainstream and the underground. Fan culture, I will argue, is a liminal phenomenon that confounds the very boundaries that define it and serves as a reminder that *not*-Hollywood is not the same thing as *contra*-Hollywood.

PREDATION

> There is definitely a possibility that I will be killed in my attempt to get Reagan. It is for this very reason that I am writing this letter now…
> This letter is being written only an hour before I leave for the Hilton hotel. Jodie, I'm asking you to please look into your heart and at least give [me] the chance, with this historical deed, to gain your love and respect.
> I love you forever.
>
> John W. Hinckley[1]

When John Hinckley shot and wounded Ronald Reagan in 1981, the incident looked at first like a political assassination attempt. But the subsequent investigation and trial revealed neither a disaffected voter nor a professional assassin; instead, the would-be killer was a disturbed young man acting out a violent fantasy built around the 1976 film *Taxi Driver*. Obsessed with actress Jodie Foster, Hinckley had been stalking her for some time before he finally tried to gain her attention and love by enacting his own version of *Taxi Driver*'s fictional Travis Bickle's (Robert De Niro) attempt to kill a senator.

At Hinckley's trial, his defense counsel's closing argument described his actions as 'those of a totally irrational individual, driven and motivated by his own world which he created for himself, locked in his own mind, without any opportunity to have any test of those ideas from the real world because of his total isolation.'[2] In the news reports published at the time, Hinckley was represented as the epitome of the deranged loner obsessed with celebrity and desperate to turn his dark fantasies into reality. He was a Killer Fan.

The murders of American television actress Rebecca Schaeffer and ex-Beatle John Lennon by stalkers, the stabbing of tennis player Monica Seles by a deranged supporter of Steffi Graf, the mass suicide of members of the heavily *Star Trek*-influenced Heaven's Gate cult and countless similar – though usually less deadly – incidents have all been, in Henry Jenkins' words, 'explained according to a stereotypical conception of the fan as emotionally unstable, socially maladjusted, and dangerously out of sync with reality.'[3] Such events are as rare as they are extreme but, predictably, they account for almost every occasion where fandom makes the news headlines, with the effect that whenever fandom enters the public domain it seems to be in connection with madness and violence. The vocabulary and conventions used in such reports repeatedly outline a personality profile that blurs together social inadequacy, delusional psychosis and fandom, as if they were equally weighted aspects of a single psychopathology. In this paranoid, media-constructed world-view, fans are always loners and losers, trapped in a perpetual adolescence, emotionally and mentally volatile, incapable of distinguishing between fiction and actuality. They are constructed as fantasists, fanatics, obsessives, erotomaniacs, deluded individuals reacting violently against a world which refuses to conform to their fantasies. Instead of describing mentally disturbed individuals whose veering insanity has settled upon a particular celebrity or cultural text, media accounts imply 'that there is a thin line between "normal" and excessive fandom'[4] by continually recycling a stereotype of the fan whose devotion has erupted into an inevitable *telos* of violent enactment. Murderous delusion ceases to be the affliction of a particular individual and instead becomes both symptom and signifier of fandom itself, both cause and effect of fans' apparently excessive and deviant responses to cultural objects.

The sinister stereotype of the delusional predatory fan reflects not only the details of specific, isolated cases but also a wider uneasiness about fandom's unruly relation to the boundaries that regulate popular cultural consumption. Like the media scares around films such as *Child's Play* (1988) and *Natural Born Killers* (1994), which identified 'copycat crimes' as evidence of cinema's occult power over vulnerable audience members, accounts of celebrity-stalkers, killers fans and mimetic crimes reflect anxieties about the uncontrollable and unpredictable consequences of the media messages that saturate the cultural sphere. In this light, media fans seem wilfully to disregard the unwritten rules that regulate cultural consumption, engaging in aberrant practices that bespeak an irrational and excessive engagement with and investment in devalued cultural objects such as celebrities, pop music, television series, films and 'trash' genres such as science fiction, fantasy and horror.

Fandom is here interpreted as an over-attachment to the childish world of play and a refusal of fully committed participation in the 'proper' and 'serious' adult world of responsibility, pragmatism and economic productivity. As Jenkins observes:

> Whether viewed as a religious fanatic, a psychopathic killer, a neurotic fantasist, or a lust-crazed groupie, the fan remains a 'fanatic' or false worshipper, whose interests are fundamentally alien to the realm of 'normal' cultural experience and whose mentality is dangerously out of touch with reality.[5]

Not content simply to passively consume what commercial culture provides, fans make unauthorised and 'inappropriate' uses of cultural texts, reading them in ways that seem alien to non-fans and threatening to a culture industry that has a vested interest in controlling the meanings that consumers make of its products. Fans combine conspicuous, enthusiastic consumption of official texts and spin-offs with their own creative and interpretive practices. Fans are viewers who do not merely watch films or television programmes but also write fan fiction and cultural criticism, produce fan art, scratch videos, websites and so on, and who seek out other fans with whom to share their enthusiasm. Such activities violate culturally constructed and carefully policed distinctions between make-believe and reality, play and work, childhood and adulthood. Fans are distanced from 'ordinary' consumers because their modes of consumption are considered excessive. Fan-producers do not qualify as 'genuine' artists or auteurs because their creativity is regarded as derivative, amateur and non-profit-making. No matter how great fans' expertise, they are not considered aficionados because their specialised knowledge accrues to demeaned popular cultural objects rather than to the valued high culture of opera, literature or art. Fan critics are not considered scholars because their subject matter is deemed trivial, their expertise subjective rather than critical and their knowledge and analyses valueless without the validation of formal training and a formal context. Fans dedicate their time, energy and resources to activities that bring no financial return, no tangible outcomes or benefits, but are rather an end in themselves.

There is also a wider narrative of anxiety at play here that reflects a growing uneasiness about the ubiquity and ungovernability of communications technologies. As digital technologies increasingly put the tools of production and information-access into the hands of the public at large, so come spectral and sinister forces to haunt the outer reaches of commercial and governmental control – the shadowy high-tech ranks of cyberstalkers, hackers, crackers and hacktivists, cyberterrorists and virus-writers. While the objectives and practices of these groups differ, all apparently possess both an illicit expertise and an agenda that is neither contained nor sanctioned by the ordinary channels of commerce or government. Individuals and groups that make 'unauthorised' uses of technologies, cultural texts and information occupy a volatile cultural space. They exhibit a mastery of technologies and information whilst remaining mobile and unaccountable. Fans also merit a place in this catalogue of liminal and contrary interventionist subcultures which disregard cultural and legal prescriptions that dictate and police who should make use of what resources, how and for what purposes.

The liminality of fandom renders it conceptually transparent and uncertain, its epistemological evasiveness a vehicle for fearful and/or political fantasies projected upon it from without. Its liminality is seductive, a quicksilver play of possibilities allied to the subversive glamour of transgression. But, like all transgressive phenomena, its endless deferral of final meanings renders it susceptible to meanings imposed upon it from without. Its ambiguities attract interpretations dedicated to categorisation; it must be diagnosed, fixed, brought into certain relation to the categories it confounds. It must be contained within the formal binaric structures that organise and fix hierarchies of production and consumption.

SEDITION

The 1990s saw the publication of a number of studies of fan cultures by scholars such as Penley and Jenkins, whose analyses explicitly reject notions of fandom as psychopathology and instead emphasise and celebrate its unruly creativity. Drawing upon wider associations of fandom with unauthorised, illicit engagements with popular cultural texts, these writers reconstruct the 'deviant' fan as a maverick folk hero whose creative and interpretive interventions constitute strategies of resistance against capitalism's colonisation of and control over popular culture. Penley draws upon de Certeau's 'politics of the everyday' to argue that the fan practices of interpretation and creative intervention are 'tactics' which 'are not designed primarily to help users take over the system but to seize every opportunity to turn to their own ends forces that systematically exclude or marginalize them.'[6] Fandom retains something of the edginess and danger attributed to it by the 'deranged fan' model, on;y here its 'violence' is not directed towards the bodies of celebrities but rather is an activism directed at the authority, if not the systems, of commercial producers and texts. In order for this formula to work, fans must be positioned outside the gates of official culture, where they are at once disempowered and rebellious subjects. The twin themes of agency and powerlessness run throughout Jenkins' *Textual Poachers*:

> Fandom constitutes a base for consumer activism. Fans are viewers who speak back to the networks and the producers, who assert their right to make judgments and to express opinions about the development of favorite programs. ... Fandom originates, in part at least, as a response to the relative powerlessness of the consumer in relation to powerful institutions of cultural production and circulation.[7]

Fans remain 'losers', trapped at the wrong end of a massive power differential; but here they are at least *valiant* losers, doomed Davids firing their slingshot at an imperturbable Goliath. There is an old

173

mythology at work here, a romantic re-casting of the fan as heroic underdog engaged in pitched battle with more powerful enemies. This story of fandom is part Beowulf, part Class War.

Just as the work of Penley, Jenkins, *et al.* retains a sense of fandom as 'deviance' by setting fandom apart from 'legitimate' modes of consumption (i.e. those sanctioned by a broader cultural consensus about how texts are to be received and used), so too does it reassert boundaries between fandom and the culture industry, consumers and producers, between amateur enthusiasts and the slick machinery of professional commercial production, readers and unassailable texts. It is a widely accepted tenet of cultural studies that category boundaries are artificial constructs that dissolve under scrutiny, false and rigid structures inscribed upon continuums in order to fix hierarchies and inhibit movement across them. But in 'resistant' models of fandom, these boundaries and categories are restored in order to project a radical politics of opposition onto fandom. Fans, according to this model, cannot *interact* with fictions generated and circulated by the culture industry. Rather, they must *react* to texts already constituted and fixed in their final form, always exterior to the objects with which they seek intimate connection, able to participate in cultural production by 'scribbling in the margins' of the text but not to affect its substance since the text is always already complete in itself before it enters the public domain. It may be 'poached' or 'scavenged' from only after the fact, its constituent elements appropriated as the raw materials for fans' own visions, but the text itself remains discrete and inviolable. It must remain intact if is to be opposed; resistance requires an inflexible object to push against.

John Fiske notes a contradiction at the heart of 'resistant' models of fandom:

> Fandom … is a peculiar mix of cultural determinations. On the one hand, it is an intensification of popular culture which is formed outside and often against official culture, on the other it expropriates and reworks certain values and characteristics of that official culture to which it is opposed.[8]

Fandom is here constituted as a collision of the ideological meanings ascribed to it. Ascriptions of 'resistant' or 'oppositional' motives to fans serve to snatch fandom back from its boundary-confounding liminality, harnessing it to a politics that prefers subversion to collusion. The object is to instate fandom as a species of counterculture, with fandom clearly positioned as the desirable 'other' set against the bad object of commercial cultural production.

PHANTOM MENACES AND DIGITAL CINEMA

There's a city in the clouds
Where they're keeping my crew.
A Jedi's gotta do what a Jedi's gotta do.

Darth Vader, I'm coming for you.　　　*Star Warz Gangsta Rap* (2000)[9]

Fans have always produced creative and critical texts of their own. Penley describes this phenomenon in terms of an active, dynamic folk culture that refuses a passive relation to commercial culture and goes beyond a politics of interpretation. Making a case study of *Star Trek* 'slash fiction' (i.e. fan fiction that proposes an erotic relationship between two characters of the same sex, taking its name from the slash in 'Kirk/Spock' or 'K/S' erotica), she argues that fans

> are not just reading, viewing or consuming in tactical ways that offer moments of resistance or pleasure while watching TV, scanning the tabloids, or selecting from the supermarket shelves. … They are producing not just intermittent, cobbled-together acts, but real products (albeit ones taking off from already-existing heterogeneous elements) – zines, novels, artwork, videos – that (admiringly) mimic and mock those of the industry they are 'borrowing' from while offering pleasures found lacking in the original products.[10]

Penley's suggestion that slashers respond to a 'lack' in the original products, answering it with products of their own, is a telling one. As in other studies of fan cultures, fan productions are interpreted entirely in terms of fandom; they are creative *responses* that owe their genesis solely to their creators' devotion to the source text. Official cultural products remain at the heart of this 'shadow cultural economy',[11] which evolves around, draws upon and responds to them. However, as I will suggest below, it is equally possible to argue that fan productions are not an attempt to address failings and 'lacks' in official texts but rather are a reflection of the *possibilities* presented by them.

The nature, quality and dissemination of fan-produced texts have depended, in large part, upon the technologies of production and systems of distribution available to their creators. In *Textual Poachers*, Henry Jenkins describes how, in pre-Internet days, print copies of fan fiction and fanzines were distributed among fans by ordinary mail. Penley observes how, at one time, an anti-professional fan ethos upheld an ideal of amateurism: 'the strong pull towards "professionalism" is described by fans in terms of getting "hooked" or "contaminated" by the writing and editing process.'[12] But times and technologies change. Most fan-producers use the best of whatever equipment is available to them in order to create the most polished products they can. The arrival of affordable VCRs, portable video cameras and basic home editing suites allowed fans to tape, re-edit and dub films and television series. Video technologies proved both cheaper and far easier to use than the old Super-8 film cameras that preceded them as domestic production tools. From the outset, 'scratch' videos (in which clips are edited together to form a new mini-narrative, essay or themed compilation over which, usually, a music soundtrack is dubbed) have been the most common form of fan 'film' production. These were screened at conventions and other gatherings and copies sent out, usually at cost price, to fans who requested them. For obvious reasons, they achieved only very limited circulation.

For Fiske, the key differences between official culture and the 'shadow cultural economy of fandom' are

> economic rather than ones of competence, for fans do not write or produce their texts for money. ... There is also a difference in circulation; because fan texts are not produced for profit, they do not need to be mass-marketed, so unlike official culture, fan culture makes no attempt to circulate its texts outside its own community. They are 'narrowcast', not broadcast, texts.[13]

The two major distinctions identified by Fiske are, then, the amateurism of fans versus the profit-making imperative of the culture industry, and the means and breadth of their circulation and distribution. Once again, the liminality of fandom is contained through the imposition of binaries (amateur versus profit-making, narrowcast versus broadcast) that uphold ideologically inflected and clear-cut oppositional distinctions between different zones of cultural production.

Digital technologies represent a quantum leap in the domestication and democratisation of the means of production and distribution. For a relatively tiny amount of money, anyone can potentially become both producer and distributor of their own films. Equipped with a reasonably good PC, a video card, some editing software and a basic level of expertise, fans can upload official films or television series from an ordinary VCR and digitally rework them to produce an original variation on the source material. More sophisticated creations – involving animation, or special effects or scripted, live-action filmmaking – require only some additional software or a digital video camera. Of equal consequence are the distribution and promotion possibilities presented by the Web. Where once fan-produced films reached only a tiny audience of other fans, the Web and streaming technologies such as Realplayer and Quicktime now allow fan-producers to archive their films on websites where they can be accessed and downloaded by anyone. Digital technologies have immeasurably increased the size of the audiences for such films. While these audiences are still nowhere near the hundreds of millions who watch blockbuster Hollywood films or syndicated television series, they are nevertheless substantial, as are their implications for clear-cut binaric distinctions between 'producers' and 'consumers'.

Successful crossovers from fan to professional production are of course rare, but by no means unheard of. Alan McKee describes how a number of fans of the British cult television series *Doctor Who* went on to write the official series' novels, edit the official magazine, script episodes and, in one case, even produce the series.[14] Melissa Good, a popular author of *Xena: Warrior Princess* fan fiction, has achieved success on a number of levels. Her 'über-*Xena*' novel *Tropical Storm* has been published and film rights purchased by a production company. ('Über' fan fiction draws inspiration from 'official' texts but radically transforms their fictions, changing characters' names and identities, relocating them to different times and places and engaging them in original storylines.) In 1999,

Good was contracted by Renaissance Pictures to script three episodes of *Xena: Warrior Princess*. She now works full-time as a professional television scriptwriter in Hollywood. Rap artist Bentframe's *Star Warz Gangsta Rap*, for which Allergic to Life Productions made an animated music video, attracts thousands of visitors to his MP3 site, earning him revenue both from the number of downloads – for each of which Bentframe earns a small MP3 royalty – and through sales of CDs of his music advertised on the site.

Troops (1998) is a *Cops*-style *Star Wars* spoof which documents an ordinary evening on the Tattooine beat for Imperial Stormtroopers, complete with droid-stealing Jawas and a domestic dispute involving a young runaway named Luke.[15] Created by cel-animation archivist Kevin Rubio for $1,200, *Troops* proved a massive hit when *Star Wars* fan website theforce.net archived it for download. Drawing upon characters, settings and events from the *Star Wars* films, *Troops* is precisely the sort of text that gets described as a creative reworking of a beloved cult object: a *fan* film, a creative engagement born of love and shared with other fans. However, Rubio himself reveals a rather different and more worldly motive: 'It was designed to get us attention and to get us some work.'[16] In Rubio's case, the bid for professional recognition paid off:

> George Lucas, the Jedi Master himself, is a fan. Mark Hamill called to set up a personal screening with Rubio . ... After *Troops* was posted to the Star Wars fan page www.theforce. net, traffic to the site increased by 500 per cent. All of which explains why three talent agencies and six production companies, including DreamWorks, have called to set up meetings with Rubio. 'It's brilliant for the money,' says Roy Lee, director of development for the production house Alphaville (Michael). 'If he could do this with $1,200, what could he do for a million?'[17]

Matthew Ward, the 21-year-old writer/director of another *Star Wars*-inspired short film, presents a similar case. Ward's *Death of a Jedi* (1998) was made for an Introduction to Film and Video class he took at college.[18] Its success won Ward an internship with Industrial Light and Magic (an affiliate of Lucasfilm). Tellingly, Ward explains his film not in terms of his *Star Wars* fandom but in terms of his love of filmmaking:

> *Death of a Jedi* wasn't made to make a statement about film-work but instead to show how a couple of guys could tell a story. ... After you've worked so hard creating the idea, placing the actors, shooting the scene, editing, post, etc ... seeing the piece in its final state, as you once imagined it, to see the idea come to life ... that's the most gratifying part of all of it for me.[19]

To those motivated to see it, and who make a point of looking at it from particular angles and in the right light, these short films may be interpreted as instances of guerrilla cinema, constructed from the illicit booty of smash-and-grab tactics that raid popular culture for resources. But such interpretations, which seek to valorise fandom as a species of counterculture, emphasise fan creativity as acting both through and *against* official culture and constituting an alternative to it. They uphold notions of official and unofficial, insiders and outsiders, 'them' (the producers) and 'us' (the consumers), the exploiters and the exploited, commercial culture and folk culture. Such binaries obligingly position capitalism as something 'they' (the producers) do; they attribute motives of cynical profiteering to Hollywood and of pure love to fans, as if there could be no middle ground, no interactivity and no movement or affinity between the realms of commercial and underground production.

COMPLICATIONS: THE CONTINUED UNRULINESS OF FANS

How one reads the status of Rubio, Ward and their *Star Wars*-inspired films depends upon how much weight one attributes to their fandom and how much to their filmmaking. Are these primarily fans who have made derivative films and crossed over into the mainstream, or are they rather aspiring filmmakers whose fandom suggested the subject matter of their films and the direction of their careers? It hardly needs to be said that most of the 'creative talent' working in the culture industry consists of people who chose their careers because they had a love of film or television – because they were, in some sense, 'fans'.

Producers who operate outside the mainstream of commercial culture – whether they be fans, independent filmmakers or any other of the myriad practitioners and creators commonly described as 'alternative' or 'underground' – frequently become the objects of romantic valorisations by scholars, who heroise and celebrate them as Robin Hood figures whose practices and works rescue popular culture from the greasy grip of capitalist enterprise and restore it to 'ordinary people'. It is no surprise that some of the creators of so-called 'alternative' cultural objects choose to see themselves in the same flattering romantic light, as cultural outlaws, rebels, freedom-fighters, agents of 'underground' and 'resistance' movements, as if making a low-budget film were somehow equivalent to smuggling Jews out of Nazi-occupied France. Online fans, in particular, are not disempowered radical outsiders but – like Net users in general – a demographic that is predominantly white, middle-class, technologically literate and educated to degree level or above.[20] They represent a population group that is neither capitalism's detritus nor its *bête noir* but rather its bedrock.

One question that emerges from cultural studies' conflation of disparate concepts, interpretations, ideologies and practices under the banner of 'fandom' is whether the term 'fandom' itself remains of any use. What, exactly, is described by a term that equally embraces crazed celebrity-stalkers, insatiable consumers, obsessive collectors of trivia and merchandise, cultural dupes, textual poachers, nerds, resistant readers and consumer activists? What use is it to talk about 'fan practices' when this concept accommodates a catalogue of 'activities' as diverse as cultural criticism, web design, story-telling, socialising, shopping, quasi-religious worship, filmmaking, stalking and murder?

Ien Ang writes of

> the fleeting and dispersed tactics by which consumers, while confined by the range of offerings provided by the industry, surreptitiously seize moments to transform these offerings into 'opportunities' of their own, making 'watching television', embedded as it is in the context of everyday life, not only into a multiple and heterogenous cultural practice, but also, more fundamentally, into a mobile, indefinite, and ultimately ambiguous one, which is beyond prediction and measurement.[21]

The problems that Ang identifies in concepts such as 'the television audience' and 'watching television' extend to the production and consumption of popular culture as a whole. Our relation to commercial culture is neither monolithic nor binaric but complex, fluid and contradictory. Commercial culture is not exterior to our lives but woven into their fabric in countless ways; the strategies we use to negotiate its omnipresent and multifarious influences are not inherently strategies of resistance, which require us to take an impossible position outside our culture-saturated realities, but those of interactivity and informed involvement.

This is not to suggest that different zones of cultural production do not exist, or that 'power' is not unevenly distributed among them. But 'culture' is volatile and dynamic in ways that confound the stasis of the binary models that structure so much of our understanding of it, and which wishfully identify the 'phantom menaces' of resistance movements, countercultures and undergrounds wherever cultural production occurs outside the mainstream. As stated in the introduction to this chapter, not-Hollywood is not the same thing as *contra*-Hollywood.

CHAPTER 15

FILM CO-OPS: OLD SOLDIERS FROM THE SIXTIES STILL STANDING IN BATTLE AGAINST HOLLYWOOD COMMERCIALISM

Jack Stevenson

UNDERGROUND MANIFESTOS

Some revolutions seem to be eternal, with omnipotent protectors of the status quo never quite able to defeat the out-gunned rebel hordes, the true believers who live off the land and want to turn the whole system upside down. The battle waged by lone, independent filmmakers against the hegemonic power of Hollywood is one such battle. It pits Davey against Goliath, and it is a fight for the very soul of cinema.

Although the battlefield, in a technical and to some degree aesthetic sense, has changed over the years, the struggle to define film as a medium of personal expression instead of corporate claptrap continues to this day. The proliferation of 'underground film festivals' in various American cities (New York, Chicago, Los Angeles, Boston, Honolulu, et cetera), which began in the mid-1990s, is one such indication of the continuing need for opposition viewpoints, as is the continued viability of established independent festivals like Ann Arbor and Olympia. This spirit of independence is also manifest by the existence of gay and lesbian festivals outside the traditional bastions of San Francisco and New York, and by the establishment of foreign movements such as Dogme 95.

But the first shot in this holy war was fired across Hollywood's bow over forty years ago, on 28 September 1960, when 23 independent filmmakers – among them Peter Bogdanovich and Emile de Antonio – gathered in New York to declare the formation of the New American Cinema group. They called the masses to arms with an angry nine-point manifesto published in *Film Culture* magazine in the summer of 1961, which declared 'the official cinema' to be dead: 'We don't want false, polished, slick films – we prefer them rough, unpolished, but alive: we don't want rosy films – we want them the colour of blood.'

Point five took the following position:

> We will take a stand against the present distribution-exhibition policies. There is something decidedly wrong with the whole system of film exhibition; it is time to blow the whole thing up. It's not the audience that prevents films like *Shadows* or *Come Back, Africa* from being seen, but the distributors and theatre owners. It is a sad fact that our films have to open in London, Paris, or Tokyo before they can reach our own theaters.[1]

The good fight was on. Several theatres had pledged to exhibit their films and co-operation was also expected from The American Federation of Film Societies. The following year, The Filmmakers' Co-operative was established by the group on Park Avenue South. It was an organisation run by and for filmmakers and it was designed to distribute their films in a 'non-commercial' manner. The Co-op soon took on a spiritual as well as a physical dimension and became a place where energies, ideas and visions were exchanged. As Paul Arthur, filmmaker and President of The Board of Directors for the Co-op in 1989, recalled:

> The Co-op office was an ad-hoc dormitory for visiting artists. It functioned as the editorial space for *Film Culture* magazine. In a small back room, Gregory Markopoulos and Jonas Mekas, among others, edited their work. Itinerant political groups often found a safe haven for meetings. After The New York City police department shut down screenings at The Filmmaker's Showcase, the Co-op took over the 'unlicensed projection' of new work. Part storage depot, part urban guerrilla headquarters, it was a quintessentially Sixties American dwelling.[2]

It was an age in America when movies still needed to be licensed and censorship was rampant. Shows could be raided by the police, prints seized and theatre staff hauled off to jail. Films were routinely confiscated at the border by US Customs agents. It was a time when a 16mm camera was potentially considered to be a weapon of provocation and subversion. In this setting, the Co-op functioned as a genuine liberation movement. Their actions on occasion took the form of pitched street battles, their members risked jail and their rhetoric was impassioned. They were not rebelling against the kind of entrenched social and political orders that people rebelled against in Europe, but rather were striking out at the omnipresent sense of conformity and complacency that was uniquely American. They were taking aim at the false values fabricated by the corporate mass media which dominated popular culture and which suppressed individual expression through commercial and legal mechanisms. That mass media also, of course, included the film industry.

In short, the Filmmaker's Co-operative put the politics of the New American Cinema group into a functional form. Any filmmaker wishing to join did so simply by giving a print of his or her film to the Co-operative along with a synopsis which they wrote or otherwise supplied. They set their own rental prices and received 60 per cent of all income, with 40 per cent going to support the operation of the Co-op. No rights were purchased or assigned. It was a non-contractual agreement, and filmmakers were also encouraged to seek out additional avenues of distribution for their work with the catalogue itself listing many of these alternative sources of distribution.

The Co-op sought to put the democratic, egalitarian ideals of a true collective into practice in the normally aggressively commercial realm of film distribution. It was an approach that fit the times, since many of the avant-garde filmmakers of the day had come from other arts and their motivation was to explore the creative process on film, not to create a marketable product or launch their careers. Some of the films they made were in any case unmarketable to general audiences because they were, by orthodox standards, fairly incomprehensible. Many were experimental films. Others contained pornographic content. Furthermore, most of them were short films made on very low budgets, and it has always been tough to get short films screened in commercial theaters.

There was no official ideological slant to the Co-operative. While in practice it represented the works of the 'underground' movement, in theory any type of film could be given life at the Co-op. There were no 'gatekeepers' – nobody passed personal judgement on a film. The stance was adamantly non-selective. The Co-op also espoused non-promotion: no specific film was ever promoted over another, and they were listed in the catalogue in alphabetical order. Only the organisation of the Co-op as a whole could be promoted. No competition, no promotion and no value placed on profit: Co-ops proudly presented themselves as the antithesis of the commercial film industry.

The New York Filmmaker's Co-operative served as an inspiration and basic model for the film co-op movement that spread across America and Europe through the 1960s. It gave exposure to some very obscure films and filmmakers who were never able or never wanted to make a career out of it. But it also gave a start to filmmakers who would go on to become better known. John Waters had films in the Co-op until he became a commercially viable commodity and withdrew them, turning them over to New Line Cinema to distribute. Paul Bartel and Paul Morrissey still have films from the early 1960s on deposit at the Co-op.

OTHER UNDERGROUND MODELS

In 1963, Bruce Baillie and a loose-knit group of fellow filmmakers founded Canyon Cinema in Berkeley, California. They staged free public screenings and edited the *Canyon Cinema News*. In 1966, Canyon moved to San Francisco and set up their own distribution on the co-op model. The London Filmmakers Co-op was also launched in 1966. Both were based on the New York Co-op formula, but each had its own distinct personality.

Malcolm Le Grice, a founding member of the Arts Laboratory Group, wrote in 1986 that:

> The London Filmmakers' Co-op drew heavily on the precedent of The Filmmaker's Co-operative in New York, but, through its merger with The Arts Laboratory Group, took on a much wider set of objectives. Though it was not fully appreciated at the time, even by those of us most involved, as well as having more ambitious aims, it always had a more strongly developed set of social and political objectives than had motivated the New York Co-op.[3]

The Arts Lab, founded in 1966 by Jim Haynes, was a multi-purpose exhibition venue in Covent Garden where performances, film screenings, readings and 'happenings' took place. It served as a social axis for the two groups, and inspired the foundation of similar activist venues throughout Britain.

Back in San Francisco, Canyon was to pass through various stages of existence in different locations, but it always manifested the flamboyance and rebelliousness of The Bay Area. At one point in the early 1970s, a cadre associated with Canyon stormed the projection booth at The Cinematheque in The San Francisco Art Institute, 'occupying' it for days in an attempt to get more local films shown there. This group later formed The No-Nothing Cinema, a rough-hewn but technically fine venue in the China Basin neighbourhood. Out in the courtyard there was a basketball hoop and a barbecue pit, and in adjacent rooms one of the founders, Rock Ross, ran a film-titling lab. The cinema was eventually demolished to make way for the construction of a baseball stadium but recently re-emerged as the 'New Nothing Cinema' in a new location in the South-of-Market district. The No-Nothing did for exhibition what Canyon did for distribution: any person could theoretically screen any film in a non-commercial context (no admission was allowed to be charged). They were both part-and-parcel of the very activist San Francisco scene, which even today remains one of the most vital in the country.

Other Co-op distribution organisations were formed in Paris, Vienna, Hamburg, Rome, Amsterdam, Toronto (co-founded by a young David Cronenberg) and elsewhere. But in spite of all the noble talk about 'non-promotion' and 'non-selection', there were fundamental problems with this approach. Curious potential exhibitors had few clues as to what most of these films were like – films that in many cases really needed to be contextualised beyond the often-cryptic descriptions provided by the filmmakers themselves. And when presented with a huge catalogue listing thousands of films, choice by any definition became necessary. To discourage promotion of films seemed anti-movie and certainly anti-American, and appeared to hamper the most fundamental aims of the co-ops: to give films life.

The Filmmakers' Co-operative in New York was the most rigid about non-promotion, and did not even print photos in its main catalogue, apparently in the belief that doing so would give certain films an edge. (Their 1993 and 1996 catalogue supplements, however, are full of pictures.) Length of film descriptions depended on whether a filmmaker was an 'active' member of the Co-op, and if a person left a film on deposit but no longer communicated (or contributed financially before a printing), only the title of the film was listed.

Co-ops are by nature passive rather than active distributors, and this leads to complaints from some filmmakers who argue that the places are just dead storage. Predictably, the famous underground film titles get rented a great deal more than the others. Canyon Cinema, for its part, publishes photos in its catalogue, encourages filmmakers to package their shorts into more bookable feature-length theme shows and has presented public screenings of its films sporadically over the years – all things that involve selection.

The London Filmmakers Co-op addressed the issue head-on at a meeting in 1989, and with rare accord voted to amend their non-promotion clause to 'Promotion combined with active open access'. This meant, according to Tony Warcus, who headed the LFMC-distribution from 1989–1992, 'encouraging filmmakers to assist LFMC distribution by providing preview videos, stills, and reviews of their work'.[4] In other words, ideally, *all* films should be promoted and the spirit of equality would be preserved, at least in theory.

The issue of 'non selection' is more relevant today than ever amid predictions that soon all film will be transferred to and viewed on digital mediums, and that celluloid will cease to exist. But which films will be put on tape or disc and which will be passed by? Who will judge what is worth preserving, and, by extension, what should be left to perish? Who will the new gatekeepers be? Most people would not want someone else deciding for them what they should watch and it seems to go without saying that every individual should have the freedom and possibility to search out, to explore and to discover. In this respect, the philosophy of non-selection – or rather, selection by the individual – seems visionary rather than dogmatic.

AN UNDERGROUND UNDONE: NEW CHALLENGES TO EXHIBITION

Despite efforts to stay modern, changing times have effected all three co-ops in very different ways. For instance, in the mid-1990s, America's politically driven controversy over public arts funding caught up with Canyon, and it had its NEA (National Endowment of the Arts) grant cut off over the alleged obscenity of one of the films it distributed. But a bigger threat to Canyon's existence was the skyrocketing value of San Francisco real estate. Indeed, their impressive new catalogue comes complete with a letter explaining that 'due to the rising costs of doing business in the San Francisco Bay Area, the rental fees on many films listed in the Canyon Cinema catalogue 2000 have risen in price.' Yet they seem set to remain in their current location, an industrial loft space on 3rd Street by the inner harbour, for the foreseeable future.

The Filmmaker's Co-operative until recently dwelt in a somewhat decrepit, reconverted residential building at 33rd Street and Lexington Avenue in Manhattan, but lost its lease for that site, and in January 2001 relocated downtown to the P.S. (Public School) 1 Clock-tower lofts. Prior to that, on 15 December 2000, a benefit had been held at The Millennium screening space on the Lower East Side to help raise funds for the Co-op's move. New acquisitions to the Co-op's archive were screened and film equipment was raffled off. M. M. Serra, who has managed the Co-op for many years, says she actually likes the new site better, but it was not a voluntary move and the financial health of the Co-op remains as fragile as ever.

Fragile was an apt word to describe the very state of their existence on 11 September 2001, when the World Trade Center towers collapsed only blocks away. While not directly damaged, the Co-op found itself without fax, phone or e-mail and in a no-go zone for weeks. Today it is more or less back to normal as Serra and several interns once again take orders, send out films, and check, clean, and re-shelve incoming prints. Whether the Clock-tower lofts will finally afford the Co-op the screening space it wants to accompany its archive remains uncertain, but in any case benefit screenings seem to take place with some regularity, often at the Anthology Film Archives.

The London Filmmakers' Co-op has recently found itself facing a very different set of challenges. Thanks to the funding that the National Lottery pumped into the arts in the UK in the mid-1990s, its future seemed assured. Prior to this the Co-op had experienced decades of revolving management (a policy that had logically enabled the most committed members to have the most input). It occupied a nomadic existence in a series of run down temporary-lease buildings on Robert Street, the Prince of Wales Dairy, Fitzroy Road and from the mid-1980s to the mid-1990s, on Gloucester Avenue. In September of 1997, the LFMC moved into the new Lux building in London's Hoxton Square.

However, on 1 January 1999 the Co-op was forced to consolidate with its co-tenant, London Electronic Arts (LEA), at the direction of its state arts funding bodies, and ceased to exist as such. Now both entities were simply known as The Lux Centre. It turned out that Lottery money could only be spent on *things*, not people (wages et cetera), and ironically the Co-op found itself unable to afford its new site. The Co-op gained its own cinema, gallery and state-of-the-art post-production facilities in film and video through the merger, but lost its identity – though in fact its identity had always been in flux. Ongoing modifications to the rules of how Lottery funding could be applied raised hopes that the Co-op might resurface in the future as an autonomous organisation, but those hopes were dashed on 2 October 2001 when the Lux was suddenly and unceremoniously shut down and all the employees fired! It was a devastating blow to the London independent film scene. (Why this happened would require elaboration in a separate article.) At the time of publication it is unclear if and how the various groups housed in the Lux will rise from the ashes, but specifically regarding the Co-op, the archive still exists and maybe it is time for this organisation-in-limbo to return to its roots and find another rough space.

AN UNDERGROUND REMADE: NEW CONSOLIDATIONS AND DIRECTIONS

The 'marketplace' for short film exhibition has changed a lot since the 1960s, and the ramifications of this have been felt by the co-ops. Their traditional renters have grown scarce with art-house and repertory theatres closing down *en masse* or adopting more conservative booking policies. Many theatres that once showed 16mm films have dismantled their 16mm equipment, and some venues still willing to show 16mm film now charge the filmmaker upwards of $1,000 to install 16mm projection for a specific run. And, at least in America, bookings from university film societies and film clubs have fallen off significantly.

All traditional film co-ops struggle to function in a modern environment where short, independent work is increasingly shot and distributed on video, and where the public can now *own* copies of most films. While Canyon has attempted to a limited degree to distribute on video, the filmmakers often opt to handle this themselves by advertising over the Internet or via the plethora of filmmaker magazines and fanzines. Commercial distributors like Mystic Fire Video, for example, also play a roll in the distribution of independent short films and by extension compete with the co-ops. In any other business, such a realignment of the marketplace would simply put traditional suppliers out of business, but film co-ops cannot 'go out of business' precisely because they never were 'in' business, in the classic sense, to begin with.

Today short films and 'underground films' get most of their theatrical exposure on a loose circuit of festivals that include the aforementioned American underground festivals as well as the European, primarily German 'Kurzfilm' (short film) festivals in cities like Hamburg, Stuttgart, Weiterstadt, Oberhausen, et cetera. Technical, linguistic and cultural borders become blurred as these festivals screen the works of filmmakers from all over the world in all film and video formats. These festivals also rent films when presenting retrospectives of acclaimed filmmakers, and along with film museums and educational institutions, comprise the bulk of the business that co-ops do today.

Yet to a new generation of young filmmakers, the notion of film as a non-commercial form of personal expression seems hopelessly antiquated. All too often the short film is considered a mere 'calling card' by which to get one's foot into a producer's office. For their part, film schools, which did not exist in the early 1960s, are increasingly being geared to function as portals into 'The Industry'. While there were some monumental 'commercial breakthroughs' in the underground 1960s (Warhol's *Chelsea Girls* et cetera), today the gospel of the commercial breakthrough has become holy writ to a generation of young filmmakers trying to get into Sundance, repped by John Pierson and signed by Miramax or Fineline. As for the proliferation of glossy magazines aimed at independent filmmakers, they seem to offer little besides endless variations on how to assemble an effective press kit. It is hard to believe, but there was a time when 'careerism' was uncool. Today it is an epidemic.

Yet if the 1960s mindset out of which the co-ops sprang seems to be the stuff of nostalgia, the service they provide would appear to be more urgently needed than ever. More 'underground films' are being made today than ever before. As to whether 'non-competitive' distribution has any hope of survival in today's environment, one should definitely hope so.

Much is at stake, as any perusal through the co-op catalogues or a stroll through their print archives will reveal. They are the preserve of a largely 'secret cinema' – a treasure trove of undiscovered jewels (and of course plenty of lard too) that will in essence be lost if they cease to exist. In this computer age, where the power of 'personal access' is worshipped seemingly above all else, they offer access to a body of work that is in large measure available nowhere else. In an ara when every new movie is pre-digested a hundred times in the print and broadcast media by journalists, pundits and television celebrity chat hosts, co-ops offer people the chance to discover something rare. Strangely enough, for all the technological obsolescence of the 16mm format, this 'secret cinema' constitutes a new frontier.

CHAPTER 16
'GOUTS OF BLOOD': THE COLOURFUL UNDERGROUND UNIVERSE OF HERSCHELL GORDON LEWIS

Interview by Xavier Mendik

Prior to the gruelling cinematic excess of *The Texas Chainsaw Massacre* (1974), in a time before splatter auteurs such as George Romero and Wes Craven turned the human body into a disposable art-form, there was Herschell Gordon Lewis. The original pioneer of the American gore film, Lewis revolutionised underground horror with a series of lurid titles such as *Blood Feast* (1963), *2000 Maniacs* (1964) and *The Gore-Gore Girls* (1972).

For those fortunate to have seen any of Lewis' productions, it is specific (splatter) scenes rather than the narrative as a whole which imprint themselves on the viewer's memory. In the case of his most infamous movie, *Blood Feast*, it is the forced extraction of a female victim's tongue by a crazed killer that gained the film instant notoriety, as well as securing its long-time outlaw status on the UK 'video nasty' list. *2000 Maniacs* went further, with Lewis even concocting a series of fiendish torture weapons to be used by the crazed country bumpkins who populate the film. Most famously, these included a barrel full of spikes in which one poor unfortunate brylcreemed beefcake is forced to lie, before being rolled down a hill in order to maximise his suffering.

Although Herschell Gordon Lewis' films were clearly saturated with gouts of blood, they also contained a startling film style where bodily dismemberment jostles for attention alongside crimson clad film frames. In this respect, it comes as little surprise to find the title of his 1965 film as *Color Me Blood Red*. Although this tale revolves around a crazed artist who starts using blood instead of paint to create his works of art, the title applies as much to Lewis as to any of his crazed creations. While the typical Lewis production pushed the image track into frenzied and gruesome overload, his productions were also marked by high-pitched and hysterical soundtracks that the director frequently scored himself as a way of keeping production costs to a minimum. For instance, in *Blood Feast*, he composed a near tuneless, experimental bass drum score to accompany the devilish crimes of Fuad Ramses, an 'exotic Egyptian caterer' who is using prime slices of American womanhood to revive his long dead love. For *2000 Maniacs*, Lewis turned in a high-tempo, high-tension, hillbilly theme entitled 'The South's Gonna Rise Again'. This perfectly fitted the tale of a set of suburban thrill-seekers who get waylaid and wasted by a town of Southern degenerates celebrating a centenary of local carnage.

Although Lewis' maverick production tendencies and quest to expose the viewer to new heights of visceral overload made him an easy target for critics, his movies do retain an archaic charm lacking from many recent splatter productions. Indeed, despite their Swinging Sixties locations, moods and design, the films appeared curiously dated as soon as they rolled out from the production lines of Lewis' long-time producer and associate David F. Friedman. Arguably this is because in a period where American cinema was shifting towards increasing characterisation and complexity, Lewis' work was rooted in the very different traditions of theatrical excess and narrative suspension that defined 'primitive' silent cinema. For instance, *Blood Feast* contains many of the features associated with very early silent film: camera movement is minimal (an effect that is most marked in the atypical construction of dialogue scenes), while characters frequently break the film's fictional illusion by looking directly into the lens. Equally, in his frequently grotesque and contorted realisation of the gestures of Fuad Ramses, actor Mal Arnold even emulates the 'facial expression movie' popular in the silent years. (As with Lewis' other films, *Blood Feast* 'silences' the narrative's soundtrack and dialogue as if to underscore its basis in the traditions of early cinema.) While these features effectively doomed Lewis to the vanishing underground ghetto of exploitation and B-movies, his work retained a shocking vitality which he discussed in the following exclusive interview.

Xavier Mendik: *Your films are long associated with the underground American exploitation cinema. Do you think being outside the mainstream is central to an 'underground' status?*

Herschell Gordon Lewis: Well, let me give you the example of *The Blair Witch Project*. Is this an underground film? Well, clearly yes it is. It has every identifying characteristic: hand-held camera, no star names, poor colour and production values that are close to zero. All these features are

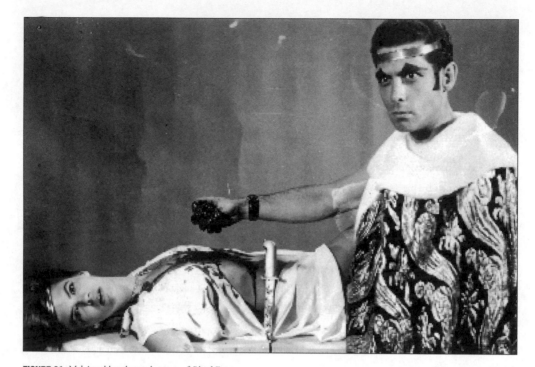

FIGURE 21 Mal Arnold as the mad caterer of *Blood Feast*

professionally exploited; in this sense it is a masterpiece of exploitation. So what does that indicate? It indicates that what is actually on film is secondary to an audience perception of what they expect to see. Now the flip side of that is what happened when they made *Blair Witch Project 2*. Why was that a resounding failure? It was a resounding failure because the first film depended so much on hype. People went to see it because of hype and they came out of the theatre saying 'I don't know what I just saw, what was there to that? It was horrifying.' Really, the plot can at best be euphemistically described as primitive. When the second one came along, they said it's probably going to be the same as the first, so the hype could no longer apply

Was the failure of Blair Witch 2 not also associated with the fact that it had a bigger budget and a more mainstream basis to it? It does seem to be the case that horror is never fully satisfying when its safe.

I would certainly agree with that. But from a filmmaker's point of view, we writhe in envy when we see big budget effects we could never have been able to afford. I look at some of the special effects that, say, George Lucas' company can do and I think 'Oh where was that when I was making my movies?' Now it's possible to make a movie without people, it is possible to do all that and never have an actor on the set. The whole thing is now done in some computer world.

Is that a good or a bad thing?

Well, actually, those are the wrong adjectives to use. Is it effective? It's effective until like everything else it's overused. One reason why *Blood Feast* has survived was not that it was well made.

No one can say that the acting in the film is very good, or indeed the special effects are good. But for its time, it was a breakthrough. For its time, it trod new ground. For its time, it provided effects that had not been seen before. Aristotle once said that drama provides a catharsis of the emotions and I sometimes think that our movies just provided a catharsis! Forget about the emotions!

Do you feel that being at the margins of film production assisted in making Blood Feast so disturbing?

If you can disturb an audience, without outraging the audience, then you have an absolute winner! If you outrage the audience, the word of mouth will kill you second time around. It is possible to disturb the audience; we did with *Blood Feast*. Here, the viewers did not come out of the theatre saying 'What terrible acting!' What they said was 'Did you see that tongue scene, I can't believe it!' I was talking to one fellow named Charlie Cooper. He owned a theatre in the ghetto section of Chicago. He made what I regard as the penultimate comment on *Blood Feast*. He said, 'I showed your picture, and there were these guys sitting there slashing the seats and shooting bullet holes in the screen. But up came that tongue scene and all I saw was a bunch of white eyeballs!' The ultimate comment on *Blood Feast* is that even after all these years, it's still showing! People are still buying the video. It has not become just a museum piece. And all the expensive films that have come after, where are they? I don't think that it was just the fact that it was the first kind of movie to do what it did. Also, there is a raw, primitive aspect to it, which is hard to duplicate today.

The acting style of the movie is quite bizarre, some critics have argued that it has an almost 'otherworldly' feel to it.

Well, I don't mind being otherworldly or surreal! But to be honest, I am beyond critics. These were not critics' pictures to start with. If I were to make a picture for critics, the public would not go. That is because most critics look for elements about which they can write and show off their interpretative skills. That may be an unfair comment, but I have been treated unfairly by them, so it's my turn! I don't see that there is a great disparity between what we did then and what we do now in terms of generating an audience reaction. The key difference is that audiences of the twenty-first century have become so sophisticated that it is increasingly difficult not to scare them, but to surprise them. They're not surprised by any big-budget effect: such as when drops of mercury form themselves seamlessly into a person, the audience are likely to respond by saying 'Oh yes, well we expected that.' Rather, what should happen in movie-making, is that you have got to hit the audience in the gut! One benefit of low-budget primitivism is that it is more 'gutsy'.

It is interesting that you link the film to cinema's primitive tradition. This is a tradition that relies on spectacle and theatrical excess rather than any strict narrative drive. Is this a tradition that you feel your own underground work belongs to?

I will leave that definition to you! I am interested in primitive cinema, but equally did not want to align myself in any one direction. Please understand that we made one movie after another, grinding them out like hamburgers. This is the way that underground and exploitation cinema works. So by the time we came to *The Gore-Gore Girls,* some of the effects in that film were far beyond what I could ever get away with in *Blood Feast.*

Does the gutsy approach you used with special effects also apply to the colour coding of Blood Feast, which seems somewhat exaggerated?

Well, the question of colour did come up early in my career. We had made a movie called *Scum of the Earth* (1963), which was a rough, tough little picture. Here, we had one frame in colour to correspond to the scene where a heavy sticks a gun in this guy's mouth, and then we have this red frame which had been hand painted. But when it came to a 'blood film', I remember making a movie called *Living Venus* (1962), which was black and white and in it we used stage blood. I remarked how purple and unrealistic it was – even in black and white. For *Blood Feast,* which was the first ever gore movie, I insisted that the blood look like blood. So, we went to a cosmetics laboratory and compounded this stage blood, which we put together by the gallon. In fact, I understand that they are

FIGURE 22 Coming attraction: *Scum of the Earth*

still selling it! This was because I wanted saturation of colour, which meant that the blood could flow as red as blood could flow. The idea was that gouts of blood, which was a phrase I picked up from Shakespeare, are more effective if they are more colourful.

Along with your surreal and extreme images, films such as Blood Feast and 2000 Maniacs demonstrated your skills at scoring. How important was music to these productions?

Very important, both artistically and economically. When I lost all ownership rights of these movies, I didn't even know that film music operated under its own separate sets of rights, which came back to me. When I wrote the music for *Blood Feast* and *2000 Maniacs,* it was not because I wanted to be a great musician, I just didn't want to pay someone else to do it! It was such a chore and that was even with me having something of a musical background. However, I just knew instinctively what I wanted: a cello and an added trombone and a set of kettledrums as in the case of *Blood Feast*, and I thought I just don't want to pay someone else, by the time I have described it, I could do it myself. Similarly, the vocals on the opening track of *2000 Maniacs* is actually my voice. I had already hired a singer to do that track, but his vocal range was far too high to deliver what I wanted, so I did the vocals myself, Rex Harrison fashion! So, the music of these films gave me a position of power that I didn't know I had. It was only years later that I learned that the only part of these movies I still owned were the musical rights, but they are a crucial part.

In many respects Blood Feast and 2000 Maniacs are very much ahead of their time, yet the monsters which they depict are curiously out of step with the 'Swinging Sixties' period in which they were produced. Would you agree that they seem to hark back to a much earlier tradition of movie monster?

Well spoken! Yes I definitely agree with you. We did not want them to be mainstream people. The Fuad Ramses killer from *Blood Feast* is a throwback to the very earliest days of cinema: with his bushy eyebrows, exaggerated limp and overacting. This was because he was supposed to be a caricature. Once again, this was because I was not making the movie for critics, but I knew the audience would be quite comfortable with that. When we were making *The Gore-Gore Girls*, I think you see far more subtlety in deciding even who the evil person is in that movie. That was because the whole genre had advanced to such a point that I could not longer get away with bushy eyebrows and dragging one leg!

The Gore-Gore Girls is both subtle and European in flavour. I wondered if Italian genres such as the giallo were in any way an influence on your work here?

The film was different to what we had done before and this was mainly because I felt that we had better go that one step beyond what we had done before. In terms of extremism, yes that is where you find it. Italian cinema was never afraid of going to extremes. Going way, way back to films like *8½* which although were not horror movies, would do something that while not impossible was unexpected.

The other thing about these European genres was that they were not afraid of showing nudity. In many respects, beyond your gore reputation, you also pioneered much of the erotic imagery associated with early

American underground cinema.

Yes, but in no film did I ever have full nudity. I had bare breasts in one, that was in *The Gore-Gore Girls,* because by that time it had become acceptable. But I never had four-letter words in these movies. But these days films are loaded with them.

Do you think this is unnecessary?

Well, good God, I am certainly the last person who would want to appear prudish! I just think it's often thrown in artificially, as a way to make it contemporaneous. But there are ways of doing this without having to resort to that, so I just don't see the need for it.

Moving away from horror to some of your other famed productions, these included She-Devils on Wheels (1968). This movie seems very innovative for a genre movie in terms of its representations of strong, independent women.

It was a big breakthrough. Up until that point there had been a lot of biker movies, but they always depicted women as hanging on to the back of the man. It was an attempt to change that kind of image that inspired the film. I said 'I would prefer women who can really ride those big Harleys and Nortons and BMWs instead of having women who are actresses alongside stunt doubles. Instead, we will teach them how to ride.' I think this was a gamble that paid off really, really well. This was because these were women who looked the part they really were. They were bikers first and actresses second.

You have talked about the so-called unrealistic nature of your movies, but there is that tradition in the American underground that exploited 'documentary' ideals for salacious intent. I am thinking here of the social hygiene genre that used a pseudo-moral examination of contemporary ills to provide titillation. I know that Doris Wishman uses these tactics and you also seemed to employ them in an early movie you did called Alley Tramp (1966).

Yes, but you have to understand that *Alley Tramp* was not my movie, it was Tom Down's. I did direct it, so I guess I am guilty by reason of insanity. That kind of movie which has almost a documentary overtone to it was the kind of film that Tom Down loved to make. He owned a theatre in downtown Chicago called 'The Capri', which played this kind of picture. Tom was in an unenviable position because there was this group of theatres that played this kind of film and he would agree to play your picture if you would agree to play his. So when he would make a movie, no matter what it was, he knew that there were around twenty-five to thirty theatres across the country that would play that movie. And with the budgets he had, he operated in total safety. So *Alley Tramp*, which was very easy to shoot because it was linear, was the kind of film that nobody took a chance on, it was home free before we shot the first frame. Tom also made a movie called *Linda and Abeline* (1969), which we shot in California. This was because he wanted to make something with a western theme to it. But as I said, Tom had an advantage that the rest of us didn't: namely whatever he played would get played. So his films could be more explicit. I am sure that you recognise they had a good deal more sex in them than mine, which meant that they were a lot of fun to shoot. However, if someone outside this circle had made them, it is questionable whether they would have had the costs of the movie covered,

FIGURE 23 Rural perversity in *2000 Maniacs*

Sticking with this titillation and pseudo-documentary theme, it is a strategy often used by underground directors such as Doris Wishman.

Well, what can I say about Doris Wishman, other than she is a lovely lady. She made that movie *Nude on the Moon* (1962). I made a movie in that very same location, it was called Coral Castle. But it was a very different kind of picture. It was a children's movie called *Jimmy The Boy Wonder* (1966), which had some animation in it, so that is as close as our paths have crossed.

Some of your early films, such as 2000 Maniacs and Moonshine Mountain (1964), have a clear theme of rural perversity running through them. I wondered if that was a feature that particularly interested you?

Yes, it does. *Moonshine Mountain*, for instance, was a labour of love. I have always been a fan of what people call 'Hillbilly music' and unsophisticated people. I do think it is easy to project the notion of evil as one becomes more and more bucolic. And that explains part of the success of *The Blair Witch Project*. If that had been shot in midtown London or Manhattan, there would be nothing to it at all.

Some people have said that the idea of rural perversity pops up in many seventies American horror films such as The Texas Chainsaw Massacre (1974). Do you see 2000 Maniacs as a blueprint for these films?

Yes I do. I have been told that its theme has been used a great number of times. I think this is because it's easy for an audience to identify with someone from a highly civilised background, riding in an open convertible, to wind up in an area where all of this is foreign. So these individuals find themselves on a different planet. If you land on the planet Mars you are never quite sure what its inhabitants are going to do, because they don't have that same element in their background. So this provides an automatic plus for the suspense factor.

Here of course is an interesting paradox. How can anyone feel alien within the United States? What is there about the collective American imagination that allows this to happen?

Well spoken! Someone can go from New York to Chicago, to Los Angeles, to San Francisco, to Miami and not be in the least bit uncomfortable. But if your automobile breaks down in the middle of some rural area and some local comes along and says [adopting Southern accent], 'Help you with your car mister?' At that moment, fear suddenly emerges.

So are we saying that the true source of horror is that of geographical perversity? Whether it's city folk breaking down in 2000 Maniacs, Hicksville or Egypt invading smalltown USA through the catering of Fuad Ramses?

Yes we are. Geographical perversity is as old as civilisation itself. We have evidence of geographical perversity still surrounding us today. Here, prejudice based on geography is flourishing in a way it never has before. You can cross a border from one country to another and the geography may seem to be the same, but there is still a border. Whether it's the border that separates the ethic Albanians or the people in Cuba. Once you cross that border you are in never-never land and you are never quite sure what is going to come up against you.

Your films always attempted to be stylish, despite their modest budgets. Were you ever afraid of compromising what you wanted to do?

With my movies, I tried to get every dime into the production itself. Which is admirable in one respect and despicable in another. It's admirable in that the film gets finished – that has to be the goal. And if you run one dollar short the film doesn't get finished. Yet, it's despicable in that there were times when I knew that we needed a second take to get a second effect, and so I had to settle for less than I know could be done. But in guerrilla filmmaking there is *always* compromise.

The Gore-Gore Girls was your last movie and it came at the time that the gore period of horror was really taking off. Why was this?

It was not intended as an ending. I had not known when I made *The Gore-Gore Girls* that it was going to be the last film I was going to make. At least up until now. That's the way life went and as the Bard said, 'Sweet are the uses of adversity'.

We hear many rumours that there may be a second Blood Feast movie. Could you tell us the latest?

For years I have been waited upon by people who have said, 'Let's make *Blood Feast 2*'. However, in the film business, the gap between 'let's do this' and 'I have the wherewithal to do this' is light years apart. Over all these years I have learned to treat that kind of suggestion with profound scepticism. To my surprise, a producer named Jackie Morgan came to me about three weeks ago complete with a 100-page script for *Blood Feast 2*. This was written without me. He had already negotiated with the current owners for the rights. He had a 21-day shooting schedule and he asked me to direct this. What caught my attention was the difference between someone who shows up with a script and a shooting schedule and the claim of backing and distribution, which is the key. All of these people used to approach me and say 'Let's make a movie'. Jackie Morgan tells me that he wanted to shoot this in July and this is so specific that it is hard to discount. It is not the treatment of *Blood Feast 2* that I would have necessarily made; this one is a fairly faithful sequel to the original, which he has obviously studied. But he is a serious and professional producer, and he insists that this film will be made. This is not the only one of my films which was going to be remade. There was also a project that was going to be called *2001 Maniacs*. In that case, I knew very little about the project except that I would get a certain amount of money as the prime mover, but I am not involved in the project at all. So who knows, this may not be the end, but a new beginning for my underground horrors!

I wish to thank Herschell Gordon Lewis for his time and patience, as well as the staff of the International Festival of the Fantastic Film in Brussels for organising the above interview.

CHAPTER 17
THEORY OF XENOMORPHOSIS

Nick Zedd

Xenomorphosis is the process through which negation of the fraudulent values, institutions, mores and taboos of consensus reality is accomplished. It is the key transforming moment in the transgression of mass media.

The unlocking of the unconscious triggered in the darkened theater by the flickering light and the seduction of the irresistible through the illusion of motion forms a magic wherein psychological and environmental factors combine to dilate chains of association. Amos Vogel has said 'The essence of cinema is not light, but a secret compact between light and darkness.'[1] Half the time we spend viewing movies is spent in total darkness. With the psychological complicity of the viewer, persistence of vision occurs.

The initially demoralising effect of xenomorphosis, wherein alienation and transformation occurs, can be frightening, infuriating and shocking to those who have been indoctrinated by an exploitative and hierarchical system. But it is only through this experience of transformation wherein one's cultural conditioning is subverted, that mutation occurs.

Xenomorphosis, triggered during persistence of vision by the use of diametrically opposing variables, e.g. libido excitation versus mutilation revulsion, results in a form of cognitive dissonance. The subconscious reconciliation of the matter/anti-matter equation is a union of opposites. The life/death, win/lose, right/wrong dichotomy imposed by the dominant hierarchy is revealed to the xenomorphic mind as a false equation.

This false dichotomy is the method by which social control is maintained. Its subversion is the final step in the process of transgression to what Nietzsche called beyond good and evil.

Xenomorphosis occurs when the empirical elements of projected sound and image conspire to negate and destroy, through the retina, neuro-pathways designed to domesticate and tranquilise. A primordial atom of unthinkable mass, in one trillionth of a second, during xenomorphosis, will explode, forming protons, neutrons and other subatomic particles, resulting in a dense fog of matter and radiant energy. In one hundred seconds, helium and other light elements will form. In three hundred thousand years the universe becomes transparent and all illusions disperse.

The moment of subversion wherein the viewers' prejudices and conditioning are completely eroded, usually occurs at the moment of laughter. It can be nervous laughter, a belly laugh or a procession of giggles. The important point is, this moment of elation is based on derision and can be likened to a big bang.

According to this theory, immediately proceeding the bang, the false vacuum of audience expectation was spinning in some kind of nether state. Occasionally it underwent routine fluctuations, most of which, like most quantum changes, were minor.

But quantum fluctuations can be sensational also and over the aeons of movie viewing, a sensational fluctuation struck the false vacuum, causing everything to come unglued. Splicing tape was then used, reversing images, turning them upside down and projecting pictures one frame at a time, surrounded by other images. Fantastic levels of gravity were set free, momentarily curving nucleotide templates activated by radiation to evolve new nervous systems, these particles materialising in astonishing numbers. The gravity repelling force of these restructured motion pictures was also released, rocketing everything outward. So much energy and particles were created that a new universe occurred.

Xenomorphosis is what happens when the domain wall of an alternate universe crashes into your reality. Neurological re-engineering occurs.

An essential element in the transgressive paradigm is danger. Throughout human existence, when the bio survival brain flashes danger, all other mental activities cease. This is of key importance in brain programming: to create a new imprint, first reduce the subject to the state of infancy, also known as first-brain vulnerability. The first step is isolation in the darkened theatre. The longer the isolation is, the more vulnerable to new imprint the audience member becomes. It is in this alien environment that the viewer willingly permits himself to be invaded by images and sounds manipulated by the xenomorph/director/magician.

All vision, as Rudolph Arnheim has pointed out, reflects an invasion of the organism by external forces which upset the balance of the nervous system. There is a dialectical wavering between self-absorption (personal associations triggered by the images) and self-abandonment. Closest to between waking and sleeping, the viewer, upon seeing the movement of shocking images become atavistic and in such a state, vulnerable to new imprint, hooks to whatever external entity comes closest to the mother archetype.

The basic principle of xenomorphosis is beyond revolutionary. It is super-evolutionary. Our human evolutionary process points to mutation through the injection of an alien genetic code to metamorphosis (rejuvenation) resulting in xenomorphosis.

The evolution from taboo into freedom comes through xenomorphosis.

This piece first appeared in the October 1998 issue (#7) of *Fringecore* magazine, published in The Netherlands.

CHAPTER 18
VISIONS OF NEW YORK: FILMS FROM THE 1960s UNDERGROUND

David Schwartz

Oh, the helplessness of the professionals, and the creative joy of the independent film artist, roaming the streets of New York, free, with his 16mm camera, on the Bowery, in Harlem, in Times Square, and in Lower East Side apartments – the new American film poet, not giving a damn about Hollywood, art, critics, or anybody.

Jonas Mekas[1]

In film, most new waves emerge not from soundstages and studios, but from the streets. The aesthetic revolution of postwar Italian neo-realism and of the French and British new waves in the early 1960s drew their vitality directly from the teeming milieus of Rome, Paris and London. The New York avant-garde film movement of the 1960s was no exception. Rejecting the factory-style artifice of Hollywood films, whose worlds were literally built from scratch on empty soundstages, underground filmmakers found their reality in the world around them. The city's buildings and streets became a

FIGURE 24 Jack Smith in *Blonde Cobra*

vast impromptu studio in which personal, idiosyncratic movies were made – movies as eclectic and varied as the city itself.

Ken Jacobs reveled in the bohemian splendor of cheap Lower East Side tenement flats and rooftops to create *Little Stabs at Happiness* (1960) and *Blonde Cobra* (1963). George and Mike Kuchar made the Bronx a cinematic wonderland, creating tawdry and hilarious versions of the Hollywood spectacles they watched as teenagers in the 1950s at the Loew's Paradise. Working with the open-eyed curiosity of the Lumière brothers, Andy Warhol turned his impassive lens on the Empire State Building, and let the camera roll for eight hours.

Cinema, after all, is an art form rooted in photographic reality, so it makes perfect sense that the films of the New York underground provide, among their artistic breakthroughs and triumphs, a vibrant record of what life felt and looked like in the 1960s.

To create *Still* (1971), his monumental study in superimposition, in which different layers of time exist in the same frame, Ernie Gehr trained his camera on a section of a block on Lexington Avenue. A mesmerising and confounding experiment in the manipulation of time and space, *Still* is also an impressionist urban portrait that takes delight in the changing patterns of sunlight on a tree, the comings and goings of people in a small diner and the flow of traffic as it passes in front of the camera.

Of course, New York City gave its filmmakers more than just a physical setting – it also provided a culture, and a means of distribution, exhibition and promotion. In 1962, the Filmmakers' Co-operative was founded, providing distribution to any filmmaker who submitted a print. Formal and informal venues emerged around the city, offering a moveable cinematic feast to an adventurous and sizeable audience. The Charles Theater, on Avenue B and East 12th Street, presented open house screenings from 1961 to 1963. The Bleecker Street Cinema briefly attempted to cash in on the scene with midnight screenings in 1963 – including the legendary double-feature premiere of *Blonde Cobra* and *Flaming Creatures*. Ken Jacobs organised screenings in his lower-Manhattan loft; it was here that the Kuchar brothers first showed their 8mm comedies.

Interest in avant-garde films was bolstered by sustained press coverage. The quarterly journal *Film Culture*, and the *Village Voice*, with its weekly 'Movie Journal' column by Jonas Mekas, provided a public forum where underground films could be championed and discussed, and placed in the context of a thriving international film scene that included Hollywood movies as well as the foreign films playing in the city's numerous commercial art-houses.

Further enhancing the impact of the New York film underground throughout the 1960s was the fact that it fit into a much broader counterculture scene that encompassed many art forms. The spontaneity and rebellious nature of underground film echoed the beatnik writing of Allen Ginsberg and Jack Kerouac; the painting of Jasper Johns, Robert Rauschenberg and Andy Warhol; the music of John Cage; and the live performances of the Living Theater, Yvonne Rainer and Trisha Brown, to name just a few. When Warhol released *Chelsea Girls* in 1966, it became a commercial success, quickly moving from a run at the Filmmakers Cinematheque on West 41st Street to a 57th Street art-house, where it played for months, and was reviewed by *Newsweek*, which called it 'one of those semi-documents that seem to be the most pointed art forms of the day'.[2] The underground also benefited from controversy and scandal. The sexually outlandish and explicit *Flaming Creatures* was banned by New York City, which was trying to clean up its public image before the 1964 World's Fair. Warhol's epic-length movies in which 'nothing' happened became the subject of cocktail-party ridicule by people who had, of course, never actually seen the films.

The notoriety and attention that gave the New York film underground a rare moment of impact and exposure have long faded, replaced by an independent film scene today that is deeply intermeshed with the mainstream. The city, too, has changed, becoming more commercial. So in a way, this retrospective is as much a portrait of a vanished city as it is a survey of a film movement that was truly independent.

This essay first appeared as programme notes for a film series held at the American Museum of the Moving Image (Astoria, New York), 4 November – 3 December 2000.

203

CHAPTER 19
A TASTELESS ART: WATERS, KAUFMAN AND THE PURSUIT OF 'PURE' GROSS-OUT

Xavier Mendik & Steven Jay Schneider

Gross-out speaks in a voice that demands to be heard because it represents a powerful strain in contemporary American culture. And it demands to be listened to closely: in the free-form give-and-take of its licentious manner, it speaks in the voice of festive freedom, uncorrected and unconstrained by the reality principle – fresh, open, aggressive, seemingly improvised, and always ambivalent.

William Paul[1]

[T]here is such a thing as good bad taste and bad bad taste. It's easy to disgust someone; I could make a ninety-minute film of people getting their limbs hacked off, but this would only be bad bad taste and not very stylish or original. To understand bad taste one must have very good taste.

John Waters[2]

Heads are crushed, cars explode, a schoolroom full of 'special' students get massacred, and there's a scene of a dolphin-person with two masturbating superheroes against a backdrop of an American flag. The *Tromeo and Juliet* monster penis even makes a cameo appearance. Yes folks, this is quality Troma.[3]

INTRODUCING THE OBSCENE

Whether embodied by the excrement-eating transsexual Divine, the chemically-altered, melted-down figure of the Toxic Avenger or the pig-faced, penis-empowered heroine of *Tromeo and Juliet* (1996), the films of John Waters and Lloyd Kaufman have come to define the American underground's ability to shock and outrage. With films such as *Multiple Maniacs* (1970), *Pink Flamingos* (1972), *Female Trouble* (1975) and *Desperate Living* (1977), Waters pioneered an 'aesthetics of gross' that differed greatly from the Hollywood images of excess available at the time. It was not merely the vast downward shift in production values, pacing, acting and effects work that distinguished his works from mainstream attempts to offend. Rather, it was the fact that his cross-gendered, orally-obsessed filth fetishists belonged to a wholly distinct *order* of trangressiveness.

It is this same drive towards violation that also characterises the work of Lloyd Kaufman, the self-styled ambassador of bad taste whose films include *The Toxic Avenger* (1986), *Tromeo and Juliet* and *Terror Firmer* (1999). Working through his independent production house 'Troma Pictures', Kaufman has created a series of underground classics whose imagery trades on grotesque and humourous depictions of the body – notably blood, buns and bodily dismemberment – whilst also utilising established literary and cinematic motifs for parodic purposes. For instance, Kaufman's daring rendition of Shakespeare's *Romeo and Juliet* periodically disrupts 'accepted' and 'official' passages from the Bard's text with a far more bodily form of communication that sees bouts of flatulence, masturbation and mutilation interrupting the dialogue between the star-struck lovers.

Although Kaufman's version/vision of the tale ends on a far more upbeat note than its source material, these changes are made with an end to achieving obscene and distasteful comedic effect. So, Tromeo (Will Keenan) and Juliet (Jane Jensen) manage to overpower the heroine's father at the point where he threatens to 'kill and fuck her at the same time' for disrupting his plan to marry her off to 'King Meatball' Arbuckle (Steve Gibbons), a local abattoir entrepreneur. Having forced the head of the evil patriarch through a television monitor, the couple proceed to ram 'Tromalite' tampons up his nostrils and beat him repeatedly with a copy of the *Collected Works of William Shakespeare*. After defeating their oppressor, the white-trash lovers emerge into the sunlight to the shocking revelation that they are in fact brother and sister. This discovery causes a momentary pause in the lovers' plans before Juliet announces: 'Fuck it, we've come this far!' With this the pair tear away in Tromeo's car before an epilogue reveals the fruits of their blissful union: a pair of misshapen, bone-headed, toxic toddlers – the result of incestuous inbreeding.

As this brief description implies, Kaufman's 'gross-out' construction of the human form and its secretions are anchored by an anti-authoritarian, distinctly *un*-American sentiment – one that has been embraced by the marginal and dispossessed groups circulating around America's youth population through such subcultures as death metal music and underground film. For these groups, Troma productions are seen as using comically offensive, disgusting and disturbing images to examine more serious issues and inequalities within US society. As Brian Matherly notes:

> Troma isn't all about boobs, blood and goo though. Through their skewed lenses, the Troma team have tackled such sensitive issues as AIDS (*Troma's War*), parental abandonment (*Toxic Avenger 2*), incest (*Tromeo and Juliet*), and gender confusion caused by years of sexual abuse (*Terror Firmer*).[4]

Indeed, it could be argued that whereas (early) Waters utilised the independent exhibition circuit as a way of circulating his obscene images of a seriously dysfunctional America, Kaufman has taken the practices and politics of underground cinema even further. Alongside his associate Michael Herz, the pair have turned Troma Pictures into a vertically-integrated production company, responsible for disseminating images that, while fiendish and quite often 'sick', are also free from big-budget studio interference. As a result, Troma not only produces films – they also distribute a wide range of existing American underground and European cult classics on celluloid, video and DVD, and stage underground film festivals as well.

What unites the films of both directors is the use of gross-out as a means of shocking and scathing viewers in a way that separates their work from mainstream cinematic efforts to disturb. To this extent, we might hypothesise that the works of both Waters and Kaufman point to differences between underground and mainstream cinematic gross-out that are not just a matter of *degree*, but rather a matter of *kind*.

These distinctions are most evident in the commentaries that have circulated around the work of both directors. Reviewers frequently emphasise the visceral effects of the films' narratives in very bodily terms, e.g., 'This is some of the funniest shit I've seen in a long, long time'.[5] Moreover, this type of underground gross-out is often interpreted as a 'pure' effect distinct from that offered up by mainstream film culture: 'Forget all you know about what Hollywood considers 'gross-out' comedy and prepare yourself for one of the most offensive, distressing and viciously funny satires ever made'.[6]

Here we will seek to determine just what this difference in kind amounts to. Our aim is to explicate the curious pleasures of underground gross-out versus the tamer, relatively 'tasteful' Hollywood alternative, and to argue for the existence of a ' pure' gross-out genre – one that bears an essential connection to the aesthetics and practices of underground filmmaking. Using the work of Mikhail Bakhtin, we will examine the visceral quality of Waters' and Kaufman's images, as well as their films' appeal to underground audiences. One advantage of a Bakhtinian analysis is that it allows for the work of both directors to be considered via notions of the carnivalesque, grotesque body. Finally, we will show how the unruly nature of these directors' gross-out spectacles indicates the potential of the American cinematic underground to subvert the physical, stylistic and ideological norms held in check by the Hollywood system.

UNDERBELLY, UNDERGROUND

In his 1990 book, *The Philosophy of Horror; or, Paradoxes of the Heart*, Noël Carroll proposes that the spectatorial response of 'art-horror' be understood as a compound emotion directed towards onscreen entities – monsters – that strike us as being both physically threatening and conceptually 'impure'. Carroll then analyses his notion of impurity using the terms originally suggested by anthropologist Mary Douglas in her classic 1966 study, *Purity and Danger*.

> Douglas correlates reactions of impurity with the transgression or violation of schemes of cultural categorisation. ,.. Things that are interstitial, that cross the boundaries of the deep categories of a culture's conceptual scheme, are impure. ... Faeces, insofar as they figure ambiguously in terms of categorical oppositions such as me/not me, inside/outside, and living/dead, serve as ready candidates for abhorrence as impure, as do spittle, blood, sweat, hair clippings, vomit, nail clippings, pieces of flesh, and so on...[7]

By adding *impurity* (understood in the culturally-specific sense of category violation) to *threat* in his above definition of art-horror, Carroll is able to distinguish this 'sophisticated' spectatorial response from 'mere' fright or even terror in the face of something interpreted as dangerous and intending to cause physical harm. In other words, it is precisely the addition of impurity to threat that separates the complex emotion of art-horror – and the horror genre on the whole – from the simple emotion of what might be called 'art-fear' (and those other genres which aim, each in their own way perhaps, at frightening audiences). What is left unresolved in Carroll's account is the question of what impurity *without* threat, or impurity *minus* threat amounts to. That is, what can we say about those films in which particular objects, entities or events are presented to the viewer as disgusting and repulsive – in short, as 'gross' – without their also (simultaneously and independently) being presented as dangerous and intending to cause physical harm? Carroll does not perform this operation in *The Philosophy of Horror*, which is not surprising considering his focus on those films in which perceived threat is held to be at least a *necessary* condition of horror-genre membership.

The cinema of both Waters and Kaufman, in which gross bodily activities are annexed to some form of comedic effect, provides us with the basis for a generic definition of the 'pure' gross-out film. Here, disgusting depictions are just as likely to be accompanied by humourous elements as by horrific ones, making their intended responses multiple and ambivalent. For example, scenes from

The Toxic Avenger, such as the one in which a bunch of street-trash assassins holding up a fast food joint are violently turned into human taco shells, ice-cream and other menu items by a sub-humanoid superhero, is just as capable of generating howls of laughter as screams of terror.

It is precisely the ability of the human body's gross-out gestures to provoke reactions of humour and disdain that governed Bakhtin's classic study of physiological transgression, *Rabelais and His World.* In this volume, Bakhtin charted what he saw as the 'civilising' and restraining processes that had been enacted against public display of the body from the seventeenth century onwards. During this period, both official acts *and* informal sensibilities mounted an increasing regulation of the human form, its gestures, waste products and secretions that still remains at play in (mainstream) contemporary society. For Bakhtin, the battleground for accepted notions of the human form dominated the policing of popular festivals, carnivals and their related bawdy representations. For instance, he argued that the work of François Rabelais focused on unruly feasts, carnal celebrations and unruly bodily representations that used comedy, excess and physiological 'gross-out' as a way of destabilising official power structures. Whether occurring through the absurd and fantastical scenarios of Rabelais' work or the gross-out displays of public farting, belching and feasting that occurred in carnival activities across Europe, the 'carnivalesque body' points to a wider suppression of established order and physical restraint. As Bakhtin noted:

> One might say that carnival celebrates temporary liberation from the prevailing truth and from the established order; it marks the suspension of all hierarchical rank, privileges, norms and prohibitions.[8]

For Bakhtin, the social dimension of carnival practices was marked through the principle of a 'world turned upside down' – a politics of subversion that saw everyday practices temporarily suspended and parodied as a way of drawing attention to established hierarchies and dominant beliefs. Here, it would not be uncommon for a beggar to be allowed to parade as a king, while women were given a free reign over sexual and social practices, all in marked contrast to the 'normal' restrictions placed on their behaviour.

Bakhtin argued that the carnivalesque body stands in opposition to the obsessive 'aesthetics of beauty' governing Renaissance constructions of the human form. Indeed, it could be argued that if modern society privileges the clean, sculptured and co-ordinated body, then the carnivalesque emphasises the body that is overwhelmed by its own gestures and secretions. This is a physiology that is dominated by libido rather than rational thought, a human form that is beset by its own tremors and spasms rather than being restrained by order and cognitive skill. In short, this is a body that provokes both laughter and unease in the viewing spectator.

While recent theorists such as Barbara Creed have charted the gradual legal and cultural drive towards cleaning up and suppressing the more gross-out aspects of carnival, they have also outlined the various ways in which the unruly grotesque body has resurfaced in underground practices and marginal representations. Whereas Peter Stallybrass and Allon White identified a carnivalesque dimension to slum/fairground and brothel practices in their classic study *The Politics and Poetics of Transgression*,[9] for Creed, similarly grotesque and unruly representations of the human form can be seen as circulating in disreputable genres such as the horror film. Through their obscenely comic images, these marginalised but militant cultural formations ensure the continuation today of a genuine carnival spirit.

In her 1995 article 'Horror and the Carnivalesque', Creed notes that central Bakhtinian features (such as an emphasis on transgression, the grotesque body and humour) are also present in modern horror cinema. As with carnival, Creed argues that, as a genre, horror films employ a transgressive drive that 'mocks and derides all established values and proprieties: the clean and proper body … the law and institutions of church and family, the sanctity of life'.[10] The body plays a central part in these subversive strategies, as indicated by Creed's 'Twelve Faces of the Body Monstrous' criteria.[11]

However, in marked contrast to Carroll's account of threat and impurity, Creed's use of Bakhtin allows her to discuss the type of representation where an excess of impurity actually serves to downgrade or diminish horrific effect. As she notes, these are representations where the monstrous body is as much 'a source of obscene humour' as a site of terror and decay.[12] For Creed, this obscene-comedic effect is particularly prominent in self-reflexive examples of the genre, where 'postmodern horror … combined with its deliberate use of parody and excess indicate the importance of grotesque humour to the success of the genre'.[13]

A prime example of this self-reflexive gross-out horror is Kaufman's *Terror Firmer*, an obscenely outward-looking tale which finds an independent film production being stalked by a serial killer intent on ruining the latest work of the blind, babbling auteur Larry Benjamin (played a bit *too* convincingly by Kaufman himself). Kaufman's manipulation of the film-within-a-film motif facilitates not only cine-literate commentary and image-laden in-jokes – it also allows him to kill off and abuse some of his greatest Troma creations. Thus, 'Sgt. Kabukiman' is listed as a prime suspect for the mayhem, while the actor playing the Toxic Avenger is assaulted in a pool of his own excrement – his nauseous leading lady declaring that she is 'not gonna take this shit any longer'. Although one fat slob attempts to clear Toxie's crud-caked passageways with an ill-aimed kiss of life (cue shots of someone literally shit-faced), the paramedics have a swifter solution to the patient's malaise: after vomiting over the unconscious actor, they dump him ungraciously off a hospital stretcher. Other notable examples of gross-out humour in *Terror Firmer* include the scene where Benjamin's obnoxious and overweight producer is attacked with an axe while on an escalator. This unlikely demise allows the chubby character to examine the discarded contents of his own stomach (guts, gore and out-of-state car licence plates) as his innards are displayed before him.

While depictions of the obscene body as a source of comedy are by no means uncommon in mainstream cinema, films like *Terror Firmer* indicate the manner in which marginal and underground

FIGURE 25 Obscene cinema: *Terror Firmer*

genre pictures use such imagery in markedly different ways to Hollywood. Here, an intensity of physiological corruption and display not only gratifies underground audience desires, but also challenges the strength of the viewer's stomach as well as their endurance skills. In this respect, underground gross-out works in a different manner to the excessive 'Bodywood' depictions identified by scholars such as William Paul. As Paul argues in his 1994 book *Laughing Screaming: Modern*

Hollywood Horror and Comedy, the main form of pleasure offered by Hollywood/mainstream gross-out is that which comes from allowing oneself 'spontaneous' feelings that may well be undesirable if reflected upon in real-life scenarios:

> It is *fun* to indulge in feelings that in the context of the real world would give us pause, to experience the surge of vitality that comes with the sudden onset of any strong feeling. There are values in gross-out horror and comedy that have more to do with the immediacy of play than the delayed satisfaction of ultimate purpose.[14]

What is so striking about the case of underground gross-out auteurs like Waters and Kaufman is that, despite having many fans and admirers, their films seem far more likely to be *endured* than *enjoyed*. Whereas in the Hollywood/mainstream case the gross-out effect is primarily functional – a means of achieving the contrary generic ends of comedy (utopian in its message, according to Paul) or horror (dystopian) – for Waters and Kaufman the cinematic gross-out is often an *end in itself*. One regularly reads or hears about the latest 'gross-out comedy' or 'gross-out horror movie', but the possibility of a 'pure gross-out' film has remained purely underground. According to Paul,

> Gross-out aesthetics must seem an oxymoron since aesthetic means the beautiful, implying a sense of decorum and proportion singularly absent from most of these films. This more usual definition was in fact a main ambition of earlier mainstream Hollywood films, which strove for middle-class respectability. …[N]ever before had an ambition to grossness *in itself* become such a prominent element in mainstream Hollywood production.[15]

If our thesis is correct, however, then the ambition to 'grossness *in itself*' that Paul identifies in recent Hollywood comedies and horror films indicates less a radical change in aesthetic sensibility than a radical change in the way already-existing generic aims have been strategically and formally achieved.

THE PURSUIT OF PURE GROSS-OUT: THE EARLY FILMS OF JOHN WATERS

If it is indeed the case that Hollywood cinema fails to provide genuine gross-out thrills, the successful pursuit of an aesthetics of 'pure gross-out' can clearly be found in the early films of John Waters. This is partly seen in the fact that his formative productions are not themselves generically situated in any clear manner; that is, they shift uneasily between definitions of comedy, horror and the absurd. Moreover, these productions connect a raw, even experimental, underground filmmaking style with depictions of disgusting characters, objects and events. As Jack Stevenson notes, 'Anyone could haul out stock grotesqueries and assault audiences with bucketfuls of bad taste, but Waters had mastered a certain ambiguity of intention that was the "active ingredient" in his filmmaking. Maybe he really *was* a fucked-up sonofabitch'.[16] A corollary to these two points is that Waters' films seemed to become less 'purely' gross just as they became more mainstream.

As numerous critics have observed, beginning with *Hairspray* in 1988, the dark violence, perverse sexuality and largely incoherent narratives of Waters' earlier work was replaced by sweeter, often nostalgic storylines. This sentimental affect was assisted by bigger budgets and the familiar presence of Hollywood stars (e.g., Johnny Depp, Kathleen Turner) and pop-culture icons (e.g., Deborah Harry, Patricia Hearst). Implicit in this shift towards the mainstream was Waters' move away from the carnivalesque via the courting of actors who define what Bakhtin characterised as the 'new bodily canon', i.e., those represented as possessing 'an entirely finished, completed, strictly limited body, shown from the outside as something individual'.[17]

This stands in stark contrast to the forms of physiological abnormality and transgression present in Waters' early films. For instance, although Stevenson calls it a mere 'marketing gimmick',[18] and Waters himself admits that it was 'conceived as a negative publicity stunt',[19] the aesthetics of pure gross-out are fully operative during the infamous finale of *Pink Flamingos*. Justin Frank is hardly exaggerating when he identifies this film's concluding scene as 'the most famous … in all underground cinema – the underground equivalent of the shower scene in *Psycho*'.[20] *Pink Flamingos* traces the inevitable victory of Waters' transvestite diva Divine and 'her' equally eccentric family in a battle against the self-consciously twisted and social-(anti)-climbing Marbles (Mink Stole and David Lochary) for the title of 'The Filthiest People Alive'. In the film's notorious postscript, Divine stops on a street in downtown Baltimore to pick up the freshly-laid turd of a small dog. Waters' own recollection of what happens next is as good a description as one could possibly want: '[she] put it in her mouth. She chewed it, flicked it off her teeth with her tongue, gagged slightly, and gave a shit-eating grin to the camera. Presto – cinema history!'[21]

What is it about this simple, if sick and twisted, act of coprophagy that enabled it so quickly to obtain the status of gross-out legend? (Just try entering the words 'Waters', 'shit' and 'divine' into an Internet search engine and see how many thousands of hits you come up with.) After all, the turd might have been – it surely *should* have been! – a fake. In fact, however, it may not matter ultimately whether Divine nibbled on a real piece of crap that afternoon or just an expertly-crafted shit simulacrum. What matters is that Waters succeeded in making viewers *believe* she ate shit; not in order to make them laugh (though he was happy for them to do so), and not so as to horrify them (in any but a metaphorical sense of the term), but in order to give them a pure gross-out they would not soon forget.

This success was obtained primarily through Waters' concerted effort at achieving maximum verisimilitude through the adoption of traditional documentary film technique: the scene was shot in real time, on location, using natural light, with minimal cuts, etc. This was merely an extension of the same underground aesthetic (dictated as much by budgetary constraints as by any kind of 'principle') dominating *Pink Flamingos* and Waters' early work as a whole. The shit-eating case, despite its

FIGURE 26 Divine in *Pink Flamingos*

(assumed) status as a truthful representation, is actually not dissimilar to that of such fictional/pseudo 'snuff' killings in 1970s exploitation horror movies such as *Snuff* (1976) and *Cannibal Holocaust* (1979). In both of these pictures, while the gruesome murders depicted on-screen were only staged re-enactments of the real thing, extraordinary numbers of viewers bought into the *faux* documentary charade and were convinced that they were watching actual snuff cinema. Had the production values of these films, including *Pink Flamingos*, been of a higher, more 'polished' and 'above-ground' (read 'Hollywood') standard, most viewers would not have been anywhere near so quick to buy into their signature displays of transgression.

However, unlike cases of pseudo-snuff cinema – as well as such modern 'shock-horror' classics as *Eyes Without a Face* (France, 1959) and *Suspiria* (Italy, 1977) – *Pink Flamingos* does not 'dilute' its disgust with horror, as there is no obvious or significant physical threat implied in Divine's shit-eating spectacle, save the digestive harm she might have caused herself. (Waters reports how that same evening, at the film's wrap party, Divine rang the emergency ward of the local hospital stating that her 'retarded son ... ate some dog faeces and I'm wondering if he can get sick?'[22]) Beyond this, the distinctly underground sensibility of *Pink Flamingos* can be seen in the film's raw, unfiltered, uncensored content; the haphazard camerawork and half-arbitrary *mise-en-scène*; the campy, over-the-top nature of Divine's performance; and the lack of firm distinctions between characters and the actors (often non-actors) who play them. Together these features operate as an extra-diegetic parallel of sorts to the disgusting acts depicted within the diegesis: *Pink Flamingos* is *itself* bad taste, although, as Waters would say, it is 'good bad taste' not 'bad bad taste'.

Though it might provoke a degree of awkward laughter, most viewers would hardly admit to the final scene's qualifying as particularly funny either. Arguably, the film has its amusing moments – in particular the scenes involving Mama Edie (Waters regular Edith Massey), as an old woman who spends most of her time worshipping eggs while sitting in a playpen dressed in nothing but a bra and girdle. However, even these unconventional scenes hardly fit in the 'comedy' category in any straightforward generic sense of the term. Divine's fabled act of shit-eating, though it may have been conceived of merely as a 'negative publicity stunt' to be tacked on to the end of *Pink Flamingos*, nevertheless stands as a perfect encapsulation of all that comes before it in the film. It represents a minimalist display of multiple transgression (abjection, impurity, boundary-crossing) without the distraction of mainstream genre conventions that would effectively 'impurify' the gross-out grabber.

As befitting *Desperate Living*'s relatively more polished look (it's $65,000 budget was much bigger than any of Waters' previous productions), the central gross-out scene in this film occurs midway through the story and is no longer minimalist in either style or duration. The emphasis on multiple transgressions is still in place, but now the presentation is extended, lasting several minutes, and with the disgusting displays piled on to such an extent that the sheer spectacle of the sequence serves to render the loose but inspired narrative utterly inconsequential.

Waters himself has called the scene in question 'more outrageous than any [other] in the film',[23] and for good reason. The director's characterisation of the film as a 'lesbian melodrama about revolution. … A monstrous fairy-tale comedy dealing with mental anguish, penis envy, and political corruption'[24] suffices for present purposes. The scene opens with butch lady wrestler Mole McHenry (Susan Lowe) returning home from a sex change operation in Baltimore to her ditzy, massive-bosomed girlfriend Muffy St. Jacques (Liz Renay). To Mole's dismay, Muffy is repulsed by the very sight of her partner's penis transplant, and vomits after Mole climbs on top of her in an over-eager attempt at showing off the new organ. Muffy pleads with Mole to cut it out – and cut it off – and the depressed and defeated Mole promptly obliges, using a pair of garden shears to perform the self-surgery. Showing no mercy to his audience, Waters does not end the scene with this castration operation: while Mole cries out in agony, Muffy begins to sew up her girlfriend's bleeding crotch, reassuring her 'I'll love it, Mole. I'll love it, feel it and eat it just like old times'. As for the prosthetic penis, after Moles tosses it out the front door, a dog comes along, sniffs around for a while and finally starts nibbling on it.

In his review of *Desperate Living* for the *Baltimore Evening Sun* following the film's premiere, Lou Cedrone declared: 'Waters is a little bent. No, he's twisted, maybe even broken. If you are amused by vomit, blood, cannibalism, cruelty to children, and rats served as dinner, you may want to see the film. It would be fun as low-low camp if it wasn't so sick'. R. H. Gardner of *The Sun*, another Baltimore daily, somehow managed to top Cedrone:

> John Waters specialises in works of an unbelievably gross and offensive nature. No contemporary filmmaker has presented the human race in so disgusting a light. Waters' characters are not simply hideous, they affront the soul. They exude the aroma of outside toilets. They achieve a grotesqueness for which the adjective 'repulsive' leaves something to be desired.[25]

Interestingly, it is not entirely clear whether these reviews are meant to be positive or negative in their evaluations of the film. It would be one thing if Waters, like his more mainstream contemporaries, intended for the grossness and offensiveness of *Desperate Living* to serve (functionally) as a source of humour, or perhaps of horror. Were that the case, then the striking statements by Cedrone (who comes close to accusing Waters of trying unsuccessfully to make a campy comedy) and especially Gardner could be taken as indicating the director's failure. But not surprisingly, given his long-standing efforts at creating a cinema of pure gross-out, Waters himself takes both statements as compliments: 'the[se] two leading local critics … who had given up on getting rid of me years ago, came through with just the kind of review I love to get'.[26] This offhand remark indicates something other than a desire on Waters' part for negative publicity; it signals his appreciation for those in the press who eventually learned to judge his work by its own (underground) standards, rather than according to the conventions of Hollywood genre cinema.

Besides lasting several minutes longer than the shit-eating scene in *Pink Flamingos*, the gross-out sequence in *Desperate Living* described above differs from its predecessor in giving up any pretence to verisimilitude. Instead, it emphasises – even revels in – the obvious *fakeness* of the situation: yet another underground (and avant-garde) filmmaking strategy present in the works of Jack Smith and Andy Warhol, among others. Besides the histrionic, hyperbolic performances and the see-through set design, Mole's makeshift member looks more like a dime-store dildo than a real-if-transplanted penis, and Muffy's vomiting act has nothing whatsoever on *The Exorcist* (1973). But here it is precisely the fact that there is no attempt to hide the artifice that adds to the gross-out flavour of the scene. Fully aware the whole time that what we are watching is fake – there is not even a moment of suspended disbelief – we are forced to wonder both why the director is doing this at all and why we are allowing him to do it *to us*.

BLOOD, BUNS AND BELLY LAUGHS: LLOYD KAUFMAN AND TROMA

With their uneasy blend of sick humour, bodily fluids and diverse displays of gross-out, Lloyd Kaufman's films share many of the same offensive qualities marking the early works of John Waters. Similar to the excess orality of *Pink Flamingos*, Kaufman and Herz's *The Toxic Avenger* offers up multiple images of unruly feasts, riotous gatherings and body secretions (notably blood, semen, excrement and toxic urine), as well as depictions of the grotesque body in a variety of incarnations. These unsavoury images are stitched together in a format that fuses parodic film references (e.g., to old Chaplin movies and 1930s 'cliff-hanger' serials) with nods to experimental underground techniques (including a 'toxic transformation' with colour codings straight out of Stan Brakhage). The film focuses on a deformed superhero who defends the people of small town Tromaville from political corruption and violent crime in a narrative that uses the grotesque body to parody the norms, ideals and values associated with the American dream.

By centring the film at 'The Tromaville Health Club', *The Toxic Avenger* establishes the ideal of a worked-out, toned and trimmed, pumped up and primed physical form (this being reiterated by the theme song 'Body Talk' that accompanies the gym sequences). From the outset, however, the film degrades and displaces this notion of bodily integrity. For instance, it is implied that Tromaville's corrupt Mayor Belgoody (Pat Ryan) has been allowing the illegal dumping of toxic waste in suburban areas, thus ensuring human decay and infection. In this environment, it is the grotesque, carnivalesque frame that comes to replace the body beautiful.

Indeed, *The Toxic Avenger* splits Bakhtin's conception of the grotesque, comedic body into two distinct forms. Firstly, there are the gargantuan, slob-like and food-obsessed figures such as Belgoody (whose excessive orality is signified by his insistence on eating fast food whilst receiving an erotic massage), who are clear matches for the oversized and insatiable creatures found in writers such as Rabelais. Alongside these (literally) larger than life figures exist the emaciated males – including the film's hero, Melvin (Mark Torgl) – whose meagre frames and jerky, uncoordinated gestures contradict the healthy images of masculinity that the film is seen to critique. In Bakhtinian terms, this split represents a disjuncture between the essentially open, tactile and unfinished body of carnival and the sleek, sculptured and 'closed' human ideal that came to replace it. As Bakhtin states in *Rabelais and His World*:

> We find at the basis of grotesque imagery a special concept of the body as a whole and of the limits of this whole. The confines between the body and the world and between separate bodies are drawn in the grotesque genre quite differently than in the classic and naturalist images.[27]

The distinctions between the grotesque and classical depictions of the body are present in the opening montage scene of *The Toxic Avenger*. Here, Kaufman and Herz shift between the vigorous exercises of the film's key villains, Bozo (Gary Schneider) and Slug (Robert Prichard), contrasting these physically perfect but psychotic protagonists with the misshapen misfits who circulate on the health spa's fringes. The latter include a pair of old camp queens engaged in heavy petting over an exercise machine, a grossly overweight woman eating potato chips during an aerobics routine and various male weaklings on the very edge of being crushed by their own dumbbells.

In the course of surveying this curious collection of individuals, the camera eventually settles on Melvin, the nerdy toilet attendant who is later transformed into the toxic superhero of the film's title. From the outset, this character's comic construction meets Bakhtin's criteria in several ways. To begin with, Melvin's emaciated, effeminate features provide a direct and parodic contrast to the socially-reinforced ideals embodied by Bozo's construction of masculinity. (Melvin's pitiful attempts at flexing his underdeveloped muscles before a locker room mirror provoke hysterical outbursts from Bozo precisely because they comically emulate his own, overblown gestures of machismo.) At the level of facial characteristics, Melvin's bucktoothed visage – a deformity that literally prevents him from closing his mouth – further links him to notions of the grotesque.

In Bakhtinian language, Melvin's body is perpetually 'in the act of becoming. It is never finished, never completed, the body swallows the world and is itself swallowed by the world'.[28] This is also a physique that retains a degraded, low socio-economic status (embodied by Melvin's role as the health club 'mop boy'), one that is intrinsically linked to the body's more distasteful aspects. Indeed, Melvin is associated with waste matter from the start via his role as a toilet attendant. At one point Bozo even comments that Melvin is struck with a 'shit-eating grin', and the latter's excremental stench serves to offend the 'cool kids' who hang out at the club.

Melvin's gross-out status is confirmed by the cruel trick (played on him by Bozo and his buxom girlfriend Julie (Cindy Manion)) that unwittingly transforms him into the Toxic Avenger. Here,

FIGURE 27 A grotesque carnivalesque body: *The Toxic Avenger*

Melvin is cajoled into donning a pink leotard and tutu in the belief that he is about to experience a sexual encounter with Julie in the girl's locker room. (The protagonist's comment that he can meet her at this location whilst he is cleaning the nearby toilets once again confirms his association with waste matter.) Having been led into a darkened location, Melvin begins to kiss and fondle what he believes is the object of his affections, before a blaze of light and laughter reveal that he is in fact engaging in an erotic encounter with a goat. Having been tricked by Bozo, Julie and the 'beautiful people' of the health club, Melvin attempts to escape his tormentors by jumping from an upper-level window … only to land in a vat of toxic waste that has been dumped outside the venue.

Melvin's subsequent 'toxic' transformation more than satisfies Creed's criteria concerning the gross-out nature of the carnivalesque body in underground and horror cinema. Here, the protagonist's skin turns green, pulsates and oozes slime as he jerks, spasms and finally erupts into flames before an assembled audience from the health club. The scene also confirms Bakhtin's belief that 'exaggeration, hyperbolism, excessiveness are all generally considered fundamental attributes of the grotesque style'.[29] In case the effects might be deemed *too* horrific, or his agony look *too* real, Bozo re-injects a comic angle into Melvin's suffering by informing Julie (and thereby the film's audience) that he is 'faking it'. (A similar self-reflexive comment is made in *Tromeo and Juliet* when the heroine's father derides his daughter's self-inflicted transformation into a farmyard animal as 'special effects'.)

The Toxic Avenger's semi-humourous degradation of the body in pain is reiterated when Melvin returns home to bathe and metamorphose some more. Here, the protagonist's skin erupts into a series of lesions which then expel a foul green liquid, while his hair falls out in clumps revealing a misshapen, swollen skull. Further, his torso and arms swell to body-builder proportions while his effeminate squealing is replaced by a far more masculine voice. This leads Melvin's mother (on overhearing her son's transformation through the wall) to comically misinterpret what she hears as her 'little boy' finally reaching puberty!

Melvin's alteration into Toxie confirms Creed's claim that 'the grotesque body lacks boundaries; it is not "completed", "calm" or "stable." Instead the flesh is decaying and deformed'.[30] This process of becoming also points to themes of metamorphosis within the carnivalesque and underground fictions that she analyses. In many respects, such images of transformation disturb 'not only what it means to be human',[31] but also what it means to be gendered. Although Melvin's toxic makeover results in a newly hyper-masculine appearance, his chemical fusion also results in the permanent moulding of the 'feminine' health club tutu onto his flesh. As a result, his body connotes a grotesque excess of both male *and* female signifiers that rival the transgendered glory of Divine in John Waters' early productions.

The connection between the grotesque, carnivalesque body and sexual ambiguity is not only confined to Toxie and his opponents (who include cross-dressing martial artists and over-decorated and rouged street punks), but rather forms a consistent trait in all of Kaufman's work. *Tromeo and Juliet,* for instance, features a heroine who transforms herself into a pig-faced monster with an excessively long phallus in order to avoid the advances of an amorous suitor. The protagonist's uneasy relation to traditional notions of femininity are established in an earlier dream sequence, when Juliet imagines her belly swollen and erupting with filth in a bizarre parody of the birth act. This sequence supports the notion that the carnivalesque body 'gives birth and is born, devours and is devoured, drinks, defecates, is sick and dying'.[32] Even more surreal is the figure of Casey (Will Keenan), a cross-dressing killer from *Terror Firmer*. Although Casey appears to the film's heroine in a variety of fantasised 'macho' poses, he is only able to pleasure her with the aid of a green pickle, after his father (played by porn superstar Ron Jeremy) castrates him and forces him to dress as a female.

With their outrageous content, parodic, scathing humour and emphasis on bad taste, both John Waters and Lloyd Kaufman have confirmed the American underground's ability to produce 'pure' gross-out cinema. Yet behind the muck, goo and outlandish body imagery lies a far more serious and potentially subversive message. This relates to the ability of humour and obscene human forms to be presented in challenging and unconventional ways that are capable of overturning wider social norms and values. Bakhtin argued that 'Whenever men laugh and curse, particularly in a familiar environment, their speech is filled bodily images'.[33] The films of our two underground auteurs have turned such body talk into an aesthetics and politics of gross-out, now residing in the obscene underbelly of Hollywood.

NOTES

CHAPTER 1

1 Mendik, X. (2000) 'Shooting up on Speech: the Female "Fix" of *The Addiction*', in J. Hunter (ed.) *Christopher Walken: Movie Top Ten*. London: Creation Books, 106.
2 Charity, T. (1999) 'The Addiction', in J. Pym (ed.) *Time Out Film Guide*, Seventh Edition. London: Penguin, 7.
3 Hawkins, J. (2001) 'Smart Art and Theoretical Fictions', Part One. *C Theory* Review Article, p. 50.
4 Burroughs, W. (1959) *Naked Lunch*. New York: Grove Press, xxxviii.
5 Siegle, R. (1989) *Suburban Ambush: Downtown Writing and the Fiction of Insurgency*. Baltimore and London: Johns Hopkins Press, 1.
6 Burroughs 1959, xxxix.
7 Ibid. p. xxxviii.
8 Quoted in Burroughs 1959: xix.
9 Hoberman, J. (1995) 'Youngbloods', *Village Voice*, 40, 41, 69.
10 Ronell, A (1992) *Crack Wars: Literature, Addiction, Mania*. Lincoln and London: University of Nebraska Press, 13.
11 Ibid. p. 3.
12 Derrida, J. (1993) 'The Rhetoric of Drugs', Interview with *Autrement*. Trans. Michael Israel. *Differences*, 5, 1, 13.
13 See S. Reynolds (1999) *Generation Ecstasy: Into the World of Techno and Rave Culture*. New York: Routledge. See also G. Deleuze and F. Guattari (1987) *A Thousand Plateaus: Capitalism and Schizophrenia* [Translation of *Mille Plateaus*]. Trans. Brian Massumi. Minneapolis: University of Minnesota Press.
14 Clover, C. (1992) *Men, Women and Chainsaws*. Princeton, N.J.:Princeton University Press.
15 Keough, P. 'Bad Blood'. http://www.bostonphoenix.com/a;t1/archive/movies/reviews/11-10-95/addict.html, 19 April 1998.
16 Cited in Kraus, C. (2000) *Aliens and Anorexia* . New York: Semiotext(e) [Native Agents Series], 27.
17 Auerbach, N. (1995) *Our Vampires,Ourselves*. Chicago and London: University of Chicago Press.
18 LaSalle, M. (1995) '"Addiction" in All Its Gory Detail: Vampire Tale Told Ferrara Style', *San Francisco Chronicle*, 10 November, C3.
19 Mendik 2000: 106.

CHAPTER 2

1   Schaefer, E. (1999) *Bold! Daring! Shocking! True! A History of Exploitation Film 1919–1959*. Durham: Duke University Press.

2   D'Emilio, J. & E. Freedman (1988) *Intimate Matters: A History of Sexuality in America*. New York: Harper and Row, 327.

3   Wilinsky, B. (2001) *Sure Seaters: The Emergence of Arthouse Cinema*. Minneapolis & London: University of Minnesota Press.

4   Canby, V. (1968) 'Films Exploiting Interest in Sex and Violence Find Growing Audience Here: Crude 42nd Street Fare Now Seen All Over City and Suburbs', *New York Times*, 24 January, 48.

5   Gallagher, S. (2000) 'The Libertine: Stephen Gallagher on *Score's* Radley Metzger' (Interview), *Filmmag*. <www.filmmag.com/nonink/metzger.html>

6   Ibid.

7   Randall, R. (1976) 'Censorship: From *The Miracle* to *Deep Throat*', in T. Balio (ed.) *The American Film Industry*. Madison: University of Wisconsin Press, 432–58.

8   Canby 1968: 32.

9   Wyatt, J. (1999) 'Selling "Atrocious Sexual Behaviour": Revising Sexualities in the Marketplace for Adult Film in the 1960s', in H. Radner & M. Luckett (eds) *Swinging Single: Representing Sexuality in the 1960s*. Minneapolis and London: University of Minnesota Press, 105–32.

10 Quoted in Albarino, R. (1966) 'Stranglehold on Sex Gasps: Majors Giving Indies a Lesson', *Variety*, 12 October, 7, 26.

11 Stevenson, J. (2001) 'And God Created Europe: How the European Sexual Myth Was Created and Sold to Post-War American Movie Audiences', in J. Stevenson (ed.) *Fleshpot: Cinema's Sexual Mythmakers and Taboo Breakers*. Manchester: Headpress, 17–48.

12 'Newspapers & "*Adults Only*"' Editorial. *Motion Picture Herald*, 15 July 1961, 224, 3, 1.

13 Reade, W. (1961) 'Who's For Censorship? Recent Supreme Court Ruling Leaves Problem Unsolved', *New York Times*, 9 July.

14 Albarino 1966: 7.

15 Doerfler, J. (1971) 'Radley Metzger: Let'em See Skin…', *Boston After Dark*, 9 February, 16.

16 Jancovich, M. (2001) 'Naked Ambitions: Pornography, Taste and the Problem of the Middlebrow', *Scope Film Journal*, June. <http://www.nottingham.ac.uk/film/journal/articles/naked-ambition.htm>

17 Lewis, J. (2001) *Hollywood v. HardCore: How the Struggle Over Censorship Saved the Modern Film Industry*. New York: New York University Press.

18 Hentoff, M. (1969) 'Notes from Above Ground', *The New York Review of Books*, 22 May, 19–20.

19 Doerfler 1971: 16.

20 Friedman, D. with D. De Nevi (1990) *A Youth in Babylon: Confessions of a Trash Film King*. Buffalo, NY: Prometheus Books, 100.

21 Bourdieu, P. (1984) *Distinction: A Social Critique of the Judgement of Taste*. Trans. Richard Nice. Cambridge: Harvard University Press, 56–7.

22 Gallagher, ibid.

23 Lynes, R. (1954) *The Tastemakers: The Shaping of American Popular Taste*. New York: Dover Publications. 338.

24 Waugh, T. (1996) "Cockteaser." In Doyle, J. Flatley, & J., Munoz (eds.) *Pop Out: Queer Warhol*. Durham: Duke University Press, 61.

25 Jameson, F. (1992) *Signatures of the Visible*. New York and London: Routledge, 1.

26 Gallagher 2000.

27 Bourdieu 1984: 56.

28 Turan, K. & S. Zito (1974) *Sinema: American Pornographic Films and the People Who Make Them*. New York: Praeger, 56.

29 Staiger, J. (2000) 'Finding Community in the Early 1960s: Underground Cinema and Sexual Politics', in *Perverse Spectators: The Practices of Film Reception*. New York: New York University Press, 125–60.

30 Verrill, A. (1974) 'Test for Right Sell to Wrong Sex: Audubon Finds Porno Regulars Resist Male-to-Male', *Variety*, 3 July, 17.

CHAPTER 3

1   Curtis, D. (1971) *Experimental Cinema: A Fifty-Year Evolution*. Delta: Dell, 51–3.

2   Vogel, A. (1967) 'Thirteen Confusions', in *Evergreen Review*; reprinted in G. Battcock & E. P. Dutton (eds) *The New American Cinema: A Critical Anthology*. New York: Dutton & Co, 128.

3   Quoted in C. Stephens (2000) 'Brides and Monsters: Curtis Harrington Revisits the Past', *Filmmaker*, Fall, 9, 1,

16–17.

4   Quoted from a television interview with Harrington conducted by David Del Valle on the first of a two-part episode of Del Valle's programme Sinister Image; 1987, Century Cable Public Access Studio, Santa Monica, CA.

5   Fischer, D. (1991) *Horror Film Directors, 1931–1990*. Baltimore: McFarland & Co, 502.

6   Ibid, 502–3.

7   Renan, S. (1967) in Battcock & Dutton, 87.

8   Ibid.

9   Del Valle 1987,

10 Ibid.

11 Quoted in P. Adams Sitney (1970) *Film Culture Reader*. Westport, CN: Praeger, 8.

12 The quotes attributed to Harrington come from editorial corrections and notation for S. Bissette (1992) 'Harrington Ascending: The Underground Roots', *Video Watchdog*, 14, Nov/Dec, 24–5.

13 Curtis 1971: 82.

14 Lucas, T. (1992) 'Curtis Harrington Videography', *Video Watchdog*, 14, Nov/Dec, 50.

15 Del Valle 1987.

16 Dwoskin, S. (1975) *Film Is: The International Free Cinema*. New York: The Overlook Press, 55.

17 Renan 1967: 223.

18 Ibid.

19 Del Valle 1987.

20 Anders quote from 25 August 1992, *Video Watchdog*, 14, Nov/Dec, 27.

21 Jonas Mekas cited in Sitney 1970: 102.

22 Markopoulos interviewed by J. Mekas (1972) *Movie Journal: The Rise of the New American Cinema, 1959–1971*. New York: Collier Books, 234.

23 Stephens 2000: 16.

CHAPTER 4

1   Williams, T. (1997) *Larry Cohen: Radical Allegories of an American Filmmaker*. Jefferson, N.C.: McFarland.

2   Dixon, W. W. (1999) *The Exploding Eye: A Re-Visionary History of 1960s American Experimental Cinema*. Albany: State University of New York Press.

3   Williams 1997: 329.

4   Mulvey, L. (1975) 'Visual Pleasure and Narrative Cinema', *Screen*, 16, 1, 6–18.

5   Rodowick, D. N. (1982) 'The Difficulty of Difference', *Wide Angle*, 5, 1, 4–15.

6   Mulvey, L. (1985) 'Changes', *Discourse*, 3, 11–30.

7   Marks, P. (2000) 'On TV, Crime Will Pay', *The New York Times: Weekend*, 11 May, B1, B12.

8   See Williams 1997: 100–10.

9   Rothman, W. (1982) *Hitchcock – The Murderous Gaze*. Cambridge, Massachusetts: Harvard University Press.

10 Brill, L. (1988) *The Hitchcock Romance: Love and Irony in Hitchcock's Films*. New Jersey: Princeton University Press, 242.

11 Mulvey 1985: 28.

CHAPTER 5

1   Quoted in J. Petley (2000) '"Snuffed Out": Nightmares in a Trading Standards Officer's Brain', in G. Harper & X. Mendik (eds) *Unruly Pleasures: The Cult Film and its Critics*. Guildford: FAB Press, 206.

2   Quoted in H. Millea (1999) 'Voyeurs, Guns, and Money', *Premier*, March, 62–9, 100.

3   J. David Slocum quoted in Millea 1999: 65.

4   Gloria Buck quoted in J. Yardley (2001) 'Oklahoma City: Execution on TV Brings Little Solace', *New York Times*, 12 June.

5   Wills, G. (2001) 'The Dramaturgy of Death', *New York Review of Books*, 21 June, 10.

6   Brian Lowry, television columnist for the *Los Angeles Times*, interviewed by Mandalit Delbarco on NPR's 'Morning Edition', 9 February 2001.

7   Lesser, W. (2001) 'TV's Love Affair with Death', *New York Times*, 25 March. See also her 1993 book, *Pictures at an Execution*. Cambridge, MA: Harvard University Press.

8   Schneider, S. (2000) 'The International Language of Horror: Anthony Waller's *Mute Witness*', *Central Europe Review*, 6 November <http://www.ce-review.org../00/38/kinoeye38_schneider.html>

9   Freeland, C. (1995) 'Realist Horror', in C. Freeland & T. Wartenberg (eds) *Philosophy and Film*. New York: Routledge, 126–42.

10 McDonough, J. (1991) 'Director Without a Past', *American Film* (May), 44.

11 Simpson, P. (2000) *Psycho Paths: Tracking the Serial Killer Through Contemporary American Film and Fiction.* Carbondale: Southern Illinois University Press, 141.

12 Wilkinson, P. (1992) 'Hot Director', *Rolling Stone*, 14 May, 75.

13 Freeland 1995: 129.

14 Kerekes, D. & D. Slater (1995) *Killing For Culture: An Illustrated History of the Death Film from Mondo to Snuff.* London: Creation Books, 252, n6.

15 Simpson, 147.

16 Quoted on 'American Justice: The California Killing Field' (2000). A&E video.

17 Petley 2000: 207.

18 See Conrich, I. & S. Schneider 'The Paradox of Pseudo Snuff', in N. Rombes (ed.) *From Avant-Garde to Mainstream: Post-Punk Cinemas* (forthcoming).

19 Petley 2000: 217, 209.

20 Kerekes & Slater 1995: 245.

21 Quoted on 'American Justice: Getting Away with Murder' (1999/2000). A&E video.

22 Kerekes & Slater 1995: 43.

23 Ibid.

24 See J. Brooke (2000) 'Crime Book May Become a Page in Canadian law', *New York Times*, April 10.

25 Quoted by A. DePalma (1997) 'Murderer's Sex Tapes Put Canadian Lawyer at Risk', *New York Times*, February 24.

26 Cf. Tony Williams's essay on *Special Effects* in this volume.

27 Petley 2000: 206.

28 Ballard, J. G. (1990) *The Atrocity Exhibition* [1972]. San Francisco: Re/Search, 69 (Ballard's annotation).

29 Kerekes & Slater 1995: 48.

30 Pasolini, P. P. (1988) *Heretical Empiricism*. Trans. B. Lawton & L. K. Barnett. Bloomington: Indiana University Press, 233.

31 Morrison, K. (1999) 'The Technology of Homicide: Constructions of Evidence and Truth in the American Murder film', in C. Sharrett (ed.) *Mythologies of Violence in Postmodern Media*. Detroit: Wayne State University Press, 312.

32 Eldridge, C. (2000) 'Better Art Through Circuitry – Questions for Natalie Jeremijenko', *The New York Times Magazine*, 11 June, 25.

33 Petley 2000: 219.

34 For a detailed discussion of this film, see J. Black (2001) *The Reality Effect: Film Culture and the Graphic Imperative*. New York: Routledge.

CHAPTER 6

1 Boswell, P. (2000) 'Bruce Conner: Theater of Light and Shadow', in *2000 BC: The Bruce Conner Story Part II.* Minneapolis: Walker Art Center, 39.

2 Ibid.

3 Belz, C. (1967) 'Three Films by Bruce Conner', *Film Culture*, 44, Spring, 57.

4 O'Doherty, B. (1967) 'Bruce Conner and His Films', in G. Battock (ed.) *The New American Cinema: A Critical Anthology*. New York: Dutton, 196.

5 Conner, B. (1969) 'Bruce Conner', *Film Comment*, 5.4, Winter, 18.

6 Quoted in R. Haller (1979) 'Excerpts from an Interview with Bruce Conner Conducted in July of 1971', *Film Culture*, 67–9, 193.

7 Conner 1969: 17 18.

8 Huss, R. & N. Silverstein (1968) *The Film Experience: Elements of Motion Picture Art*. New York: Harper & Row, 4.

9 Quoted in M. Caywood (2000) 'Not to the Beat: Bruce Conner Often Metamorphosizes, but One Thing Remains Consistent', *Fort Worth Weekly*, 17–24 February.

10 Boswell 2000: 54.

11 Belz 1967: 58.

12 Conner 1969: 18.

13 Mosen, D. (1966) '*Report*', *Film Quarterly*, 19, 3, Spring, 55.

14 Conner 1969: 18.

15 Brakhage, S. (1989) *Film at Wit's End: Eight Avant-Garde Filmmakers*. Kingston: McPherson, 141.

16 Conner 1969: 18.

17 Ibid.

18 Jenkins, B. (2000) 'Explosion in a Film Factory: The Cinema of Bruce Conner', in *2000 BC: The Bruce Conner Story*

Part II. Minneapolis: Walker Art Center, 211.

19 See Conner 1969: 18; Haller 1979: 193.

CHAPTER 7

1   See S. Renan (1967) *The Underground Film: An Introduction To Its Development In America*. London: Studio Vista; and R. Dyer (1990) *Now You See It*. London: Routledge, 149–52.

2   See 'Paul Morrissey in His Own Words About his and Andy Warhol's Movies' (for the Stockholm Film Festival, 1997). <http://www.filmfestivalen.se/1997/warmorkat97.html>

3   Warhol, A. & P. Hackett (1981) *POPism: The Warhol '60s*. London: Hutchinson, 252.

4   Hackett, P (ed.) (1989) *The Andy Warhol Diaries*. London: Simon & Schuster, 689.

5   Warhol, A. (1976) *From A To B And Back Again: The Philosophy of Andy Warhol*. London: Picador, 213.

6   Woronov, M. (2000) *Swimming Underground: My Years in the Warhol Factory*. London: Serpent's Tail, 30 (my emphasis).

7   Woronov, M. (2001) 'Screen Tests', *The Guardian*, 21 July.

8   Warhol & Hackett 1981: 91.

9   Mary Woronov quoted in J. Sargeant (2001) 'Mary Woronov, So Far Underground, You Get The Bends', *BBGun* 5, 77–80.

10 Warhol & Hackett 1981: 233.

11 Berg, G. (1989) 'Nothing To Lose: An Interview With Andy Warhol', in M. O'Pray (ed.) *Andy Warhol Film Factory*. London: BFI Publishing, 54–61.

12 Ibid.

13 Warhol and Hackett 1981: 51.

14 Ibid.

CHAPTER 8

1   Setlowe, R. (1967) 'Saga of Negro Director', *Daily Variety*, 13 December, 7.

2   Ibid.

3   Ibid.

4   Morgenstern, J. (1970) 'Off-Colour Joke', *Newsweek*, 25 May, 102.

5   Gillespie, C. (1970) 'Watermelon Man', *Entertainment World*, 29 May, 23.

6   Carroll, K. (1970) 'Black and White Blues', *Daily News*, 28 May, 74.

7   Gillespie 1970: 23.

8   *Newsweek* (1971) 'Sweet Song of Success', 21 August, 89.

9   *Time* (1971) 'Power to the Peebles', 16 August, 47.

10 Reid, M. (1993) *Redefining Black Film*. Berkeley, Los Angeles & Oxford: University of California Press, 79; T. Topor (1972) 'The Show That Was Supposed To Die', *New York Post*, 5 February, 15.

11 Bogle, D. (2000) *Toms, Coons, Mulattoes, Mammies, & Bucks: An Interpretive History of Blacks in American Films*. 3rd Edition. New York: Continuum, 194–266; T. Cripps (1979) *Black Film as Genre*. Bloomington & London: Indiana University Press, 128–40; Ed Guerrero (1993) *Framing Blackness: The African American Image in Film*. Philadelphia: Temple University Press, 69–112; Reid 1993.

12 Gilliatt, P. (June 19, 1971) 'Sweetback', *The New Yorker*, 68.

13 Ibid.

14 Gussow, M. (1972) 'The Baadasssss Success of Melvin Van Peebles', *New York Times Magazine*, 20 August, 86.

15 Ibid.

16 Van Peebles, M. (1971) 'A Stork Flew Over the Zoo Fence…', *Sunday News*, 3 October, S3.

17 Canby, V. (1971) '"Sweetback": Does It Exploit Injustice?', *New York Times*, 9 May, D1.

18 Riley, C. (1971) 'What Makes Sweetback Run?', *New York Times*, 9 May, D11.

19 Bennett, L. (1971) 'The Emancipation Orgasm: Sweetback in Wonderland', *Ebony*, September, 112.

CHAPTER 9

1   Heard, C. (1969) 'Sexploitation', in C. Heard & J. Lithgow 'Underground U.S.A. and the Sexploitation Market', *Films and Filming*, 25.

2   Ibid.

3   Bowen, M. (1997) 'The Many Film Bodies of Doris Wishman', *Wide Angle*, 19, 3; Gorfinkel, E. (2000) 'The Body as Apparatus: Chesty Morgan Takes on the Academy', in X. Mendik & G. Harper (eds) *Unruly Pleasures: The Cult*

Film and its Critics. London: Fab Press.

4   Oppenheim, P. (1991) 'Queen of Sexploitation Quickie: Doris Wishman', *Filmfax*, 28, 73–6; J. Renshaw (1998) 'Sexploitation Queen', *The Austin Chronicle*, 10 July, 48–50.

5   Dennis Dermody, interview with the author.

6   Wishman's testimony from numerous interviews with the author.

7   Moller, D. (1962) 'Nuderama', *Vision*, 1, 2, 18.

8   Ibid: 19.

9   Ibid.

10 Heard 1969: 25.

11 Wishman, interview with the author.

12 Heard, ibid.

13 Morton, J. (ed.) (1986) *Incredibly Strange Film*. San Francisco: RE/Search Publications, 113.

14 Wishman, interview with the author.

15 Morton 1986: 113.

16 C. Davis Smith, interview with the author.

17 Wishman, interview with the author.

18 Awesh, P. (1998) 'Nude Deal', *The Village Voice*, 43, 12, 24.

19 Wishman, interview with the author.

20 'Mamell's Story', (1975) Ecran 35, 75; McGillivray, D. (1974) 'Deadly Weapons', *Monthly Film Bulletin*, 41, 409, 249.

21 McGillivray, ibid.

CHAPTER 10

1   Thompson, H. S. (1966) *Hell's Angels: The Strange and Terrible Saga of the Outlaw Motorcycle Gangs*. New York: Random House, 1.

2   Corrigan, T. (1991) *A Cinema Without Walls: Movies and Culture after Vietnam*. New Brunswick, NJ: Rutgers University Press, 143.

3   Ibid: 146.

4   Ibid: 143.

5   Cohan, S. and I. Rae Hark (eds) (1997) *The Road Movie Book*. London: Routledge, 1.

6   Ibid: 2.

7   Laderman, D. 'What a Trip: The Road Film and American Culture', *Journal of Film and Video*, 48, 1–2, Spring/Summer, 41–57.

8   Seate, M. (2000) *Two Wheels on Two Reels: A History of Biker Movies*. North Conway: Whitehorse Press, 14.

9   Cited in J. Cott 'Anger Rising', *Sunday Ramparts*, 7 May.

10 Morris, G. (1993) 'Beyond the Beach: Social and Formal Aspects of AIP's Beach Party Movies', *Journal of Popular Film and Television*, 2, 2–11.

11 Cited in Seate 2000: 23.

12 The success of the more famous sequel, *Billy Jack* (1970), prompted the re-release of the original.

13 Martin, R. (1997) *Mean Streets and Raging Bulls: The Legacy of Film Noir in Contemporary American Cinema*. London: Scarecrow, 85. Jim Hillier also cites *Easy Rider* as a herald to more innovative filmmaking practice in mainstream American cinema. See J. Hillier (1992) *The New Hollywood*. London: Studio Vista.

14 Klinger, B. (1997) 'The Road to Dystopia: Landscaping the Nation in *Easy Rider*', in Cohan & Hark, 181–2.

15 Ibid: 184.

16 Daniel, A. (1999) 'Get Your Kicks: *Easy Rider* and the Counter-Culture', in J. Sargeant & S. Watson (eds) *Lost Highways: An Illustrated History of Road Movies*. London: Creation, 70.

17 Roberts, S. (1997) 'Western Meets Eastwood: Genre and Gender on the Road', in Cohan & Hark, 61.

18 Ibid.

19 Crane, J. (2000) 'A Lust for Life: The Cult Films of Russ Meyer', in X. Mendik & G. Harper (eds) *Unruly Pleasures: The Cult Film and Its Critics*. Guildford: Fab Press, 91.

20 Morton, Jim (1999) 'Rebels of the Road: The Biker Film', in Sargeant & Watson, 64.

21 Ibid.

CHAPTER 11

1   Sitney, P. A. (1974) *Visionary Film: The American Avant-Garde*. New York: Oxford, 398.

2   For more on Smith's epic journey, see R. Singh (1995) 'Anthology Film Archives: New York' and B. Breeze (1996)

'In Memoriam, Harry Smith', in P. Igliori (1996) *American Magus – Harry Smith: A Modern Alchemist*. New York: Inandout Press. The Harry Smith Archives maintains an extensive website at www.harrysmitharchives.com.

3 Marcus, G. (1997) *Invisible Republic: Bob Dylan's Basement Tapes*. New York: Henry Holt, 95. See also R. Cantwell (1996) *When We Were Good: The Folk Revival*. Cambridge, MA: Harvard University Press.

4 Deleuze, G. (1989) *Cinema 2: The Time-Image*. Minneapolis: University of Minnesota Press (Trans. H. Tomlinson and R. Galeta; first published in French in 1985), 20.

5 Igliori 1996: 31.

6 See Berge, C. (1965) 'Dialogue with Words: The Work of Harry Smith', *Film Culture* 37 (Summer), 2–4; N. Carroll (1977–78) 'Mind, Medium and Metaphor in Harry Smith's *Heaven and Earth Magic*', *Film Quarterly* 31.2 (Winter), 37–44; and Sitney, 232–62.

CHAPTER 12

1 Benjamin, W. (1973) *Understanding Brecht*. London: New Left Books, 94–5.

2 Walsh, D. 'Thoughts about the 1997 Toronto Film Festival: Film, Social Reality and Authenticity', *World Socialist Web Site* <http://www.wsws.org/arts/1997/sep1997/tff-2.shtml>

3 Werner Herzog interview with Harmony Korine (November 1997) 'Gummo's Whammo', *Interview Magazine* <http://www.angelfire.com/ab/harmonykorine/interviewmag.html>

4 Ibid.

5 Cooper, C. (29/09/89) 'Subliminal Messages, Heavy Metal Music and Teen-Age Suicide', *San Francisco Examiner* <http://www.reversespeech.com/judas.shtml>

6 Herzog interview with Korine.

CHAPTER 14

1 Hinckley, J. (1981) 'Letter to Jodie Foster' <http://www.law.umkc.edu/faculty/projects/ftrials/hinckley/letter.htm>

2 Fuller, V. (1981) Closing argument as defence counsel for John W. Hinckley <http://www.law.umkc.edu/faculty/projects/ftrials/hinckley/fuller.htm>

3 Jenkins, H. (1992) *Textual Poachers: Television Fans and Participatory Culture*. New York and London: Routledge, 13.

4 Jenson, J. (1992) 'Fandom as Pathology: the Consequences of Characterization', in L. Lewis (ed.) *The Adoring Audience: Fan Culture and Popular Culture*. London and New York: Routledge.

5 Jenkins 1992: 15.

6 Penley, C. (1991) 'Brownian motion: Women, Tactics and Technology', in C. Penley & A. Ross (eds) *Technoculture*. Minneapolis: University of Minnesota Press.

7 Jenkins 1992: 278.

8 Fiske, J. (1992) 'The Cultural Economy of Fandom', in L. Lewis (ed.) *The Adoring Audience: Fan Culture and Popular Culture*. London and New York: Routledge, 30–9.

9 *Star Warz Gangsta Rap* (2000), Allergic to Life Productions/Bentframe, <http://www.allergictolife.com>

10 Penley 1991: 139.

11 Fiske 1992: 30.

12 Penley 1991: 143.

13 Fiske 1992: 39.

14 McKee, A. (forthcoming) 'How to Tell the Difference Between Production and Consumption: a case study in *Doctor Who* fandom', in S. Jones & R. Pearson (eds) *Worlds Apart: Essays on Cult Television*. Minneapolis: University of Minnesota Press.

15 Rubio, K. (1997) *Troops*, <http://www.theforce.net/troops>

16 Rubio, K. (1998) '*Troops*: Whatcha Gonna Do? A revealing interview with the creators of *Troops*', *Daily Movies*, 22 April, <http://theforce.ign.com>

17 Wolk, J. (2001) 'Troop Dreams', *Entertainment Weekly Online*, 28 April, <http://www.ew.com/ew/archive/0,1798,1/22616/0/rubio,00.html>

18 Ward, M. (1998) *Death of a Jedi*, <http://mawproductions.com/deathofajedi/index2.html>

19 Young, C. (1998) 'Matthew Ward Interview', <http://mawproductions.com/deathofajedi/wardinterview.html>

20 See 'The Internet Index' <http://new-website.openmarket.com/intindex/index.cfm>; and D. Tapscott (1997) *Growing Up Digital: The Rise of the Net Generation*. New York: McGraw-Hill.

21 Ang, I. (2000) 'New Technologies, Audience Measurement, and the Tactics of Television Consumption', in J. Caldwell (ed.) *Electronic Media and Technoculture*. New Brunswick, New Jersey: Rutgers University Press, 183–96.

CHAPTER 16

1   Original source of this quotation was in *Film Culture*, 22–3, Summer 1961. The manifesto was reprinted in P. Adams Sitney (1970) *Film Culture Reader*. New York: Praeger Publishers, 81–2.
2   Arthur, P. (1989) *The Film Co-op Catalogue*. New York: The New American Cinema Group.
3   Le Grice, M. (1986) *Light Years Catalogue: A Twenty Year Celebration of the LFMC*.
4   Cited in *The 1993 London Filmmaker's Co-op Catalogue*, 163–4.

CHAPTER 17

1   Vogel, A. (1974) *Film as a Subversive Art*. New York: Random House.

CHAPTER 18

1   Mekas, J. (1961) *Village Voice*, 12 January.
2   Kroll, J. (1966) 'Underground in Hell', *Newsweek*, November 14.

CHAPTER 19

1   Paul, W. (1994) *Laughing Screaming: Modern Hollywood Horror and Comedy*. New York: Columbia University Press, 81.
2   Waters, J. (1995) *Shock Value: a tasteful book about bad taste*. New York: Thunder's Mouth Press, 2.
3   Anon. Review of *Citizen Toxi: Toxic Avenger 1V* <http://www.zombiegirls.net/citizentoxie.html> 29/6/02.
4   *Citizen Toxi: The Toxic Avenger 1V* (review) <http://www.daily-reviews.com/c/bmtoxic4.htm> 30/6/2002.
5   Review of *Citizen Toxi: Toxic Avenger 1V* <http://www.zombiegirls.net/citizentoxie.html> 29/06/02
6   *Citizen Toxi: The Toxic Avenger 1V* (review) <http://www.daily-reviews.com/c/bmtoxic4.htm> 30/6/2002.
7   Carroll, N. (1990) *The Philosophy of Horror; or, Paradoxes of the Heart*. New York: Routledge, 1990, 32.
8   Bakhtin, cited in Creed, B. (1995) 'Horror and the Carnivalesque', in Devereaux, L and Hillman, R. (eds.) *Fields of Vision: Essays in Film Studies, Visual Anthropology, and Photography*. Berkeley: University of California Press, 130.
9   Cited in Creed, 130.
10 Ibid., 131.
11 Ibid., 136.
12 Ibid.
13 Ibid., 135.
14 Paul, 421, 423.
15 Ibid., 419.
16 Stevenson, J. (1996) *Desperate Visions: The Journal of Alternative Cinema 1: Camp America (Interviews and Essays)*. London: Creation Books, 13.
17 Bakhtin, M. (1985) *Rabelais and His World*. Bloomington: Indiana University Press, 320.
18 Stevenson, 19.
19 Waters, 14.
20 Frank, J. (1997) '25th Anniversary of the Filthiest Marriage: *Pink Flamingos* Reprocessed', *Projections: A publication of the Forum for the Psychoanalytic Study of Film* 11.1 (Spring): 23.
21 Waters, 12.
22 Ibid., 14.
23 Ibid., 166.
24 Ibid., 158.
25 Ibid., 173–74.
26 Ibid., 173.
27 Bakhtin, 315.
28 Ibid.
29 Ibid., 303.
30 Creed, 136.
31 Ibid., 137.
32 Ibid., 139.
33 Bakhtin, 319.

INDEX

235

AlterImage

a new list of publications
exploring global cult and popular cinema

For further information about the AlterImage series, or any other of our publications across the field of film and media studies, please visit:

www.wallflowerpress.co.uk

other series include:

Short Cuts **entry-level undergraduate introductions to film studies**
Directors' Cuts **in-depth studies of significant international filmmakers**
Critical Guides **comprehensive reference guides to thousands of contemporary directors**
24 Frames **edited collections on the films of national and regional cinemas around the world**

 **WALLFLOWER PRESS**
LONDON and NEW YORK